Challenges to the Welfare State

Challenges to the Welfare State:
Internal and External Dynamics for Change

Edited by

Henry Cavanna

Director, Forum International des Sciences Humaines, Paris, France

Edward Elgar

Cheltenham, UK • Northampton, MA, USA

© Forum International des Sciences Humaines 1998

Published by
Edward Elgar Publishing Limited
8 Lansdown Place
Cheltenham
Glos GL50 2HU
UK

Edward Elgar Publishing, Inc
6 Market Street
Northampton
Massachusetts 01060
USA

A catalogue record for this book
is available from the British Library

Library of Congress Cataloguing in Publication Data

Challenges to the welfare state: internal and external dynamics for
  change / edited by Henry Cavanna.
Includes bibliographical references.
1. Welfare state.   2. Comparative government.   I. Cavanna, Henry.

JC479.C53 1998   97–17945
361.6'5–dc21   CIP

ISBN 1 85898 636 2

Printed and bound in Great Britain by Biddles Ltd, Guildford and King's Lynn

Contents

Contents

Contents

List of figures

List of tables

List of contributors

Philippe Bénéton
University of Rennes I

Sir Samuel Brittan
Assistant Editor
Financial Times

Henry Cavanna
Director
Forum International des Sciences Humaines, Paris

Maurizio Ferrera
University of Pavia

Nathan Glazer
Harvard University

Hans Keman
Vrije University, Amsterdam
Research Fellow, Netherlands Institute of Advanced Studies

Stein Kuhnle
University of Bergen

Egon Matzner
Technische University
Austrian Academy of Sciences, Vienna

Kenneth Newton
University of Essex
Executive Director, European Consortium for Political Research

Vladimir Rys
Research Consultant
Universities of Prague and Geneva

Peter Scherer
Head of the Social Policies Division
OECD, Paris

Introduction

The welfare state has long been considered a sort of 'miracle solution,' which, after World War II, has forestalled a true revolution in Western Europe. Economic development, both considerable and sustained, has permitted an extraordinary improvement in the standard of living and has practically eliminated unemployment. But in the 1970s, the increase in the gross domestic product (GDP) became lower than that in social spending, and the trend was reversed. The cost of social coverage has thus gone beyond the possibilities offered by the economic machine, and budgetary deficits have accrued.

Concurrently with the poor economic results has appeared a sociologically troubling phenomenon. Have we not been building a society of dependants, where the motivation to do better and more has disappeared? Furthermore, has not the State done too much, in so departing from its customary mission to undertake others for which it was not equipped? Huge bureaucratic entities have also been born that, often, defend their own interests rather than those of society.

The welfare state has thus ceased to be the solution to serious problems of integration and well-being, and can even be considered as the cause of social stagnation and economic impoverishment. It is in these circumstances and this state of mind that we will find the new solution: the market which, allowing the free play of economic agents and not subject to 'political' constraints, will likewise resolve new problems. Meanwhile, for more than two decades we observe, at least on this side of the Atlantic, that unemployment, exclusion and poverty do not cease to augment.

What, in this context, is the opinion of the experts? The Forum International des Sciences Humaines, which as early as 1981 organized a colloquium on 'The Future Functions of the Welfare State', wishes to gather today, with the sponsorship of the University of Navarra, the analyses of a group of renowned experts. They possess different ideological horizons and intellectual occupations – economists, political scientists, sociologists – and present in their essays an analysis of the economic and social problems which confront us.

As Samuel Brittan points out, 'It is a fact at any rate that in many industrial countries the budget deficit is, or has been until very lately, about 5 per cent of the GDP levels, only seen previously during major wars and in great depressions.' Dealing with existing deficits, which an ageing population cannot but make worse, will require either a considerable increase in taxation or a significant reduction of entitlements.

As explained by Mauricio Ferrara, 'Overprotection against the risks of old age is a danger, not only in Italy or in other Southern European countries, but everywhere.' The proportion of voters in the EU over 55 years old was 33 per cent in 1990; a projection for 2020 gives 42 per cent. The State will, therefore, be obliged to limit the size of future benefits.

However, as Ken Newton notes, 'Mass survey evidence shows that voters regard the core services of the welfare state – health, education, housing and provision for the old, the ill and the unemployed – as government responsibilities.' The high legitimacy enjoyed by European welfare states is, then, an impediment to the reduction of welfare responsibilities, which all experts consider necessary in Europe.

In these circumstances, we could ask ourselves whether this feature of the European way of life is not a drawback with respect to the globalization of the economy and the internationalization of money markets, and whether this legitimacy is not creating, as Stein Kuhnle observes, 'Voter expectations which are higher than government can cope with.'

We could also consider whether Nathan Glazer's view is correct, that Europe is becoming more like America, for good and ill, and whether we will begin to have a greater respect in Europe for the profit-making sector as a provider of solutions to some key problems in social policy. Today, all politicians in America preach the same message: cut taxes and public expenditure because, as even Clinton affirms, the age of big government is over.

The majority of authors concur in any event: the European welfare state faces cultural, economic and political challenges. Will European integration bring a reconstruction of European welfare, all citizens being guaranteed some basic social rights, in addition to which they would have the possibility of purchasing some private insurance? 'Would that mean', Stein Kuhnle queries, 'creating social security and welfare systems which are more dual and socially stratified than at present?'

More taxes, fewer social benefits, an older age before being entitled to pensions? Something must be done, unless we resign ourselves to present differentials in market-clearing rates of pay. According to Samuel Brittan, 'The victims will always be, the unlucky and the unskilled, with either low pay or high unemployment.'

Suggestions for the reorganization of the welfare state based on a functional analysis of the fulfilment of State tasks have largely been neglected, add other authors. It is true that alternatives to monetarist *laissez-faire* ideology have not been sufficiently elaborated. 'This is, of course', remarks Egon Matzner, 'a more demanding task than to make suggestions on deregulation and monetary discipline often based on unfounded theories.'

The political philosopher, who has followed this rather 'technical discussion', may wonder, however, in the end whether we are doing, or trying to do, good without the idea of the good. This question, some of his colleagues might say, could open a new and different debate.

Henry Cavanna

Acknowledgements

I especially wish to thank the faculty of Ciencias Economicas y Empresariales, Universidad de Navarra, and their Dean, Professor Luis Ravina Bohorquez, who hosted the symposium 'Challenges to the welfare state: Internal and External Dynamics for Change'. We greatly enjoyed their wonderful hospitality and their beautiful campus. My thanks also to Professors José Barea Tejeiro, Secretary of State at the Budget Office in Madrid; José Luis Feito, Spanish Ambassador to the OECD; and José Antonio Garcia-Duran, University of Barcelona, who all helped to enliven our debate.

1. Challenges to the welfare state

Sir Samuel Brittan

1.1 MAIN CHALLENGES

The challenges to the welfare state are easily outlined, although the detail is endless and constantly changing.

On the financial side they show themselves mainly in the crisis of government spending and public debt faced by most European countries. The typical ratio of general government outlays to GDP rose from 35 per cent in 1970 to over 50 per cent in the early 1990s.

Welfare spending of all kinds, and social security spending in particular, were the main, although of course not the only, reasons.

The slowdown in economic growth compared to the 1960s obviously had some effect in holding down the denominator of this ratio. But the changes in the numerator were even more important. Many influences were involved: improved benefits; demographic shifts and changed social attitudes which led to a greater take-up.

But probably the main reason is that benefit levels were decided on the basis of much more optimistic economic growth assumptions than would today be regarded as realistic.

We have now reached the stage where we have to run fast to stay where we are. In many industrial countries the budget deficit has approached 5 per cent of GDP, levels previously only seen during major wars and in the great depression. These have been associated with corresponding leaps in the debt ratios. So if the Maastricht critertia and the proposed stability pact had not been devised for the purposes of European monetary union, they would still have to be invented to prevent an explosive debt trap. By a debt trap I mean a position where deficits increase continuously or taxation has to rise indefinitely, not to finance increased primary spending, but simply to service debt on past borrowing.

Unfortunately dealing with existing deficits is only the beginning. Because of the ageing of the population, contributions or taxes will have to increase or entitlements be reduced, simply to close the contribution gap in the main European social security funds. This gap is put by the International Monetary Fund (IMF) at 3 to 3.5 per cent of GDP for

France and Germany, but only 0.1 per cent for the UK. These are very large sums indeed. They would be equivalent to raising personal tax rates by 7 percentage points or more.

1.2 TWO KINDS OF CLAIM

What lies behind these very high claims on resources? There are two main categories: first, the rising ratio of citizens of pensionable age to the working population. This arises partly from the ageing of the post-war baby boom, but also from an increase in life expectancy. So far this has not been matched by a later retirement age. On the contrary it has been aggravated by a trend to early retirement or departure from the working population by workers in late middle age or even earlier. It is this first pressure which leads to the most alarming statistical projections.

But I worry more about the second source of pressure, even though it produces less alarming numbers. This is growing differentials in market-clearing rates of pay. The victims are the unlucky and the unskilled. In some countries these pressures express themselves in low pay; and in others, where pay is held up by collective agreements or the law, it is expressed in high unemployment.

The effects of these distributional forces are highly pervasive. I have often canvassed the idea of some form of minimum income guarantee. The cost of such a guarantee, and its disincentive effects, are least when there is a large gap between the pay of typical low-paid workers and what would be regarded as a decent subsistence minimum. When median pay is itself very low the gap is small or non-existent. So the costs of such a scheme go up. So too does the danger that it would provide many people with a disincentive to seek paid work. This was believed to be the effect of the Speenhamland system introduced by the British magistrates in 1795 under which local justices of the peace were supposed to make payments to supplement the pay of agricultural workers.

As usual categorization is too simple, for there is an intermediate category between on the one hand, the retired of pensionable age, and people of working age either officially unemployed or working for low pay. These are the many *discouraged workers* who are not officially unemployed, but have left the labour force, usually after losing their job, at well below the normal pension age.

Such inactive middle-aged people may live on benefits such as invalidity, but very often they will have an occupational pension or be supported by a wife or husband who is at work. They will mostly have paid off their mortgages and be able to live on a much lower take home pay than younger people.

The inactivity of so many people of working age is not only a social problem. It represents an unpardonable waste at a time when the dependency ratio is in any case growing. We are, as it were, throwing away the contributions of many people who, with a little encouragement, would still like paid work.

By far the most important contribution that could be made to the state pension problem would be to *raise the age of retirement*. This takes a few seconds to say, but would have enormous implications. It would reverse many of the effects of demography and enormously reduce the burden of caring for the old. On the IMF estimate, raising the normal German retirement age to 67 would eliminate completely the contribution deficit.

But the demonstration effects might extend very much further. Private pension schemes would be bound to be influenced towards a higher retirement age. Moreover both employers and older workers would tend to have a different attitude if the reference point for retirement was 67 rather than 60. The ideal would be to have no standard retirement age and to leave it to individual decisions.

1.3 MINIMUM INCOME GUARANTEE

Intellectually more interesting than the pension problem is the problem of low market-clearing rates of pay for those of working age. I have been attracted to the minimum income idea for many reasons. First and foremost I would like to reduce the puritan element in capitalist culture by allowing everyone a choice to live on a modest but survivable income if he or she wants to opt out of the conventional rat race. Such an income would also help people in the beginning of their careers who wanted to take risks or work part time while they developed their real talents. Many such people are not eligible for conventional grants or do not know how to apply for them.

Of more immediate relevance is that if there were a minimum income it would be possible to oppose minimum wage legislation, or indeed all the collective bargaining practices which divorce an individual's pay from his or her market rate, and to do so with a clear conscience. It is surely better to supplement low pay with top-up benefits than to price people out of work and then pay them the dole for doing nothing.

Finally there are always bound to be gaps and injustices in social security schemes which depend either on contribution records or which are means tested in one way or another. An automatic over-the-counter payment would enable everyone to have a very basic minimum without having to satisfy complicated criteria or having to tell public officials about all his or her private circumstances.

Alas, one has to face the fact that when even existing welfare payments are under enormous stress, it is not very realistic to propose a highly expensive new scheme. What I did in my last book[1] was to ask in broad outline how far existing social security schemes did fail to provide a minimum income in practice and how we could fill the gaps.

Probably the harshest aspect of income related benefits is the very severe test of capital means, which could be lightened somewhat without opening the floodgates to abuse. Wherever possible there should also be a shift of emphasis from the dole to income top-up. In the UK this top up, known as 'family benefit', is available, but so far only for families with dependent children. Some experimental schemes are under way to make them more general.

I still favour a very small unconditional payment to everyone to keep the principle of a citizen income alive. Such a payment could make the difference for many people between a life full of negotiation with social security officers and one which they can call their own.

The big difference between what I recommend and the advocates of a full basic income is that payment would be cut off quite steeply as outside income rose. The full basic income ideal, under which benefits would only be withdrawn at the normal income tax rate, is not likely to be affordable for the foreseeable future.

1.4 RELEVANCE OF GLOBALIZATION

There is far more to be said on all the detail. But I do not think the main outlines of the problem will change very quickly. So I would like to end by raising a question which I did not cover in the book. That is: how far are the problems of the welfare state affected by globalization? By this I mean primarily the new freedom for capital movements and trade to go wherever the return seems highest. This is caricatured by people who dislike the supposed dominance of the bond markets. But a more straightforward way of putting it is that the world is becoming a single economy.

I shall assume that pensioners will either not wish to move from country to country to take advantage of differences in benefit or will still be prevented from doing so. So I will concentrate on the effects on those of working age.

The system which might be called the social market has been based on a simple compromise. This is that workers can be paid the market rate of return. But very adverse impacts on low incomes are in principle offset by cash transfers. This is so whether the transfers come from a conventional social security system or from some basic income guarantee.

Such transfers are of course between citizens. The state is only an agency and has no resources of its own. The nagging question is: will those who are net payers accept the loss in their take-home pay? Or will they be able to pass on the cost of their tax and social security payments so that there is nothing left to redistribute?

In a traditional parochial economy passing on has been limited. For the essential assumption is that workers are immobile between countries. In that case a skilled worker who is taxed to finance a top-up payment for other workers has not much choice but to accept most of the burden. He may at the margin work a little less, but he will find it difficult to escape the transfer altogether.

In the early stages of the global economy one may assume that mobility of labour is limited, in line with existing European evidence. In that case it will still be possible to offset some of the tendency towards increased income differentials. But that will apply only as far as they affect the relativities of different sorts of worker. The grave problems will arise in today's global economy if there is not merely an adverse trend in the pay of low skilled or unlucky workers. Let us suppose that there is also a fall in the return to labour in general relative to the return to capital. This is certainly possible in a world of capital shortage, which has so far only been a threat but may yet develop.

Capital is by definition mobile in a global economy. One country can still have higher rates of corporation tax than another. But it must allow a pattern of pay, prices and exchange rates which will enable companies working in that country to enjoy the going world net post-tax rate of return. If a government tries to stop this, not only will it fail to attract outside capital, but existing domestic companies will shift more of their investment abroad.

I have no magic answer. The only thing I can say in general is that the more ownership of capital can be spread among the mass of citizens, the less will this trend matter. For the going rate of return will be available to a pension fund holder in a small village in the mountains, as well as to an international dealer in Barcelona. Devices such as pension funds, especially when individually owned, or worker shares, are all helpful here. The problem is the bottom 50 per cent of the population who tend to be outside all such schemes.

Finally may I leave you with a vision which some will regard as a utopia and others as a nightmare. The situation, in which capital is mobile and labour is not, is hardly permanent. Developments on the Rio Grande in between Mexico and the USA are surely suggestive of what will happen in Europe. It is inconceivable that growing populations in North Africa, enjoying more and more media information on European life, will simply accept a large adverse disparity in living standards without doing something about it. Migration, whether legal or illegal, is about the most peaceful move they might attempt. The prospect of fundamentalist Moslem governments is likely to make movement even greater as there will be many millions who will prefer the rewards of this world to the consolation of the faith.

There are also likely to be many attempts to move from a chaotic and disordered Russia to countries further west. If a European single market is to mean anything at all there will have to be a common immigration policy; and the only enforceable one will be that of the country with the lowest barriers.

The equalization of net return to workers of comparable skill and motivation is a prediction of classical economic theory. It was also a traditional goal of international socialism. I have no doubt that existing European workers will engage in extensive rearguard actions to stop these ideals from being realized. But in the long run, when not all of us will be dead, we may as well face the fact that there will be such tendencies at work. Maybe the growing disparities in the return to different kinds of skill and knowhow will continue. But in addition there will be a tendency to the worldwide equalization of returns for comparable work. Can anyone give a good ethical reason for objecting to these trends? And has anyone some practical suggestions for anticipating and living with them?

ENDNOTES

[1] Samuel Brittan (1995), *Capitalism with a Human Face*, Edward Elgar, London. Fontana edition, 1996.

2. The American welfare state: exceptional no longer?

Nathan Glazer

Twice within the last decade I have addressed the question of the relative 'backwardness' of the American welfare state, compared with European states at similar levels of economic development and political maturity, and with a similar commitment to democracy and to the improvement of the condition of their populations. In 1988, as the two Reagan administrations came to an end, to be succeeded by yet another Republican administration under George Bush, I asked about the American welfare state, was it incomplete or different?[1] In 1993, at the end of 12 years of Republican rule nationally, I asked was the American welfare state still exceptional?[2]

The reasons for asking these questions are clear: social protection in the USA, of whatever type, lags considerably behind that which is available in Europe. Whether it is protection against unemployment, or ill-health, or extreme poverty owing to whatever cause, there is less of it in the USA. It is an embarrassment to the American academic, for example, that when a colleague is visiting from another country for a stay in the USA, one's first concern, as a friend, is, does that person and his family have health insurance? We are all unfortunately aware that the high cost of medical care in the USA can bankrupt anyone, and we are aware matters are very different in England, or France, or Germany. When we compare the USA with these and other countries in Europe, we find that, of all the types of social insurance and social protection, probably only one, old-age pensions, provided under the Social Security Act, give benefits that are somewhat comparable to those provided in the economically developed nations of Europe. The USA regularly stands at the bottom of developed nations in the proportion of its gross national product (GNP) devoted to social programmes or to redistribution, at the bottom in what it raises in taxation. Jostling with it at the bottom is generally Japan.

The lagging of the USA in social protection was recently illustrated when the USA celebrated, as it does every May, 'Mother's Day', when Americans are inundated with commercial messages imploring them to shower their mothers with gifts to show their appreciation. The *New York Times* asked, but what does the USA do for its mothers, compared to other countries? Very little, it appears. In an article from Rome titled 'The State of Welfare in Italy: Where Every Day is Mother's Day', one could read of the lavish, by American standards, benefits provided for mothers in Europe. The article informs us:

> Over the last five years a high school teacher here has been on the job only a year and a half, but has drawn a salary for all but a few months. Why? The answer to this riddle, laughably simple for any Italian employer is : the woman is a mother with two babies who has taken advantage of every last clause in one of Europe's most generous maternity leave packages

The article points out that Italy is not unique in its provisions for working mothers. Italy provides 22 weeks of maternity leave, but Britain provides 18 weeks, France 16 weeks, Germany 14 weeks, all with full pay or close to it. The USA had no such provision nationally until 1993, and its new legislation has no requirement for maintaining pay. (But part of salary may be replaced from disability insurance.)[3] Even so, the legislation that provided this limited benefit was fiercely opposed as imposing another cost on hard-pressed American industry.

Our modest provision for maternal leave is typical of many other programmes: America benefits in almost every field came much later than in other countries, and even so are more niggardly.

When we speak of 'American exceptionalism,' this is one of the examples of exceptionalism we have in mind. S.M. Lipset, introducing his recent comprehensive study of American exceptionalism, writes: 'European countries have devoted a much larger share of their GNP to bettering the condition of their working classes and the less privileged generally.'[4] Many explanations for this and other aspects of American difference have been given, starting from almost the first proposed, the absence of a large socialist movement, and socialist-influenced labour movement, in the USA. From one perspective, of course, this is backwardness: it is the situation we find in underdeveloped nations, where it is impossible to provide the kind of social benefits that are typical of the advanced nations. And at one time, now rather far in the past, nations were rated by how much they raised in taxation, how much they redistributed from the better off to the worst off, with the assumption that more was better, as if all the world were fated to become Sweden.

But we are less enamoured today of a single model path for the development of all nations, whether it be in economic growth or social policy. We see somewhat different paths to prosperity, as exemplified in the East Asian nations. And while the alternatives in social policy are not as clearly marked, we are more willing to accept the fact that the paths of even similar states in the development of social policy and social protection can be quite different.

I asked in the first discussion of this issue I referred to above whether the American state was 'incomplete' (which is another way of suggesting, 'backward', because to be incomplete implies that one is on the way to becoming complete). In the second discussion of this issue to which I have referred I asked whether the American welfare state was 'exceptional'. I now think that all these terms are inadequate, because with recent developments in a variety of advanced states I am impelled to ask whether the American welfare state, in its 'backwardness,' 'incompleteness,' or 'exceptionality', may not portend similar developments in the advanced European countries. This is not to deny the very substantial differences among nations and states. And yet there are some similarities that may be pressing almost all the advanced welfare states in the same direction, a direction leading to a condition which has some similarities with that we find in the USA.

In my earlier discussions of the American welfare state, I described a number of circumstances which, I argued, made America different. There were five of these which to me explained these differences. When we examine each of these distinctive circumstances today, it is my impression that the American distinctiveness is being reduced: it is not that America is becoming more like Europe as this distinctiveness is reduced, but rather Europe becomes more like America, both for good and for bad, and as a result we may see a gradual shrinking of the American–European difference.

2.1 FEDERALISM AND ITS SIGNIFICANCE

The first aspect of American distinctiveness to which I referred in explaining the special characteristics of the American welfare state was federalism. The USA was less of a unitary state than the advanced nations of Europe or of Japan. It had 50 states, with a distinctive and protected place in its Constitution, and despite the enormous growth of federal and centralized power since the Depression and the 'new deal', the states still held substantial independent power, in the power to tax, in the ability to create social policies, in the degree to which they adhered to a national standard or norm. One of the more important studies of American social policy in recent years explores in detail the role of the various states in one important area of social policy, aid for poor mothers, demonstrating the important differences among them, and the role of the more advanced states in setting a model for national policy.[5] But because states had already acted in this sphere, it made it harder to establish a uniform national policy in the period of the new deal, when a number of major national social programmes were launched.

Federalism inevitably meant that there were going to be fewer national policies in the sphere of social protection in the USA. Its most controversial social policy, the heir of the state mothers' aid discussed by Skocpol, a programme generally called 'welfare', and that was until its reform in 1996 formally titled Aid to Families with Dependent Children, has always been a joint federal-state programme. Indeed the separation of powers among political authorities in the USA involves more than two tiers. It extends to three, or four, with taxing and policy-setting powers. These lesser political governing authorities have no constitutional protection from state reorganization but they are given great independent powers by the states, which are reluctant to interfere with these powers once granted. Local democracy is not easy to transgress. And so counties and cities often have a separate role in administration or in setting benefit levels. The one million or more persons who receive 'welfare' in New York City get their benefits from a city welfare department, which can set many of its own standards, and part of the huge sums it dispenses are raised by city taxes. This is one reason why the benefits available in different states and cities vary widely.

Similarly, their national programme of Unemployment Insurance is also a federal-state programme, with different benefit levels. Their system of health care for the poor, Medicaid, the most expensive of our programmes for the poor, is also a federal-state programme, with very different benefits from state to state. Some of their key housing assistance programmes, in particular housing assistance for the poor, while funded nationally, are administered locally, by cities and counties. One of the chief characteristics of public housing in the USA – its concentration in the inner cities, its relative absence from the suburbs, is owing to the fact that suburbs, with independent powers of various sorts, can reject federally funded public housing. This of course contributes to ghettoization of the poor and in particular the black population, one of the major contributing factors to the greatest American social problem. There are some major uniform national social programmes. The largest is Social Security, which provides pensions for the retired working population, but there is also a major programme of disability payments under Social Security, which may go to non-workers and even children; and some national programmes targeted to the poor, such as food stamps and the Earned Income Tax Credit (for the working poor). But other major programmes vary from state to state, from city to city.

Federalism not only means that levels of aid will differ, and the character of programs will differ. It also means that these differing levels of aid, whether for welfare or unemployment insurance or housing, may have serious consequences for the economic development and demographic character of cities and states. The heavy participation of states and cities in funding social programmes will make them less attractive to industry subject to taxation for strong social programmes. Existing industries may migrate to states with lower taxation, new and relocating industry will look for locations with the lowest taxation. The existence of these programmes may make certain areas attractive to the poor, and serve as an incentive to attract migrants, or to retain those who under other circumstances might be impelled to seek better opportunities elsewhere. These effects have been much studied. As is so often the case in social research, to come to decisive conclusions is not easy: so many other factors come into the equation that attracts or repels industry, or attracts or repels migrants of differing economic levels. Yet it is hardly likely that these differing benefit and taxation levels are without effect.[6] It is taken for granted in political debate in the USA that these effects are significant.

To protect the benefits given by these effects the political representatives of some states will fight against the nationalization of these programmes, and against the imposition of uniformity. Thus, as Pierson points out, the South, poorer than the rest of the nation, nevertheless fought for decades against a national standard in welfare:

> Proposals for a more national system of welfare would have produced considerable net public transfers to the South, where poverty rates were highest and federal taxes were lowest. But these proposals also would have jeopardized the South's major competitive advantage within the American economy : the availability of a cheap, nonunionized work force. Southern politicians were, in short, pursuing a strategy of 'competition through laxity'.[7]

Does the development of regionalism within the national states of Europe, in various degrees, reaching to such extremes as proposals for the secession of Northern Italy, along with the rise at a supranational level of the EU, portend anything similar in Europe? Up to now, the consequences of both regionalism within national states and the growing strength of the EU have led to very different effects from those we have seen arising from federalism in the USA. The EU provides substantial assistance to the poorer areas, which mitigates regional conflict over such assistance at the national level, since the richer states of the Union pay for such aid; and the incipient rise of supranational EU standards in some areas of social policy, for example, control of migration, leads to more uniformity rather that to greater difference from state to state.

Yet developments of the kind that federalism has given rise to in the sphere of social policy in the USA cannot be foreclosed: 'competition through laxity,' in the effort to attract investment, for example. There is, I believe little of this at the present, and there are of course great differences between 'federalism' in the USA and 'federalism,' or whatever we may wish to call it, in Europe. But one does see a greater similarity with the USA developing in time. (One participant at the Pamplona conference referred to the existence of 'social dumping' as a problem in Europe.) The sovereign states of the EU are of course far stronger than the states of the USA. Can they forgeo in time the kind of competitiveness we see in the USA among the states to attract industry, leading to what has been called 'a race to the bottom'? Will these leave the uniformly high benefit levels of social programmes unaffected?[8]

2.2 DIVERSITY, ETHNICITY, RACE

When we come to the other aspects of American difference in social policy I discussed in these earlier two articles, the convergence between Europe and the USA, and its potential impact on the development of social policy, is greater. Social policy in the USA has been affected by the great religious and ethnic and racial diversity of the country. This diversity has been one reason why so much variation may exist from state to state. Mormon-dominated Utah will not be expected to have the same policies as liberal Massachusetts. The bible belt South cannot be expected to have the same policies as the Scandinavian and Lutheran states of Minnesota and Wisconsin. This diversity is why policies vary from state to state and city to city, and why so much of social policy has been left outside the realm of the state completely, and is retained in the hands of religious bodies, for example, the treatment of foster children who must be taken from their homes. In particular, social policy in the USA has been shaped by the most salient aspect of this diversity: the presence of the African Americans, the largest American minority at 12 per cent of the population, present in large numbers from the origins of the USA, whose condition, first as slaves and then as free men but subjected to severe prejudice and discrimination, has contributed to determining key aspects of the Constitution, and key elements in the pattern of governance.

The special role of the South in preventing national programmes in such areas as welfare and unemployment insurance to which I have referred was driven not only by its desire to preserve its low-wage advantage. As important, when these programmes were being designed, was the South's concern that the national government, affected by the more tolerant attitudes of the North, would set standards which would raise the economic level of the black population, still held in almost rights-less subjection during the period of the New Deal. The two motives were inextricably mixed. The low-wage advantage was in large part owing to the depressed condition of American blacks in the South. Higher welfare would mean that black mothers would no longer serve as a cheap servant class, uniform national unemployment insurance would reduce the pressure on blacks (and whites) to work at low wages, and would equalize (in this respect) the economic condition of blacks and whites. (Of course the low-wage advantage was also the result of low wages to white, non-unionized workers.) As Pierson writes:

> Race and class were inextricably entwined in this system, and both led southern politicians, who represented the ruling white oligarchy, to fiercely guard local prerogatives, particularly when it came to policies governing the labor market. Ruling interests in the South were hostile to any national policies that might weaken black sharecroppers' dependence on the labor market.[9]

Much has changed since the origin of these policies in the 1930s, of course. Black sharecroppers are no longer a significant part of the work force of the South: they were replaced by the mechanical cotton-picker in the 1950s, and blacks flowed into the central cities of the South, the North and the West. White attitudes in the North and the South have converged, under the powerful effects of the civil rights legislation of the 1960s, and the social trends reducing the difference between the South and the rest of the nation. And yet issues related to the black population still play a powerful role in the shaping of social policy in the USA. One wonders whether the growing diversity of the population of Europe under the effects of immigration from Southeastern and Eastern Europe, from North Africa, from the ex-colonial developing world generally, will not lead to similar effects on social policy in Europe.

Perhaps the most significant effect of the black–non-black divide, and of other elements of racial and religious diversity in the USA, has been to reduce the sense of a single nation, of common interests and needs, bound together as a community in some suprafamilial way. Social policy in effect means that the state takes from some to give to others. It is quite understandable that this giving would be more acceptable if the beneficiaries are people like ourselves who simply suffer some unavoidable misfortune or condition – growing old, getting sick, losing a job. The origins of national social policy in the USA are to be found in the Depression, when unemployment rates and the general misery were so high that any American could feel, in considering the more unfortunate, that there but for the grace of God go I. As President Roosevelt said in one of his most famous addresses, he saw one-third of a nation ill-housed and ill-fed.

This sense of communitiy and commonality was further fostered by the enormous national effort of World War II, in which all were engaged, hardly anyone was exempted. One of our greatest national social programmes was the provision of free college education to all the veterans of that war under the GI Bill of Rights. No one begrudged that. It was a programme that was seen as for all Americans: an entire generation, after all, had served in the war, under policies which did not exclude the wealthy or the better educated or the black or the poor. So while many could well have afforded the cost of college education, all accepted a non-income-tested benefit for all who had served. That sense of commonality I would argue also bolstered the second great epoch of American social reform, the mid-1960s, in which Medicare (health insurance for the aged) and Medicaid were established, in which a war on poverty was undertaken, in which major civil rights legislation was passed reflecting a national commitment to black fellow-citizens.

That national commitment to all our fellow-citizens began to weaken in the 1970s. A racial fissure already deep in American society, which had somewhat narrowed in the 1960s, began to widen. Certain errors in national policy contributed to that weakening: for example, policies of affirmative action, which benefited blacks as such in employment, in admission to selective institutions of higher education, in gaining government contracts. and put blacks in direct competition for whites for specific jobs.[10] Aggressive policies of school integration, in particular the bussing of blacks and white children to achieve more integrated schools, also contributed to the growing divide.

But I believe the main factor leading to the widening of the divide was the dawning recognition that the problems of the black American were not going to be solved by simply passing civil rights' laws banning discrimination and segregation.

In effect, blacks, who had been seen in the 1960s, at least by the tolerant majority, as fellow-citizens suffering under unacceptable prejudice and discrimination, whose condition would be alleviated simply by banning discrimination and segregation, began to be seen as a population not like other Americans, but peculiarly afflicted by social problems. The discrimination that had been caused by unreasoning prejudice declined; but it was replaced by a discrimination and segregation based on distaste or fear of differences that could be well documented, such as poorer behaviour and achievement in school, greater deviance from norms in sexual behaviour, a greater rate of crime. Despite the new civil rights regime some of these behaviours from which whites (and middle-class blacks) wanted to distance themselves, such as crime and childbirth out of wedlock, increased. One effect was white resistance to school integration;

another was white resistance to living in the same neighbourhoods as blacks. It became clearer and clearer that white and blacks were divided not only by race but by class.

The problems of blacks were increasingly seen by the white majority as caused by different behaviour rather than by different and unfair treatment, and this became one great source of resistance to the liberalization and nationalization of welfare standards and the expansion of other social programmes benefiting the poor, who are disproportionately black. (About 15 per cent of the American population are considered in poverty, on the basis of a national standard; twice that percentage of blacks are in poverty.) Certainly one cannot ignore the role of residual traditional prejudice in the resistance to expanding programmes that were seen not as programmes for the poor of a common community, but as programmes for others, with whom the spirit of fellowship on the basis of membership in a common nation was weak.

As against the argument that the only difference between the poor and the non-poor was that the former lacked money, the argument was now raised that more money would not change the behaviour of the poor. The opposition to higher and more uniform welfare standards, an objective widely accepted in the 1960s and 1970s, became ever more powerful in the 1980s. The Southern resistance became a national resistance. As against the claims of compassion for the poor, and the more sophisticated argument that more financial assistance to poor mothers with children would help them get on their feet, would improve the performance of their children in school, would bring them into the middle class, came a counterargument that welfare and similar forms of aid based on poverty had no such effects. What, after all, had the expanded welfare benefits of the war on poverty achieved, it was asked?

The opposition to expanded benefits became even more powerful when the argument was raised that the expanded benefits not only did not aid the poor, but that they positively harmed them. To provide aid for the dependant would simply increase their dependency. This argument was made most powerfully by Charles Murray, in his book *Losing Ground*, in 1984.[11] Murray argued that if money was provided to poor mothers because fathers had abandoned children, or fathers and mothers did not work, then more money would only encourage more abandonment by fathers, more irresponsible childbearing by mothers, less work by mothers and fathers. And there was some empirical support for such assertions in large-scale experiments conducted in the 1970s to examine the impact of greater and more liberal welfare benefits.[12]

The argument that providing for the dependant only leads to more dependent behaviour is as old as Tocqueville (at least), but it was resurrected with enormous effect by Charles Murray and other conservative and neoconservative analysts. During the Reagan years, there were efforts to restrict welfare, and to strengthen the requirements that mothers (and fathers) on welfare seek work or prepare for work. These policies surprisingly gained strength among Democrats as well as Republicans. In 1988 a Democratic Congress passed the legislation which went beyond any other in the history of welfare in requiring work or participation in programmes leading to work for adults on welfare.

In 1992, the Democratic candidate for President, Bill Clinton, asserted that he would end welfare 'as we know it', which could only mean that its character as a permanent dole for the dependant would be replaced by even stronger pressures to seek work, and by a time limit on how long persons could be on welfare. In 1994, a Republican Congress was elected for the first time in decades, and Charles Murray's heresies of the 1990s had become commonly accepted truths. The Republican Congress and the Democratic President were locked in battle over what kind of new, harsher welfare reform should be adopted nationally, but this conflict was resolved before the Presidential election of 1996, as President Clinton signed legislation that shocked his liberal supporters. The Federal openended commitment to income support for poor mothers was abandoned. The work requirement became much stronger. Even before the passage of Federal reform legislation, the states, now mostly under Republican governors, adopted measures that would not have been considered possible in the past, or would have been forbidden by the federal government: for example, some cap benefits for welfare recipients so that additional births of children bring no new benefits; or require that teenage mothers live in their parents' homes, rather than becoming eligible for an independent welfare grant; or require that the children in welfare families attend school regularly, with the welfare grant to their parents reduced if they do not.

Welfare narrowly considered, the programme that provides aid for indigent families, is hardly the most expensive or indeed the most problematic aspect of social policy in America. The rapid expansion of the cost and the number of beneficiaries of old-age pensions, as the population ages, is the most serious social policy problem in the USA, when measured by the sums and numbers involved, as is the case in other countries. The costs of medical insurance for the aged (Medicare) and medical benefits for the poor (Medicaid) expands at a phenomenal rate, and dwarfs the sums that go to the low-income population as income support. Yet welfare remains the most contested programme in American social policy. One can propose many reasons for this, but I think a central reason is that it is not seen as a programme for people like themselves by the majority, but is seen as a programme for people qualitatively different, and one reason for this is undoubtedly that blacks form such a high proportion of the people on welfare (about half, nationally).

I go into this story at this length because it raises the question of what will happen to European social benefits as they are seen to go disproportionately to immigrants, and to immigrants different in religion and race, and to fellow-citizens different in religion and race. The first step in Europe toward restricting the growth of racial and regional diversity has been to limit the number of immigrants. But the numbers of legally resident older immigrants and their families are already substantial, and many are citizens with full rights. One may well see a withdrawal in European countries from the most advanced frontier of social policy, not only because these policies are expensive, or are seen as undermining competitiveness, but also because these are seen as programmes for 'others'. Today in the USA we have new laws which restrict social benefits available to non-citizen immigrants. One reason for this is to save money; but another reason is that they are not yet seen as part of the American community. Tragically, a group that is not immigrant, American blacks, whose ancestors were settled in America long before the ancestors of most white Americans, is still seen as not fully part of the community.

2.3 THE VOLUNTARY AND PRIVATE SECTOR

In those earlier articles on the differences that characterized the American welfare state, I spoke of the great American respect, appreciation, even enthusiasm for the private sector, and indeed even the profit-making sector, as against the state and the public authorities. The state and its servants have always been less respected in the USA than in Europe. Americans generally believe no government institution can manage as well as a private one, profit or non-profit, and the general collapse of Communism has of course done nothing to undermine these beliefs. President Bush spoke of a 'thousand points of light', and he had in mind voluntary organizations which would replace or supplement governmental efforts in providing social assistance of various kinds: models for such organizations already existed in profusion (I have spoken above of the religion and ethnic-based organizations that carry out many social functions in the USA) but they had indeed been undermined by the enormous growth of government programmes. In 1996 Presidential candidate Robert Dole proposed that citizens should be able to deduct from their taxes sums they gave to agencies that assisted the poor, and the sums so lost in taxation should be made up by reducing public programmes.

The belief that non-governmental institutions can carry out more efficiently many of the functions that government undertakes, including the functions dealt with by public social programmes, becomes ever stronger.

Libertarians on the right, communitarians on the left, all seem to agree on this. Amitai Etzioni's communitarian movement, with its journal *The Responsive Community: Rights and Responsibilities,* is only one of many organizations that promote the role of voluntary organization in dealing with social problems. It is matched by the similarly titled *Re: Rights and Responsibilities,* published by the American Alliance for Rights and Responsibilities, further to the right, and many other groups could be listed. What characterizes all of them is the desire to restore a society that is not so single-mindedly committed to the strengthening of individual rights, a course which can dissolve communities in the belief that individuals have responsibilities to families and communities that must be recognized and shored up if communities are to survive and thrive. This point of view also becomes more influential in political philosophy, as can be seen in the recent book by Michael Sandel, *Democracy's Discontents: America in Search of a Public Philosophy*[13].

Even more striking is the growing respect for the profit-making sector as possibly providing solutions to some of the key problems in social policy. In welfare, one of the major issues is getting the adult beneficiaries to prepare themselves for, to seek, and to hold jobs in the private sector. Hundreds of public agencies devote themselves to this work; hundreds of voluntary organizations receive public funds to do this work; scores of major experiments in how to foster more attachment to the labour market among welfare beneficiaries have been launched. But recently there has been a good deal of publicity given to profit-making organizations which seems to have a better record in training welfare recipients to take jobs, getting them jobs and supporting them in the behaviour necessary to keep jobs than any public body.

In the field of health, profit-making organizations of all kinds, such as chains of hospitals or nursing homes, grow rapidly to the point where they dominate in more and more fields. Profit-making insurance companies insure the great majority of Americans. This complex system composed of voluntary non-profit-making health-providing organizations (community and university hospitals), profit-making health-providing organizations, a huge public sector which pays for the health of the aged and the poor and maintains chains of hospitals for veterans as well as many other institutions, a huge private insurance sector, is in marked contrast to what we find in European countries. The effort to rationalize the field of health care was the greatest social policy effort of the Clinton administration and its greatest failure. The strength of the private interests, one could argue – the hospital chains, the insurance companies., the pharmaceutical companies, the doctors committed to fee-for-service – was such that rational reorganization to cover the entire population, including that substantial part which is neither covered by private insurance nor eligible for Medicare or Medicaid, failed.[14] That is one interpretation, and there is much truth in it. But when viewed in the large perspective of American history and society, one can say something else: that Americans preferred their disorderly system, even with its large component of profit-making organizations, in a field such as health care where they would seem somewhat inappropriate. They were committed to the free market, whatever its costs and disorder.

This is another respect in which I believe one can see convergence between America and Europe, and yet another respect in which American exceptionalism becomes less exceptional.

2.4 THE PRESENT MOMENT IN THE AMERICAN WELFARE STATE

Today, after Reaganism, after Bush, after the great Republican victory in the Congressional elections in 1994, and despite President Clinton's victory in gaining a second term, scarcely anyone expects we will be expanding public programmes, adding new ones, increasing public expenditure. Public expenditure increases inexorably, as the population ages and the cost of medical care expands, but all attention is devoted to reining in public expenditure. The most popular line of any politician, Republican or Democrat, is that he or she will cut taxes and public expenditure, even though the USA still lags well behind Europe both in the level of taxation and the level of expenditure. Innovation in public policy is to be found only at the state level, and there the innovations consist of ways of cutting back on welfare and Medicaid, programmes over which the states have some control.

The states compete in ingenious approaches to remodelling welfare – limits on how long one can receive welfare, whether in single spells or for a lifetime, new forms of pressure on recipients to train for jobs or take jobs, new forms of punishment – such as deprivation of drivers' licences – if recipients do not meet certain state requirements and so on. State governors' requests for 'waivers' – exemptions from federal requirements – pour into Washington.

Many have noted President Clinton's assertion in his State of the Union address to Congress in 1996 that 'the age of big government is over'. This was a remarkable assertion from a democratic president, since Democrats have presided over the creation and expansion of the American welfare state since they become the dominant party in the 1930s under Franklin D. Roosevelt. What replaces 'big government' is not so clear. We see drives particularly at the state level, whether their governors are Republicans or Democrats, to resort to those aspects of the American approach to social policy that have always been distinctive – federalism, dependence on the voluntary and profit-making sector, a substantial degree of harshness, all contrasting with European centralism, statism, liberalism. Whether these new approaches will only increase hardship – they certainly will to some extent – or strengthen yet another aspect of American distinctiveness, individual reliance to make good in the face of adversity, remains to be seen.

ENDNOTES

1. 'The American Welfare State: Incomplete or different?', ch. 10 in *The Limits of Social Policy*, Harvard University Press, 1988.
2. In a paper available only in Italian: 'Il welfare state statiunitense: ancora un'eccezione?', in *Stato Sociale e mercato mondiale*, a cura di Maurizio Ferrera, Torino, Edizione della Fondazione Giovanni Agnelli, 1993.
3. Celestine Bohlen, 'Where Every Day is Mother's Day', *New York Times*, 12 May 1996, Section VII, pp. 1, 5.
4. Seymour Martin Lipset, *American Exceptionalism: A Double-Edged Sword*, Norton, 1996, p. 22.
5. Theda Skocpol, *Protecting Soldiers and Mothers: The Political Origins of Social Policy in the United States*, Harvard University Press, 1992.
6. See Paul E. Peterson and Mark C. Rom, *Welfare Magnets: A New Case for a National Standard*, Brookings, 1990.
7. Paul Pierson, 'The Creeping Nationalization of Income Transfers in the USA, 1935–94', in Stephan Leibfried and Paul Pierson (eds), *European Social Policy: Between Fragmentation and Integration*, Brookings, 1995, p. 307.
8. On this whole question, see Leibfried and Pierson, op. cit.
9. Pierson, op. cit., p. 307.
10. It would take us too far afield to consider the ramifications of the issue of affirmative action, which has now moved to the center of American politics. An early book, critical of this policy, was Nathan Glazer, *Affirmative Discrimination: Ethnic Inequality and Public Policy* (originally published by Basic Books, 1975, now in print by Harvard University Press).
   Recent books on the controversy include: Barbara Bergmann, *In Defence of Affirmative Action*, New Republic/Basic Books, 1996; Terry Eastland, *Ending Affirmative Action: the Case for Colorblind Justice*, Basic Books, 1996.
11. Charles Murray, *Losing Ground: American Social Policy, 1950–1980*, Basic Books, 1984. For some of the scholarly controversy around the book see Nathan Glazer, *The Limits of Social Policy*, op. cit., ch. 1, footnote 4.
12. Glazer, ibid., Ch. 2.
13. Harvard University Press, 1996.
14. See Theda Skocpol, *Boomerang: Clinton's Health Security Effort and the Turn Against Government in U.S. Politics*, New York, W.W. Norton, 1996; Haynes Johnson and David Broder, *The System: the American Way of Politics at the Breaking Point*, Boston, Little, Brown, 1996.

3. The waning of solidarity? Securing work and income and welfare statism at present

Hans Keman

3.1 INTRODUCTION: CRISIS AND GROWTH OF WELFARE STATISM

In their seminal book on the development of the welfare state, Peter Flora and Arnold Heidenheimer put forward a number of pressing questions with regard to the 'growth and crisis of the variety of publicly financed programmes that have come to be placed under the welfare state rubric' (Flora and Heidenheimer, 1981: 5). The questions raised were – among others :

– Is there really a crisis?
– Is the crisis a product of programme growth?
– Or is it rather a crisis within growth?

Now, 15 years later one can observe that these questions are still relevant ones and remain hotly debated (see for an overview: Esping-Andersen and van Kersbergen, 1992; Keman, 1988; Schmidt, 1989). What is clear by now is that we have indeed a crisis at hand in the Organization for Economic Cooperation and Development (OECD) world. The economic side of the crisis has to do with the 'oil-shocks' (in 1973 and 1979) and the manifestation of the 'stagflation' type of crisis. This situation could not be offset any more by means of Keynesian types of counter-cyclical public policy formation (Scharpf, 1992; Keman, 1993a). In addition, another side of the crisis has been, given the establishment of welfare entitlements in statutory terms, that in almost all advanced capitalist democracies 'programme growth' was inevitable and has led to a growth in public expenditures (see Castles, 1989; Keman, 1993b).

Hence, the questions raised in the Flora and Heidenheimer volume were not only pressing 15 years ago, but remain vital ones to be answered in the 1990s. Firstly, because there is still an economic situation at hand which is characterized by high levels of unemployment and a growing part of the population that is in need of social welfare. Secondly, the growth of welfare-state-related expenditures, which has generated a fiscal crisis due to a lack of economic growth and an increase of servicing public debts, induces political instability and tax-welfare backlashes.

For these reasons, but also in view of the observations made by Flora and Heidenheimer in 1981, it is important to ask ourselves a related – and in my view – very important question:

How have existing welfare states coped with the crisis and in what way have the various systems reshaped their public welfare programmes over time?

In order to answer this question I shall present a concise *contemporary quantitative history* of the political economy of welfare statism. This implies that various models of welfare statism will be scrutinized by means of cross-national data over the period 1960–90. These models will be introduced and analysed in sections 3.2–3.4 and serve the purpose of tracing which factors are still important or even more important in explaining welfare statism today.

Welfare statism is conceptualized in this paper in accordance with the three basic means by which welfare states pursue their goals as described by Flora and Heidenheimer (1981: 25–26). These policy instruments are:

1. Direct payment of cash benefits, that is *transfer payments* (to households) in order to secure income maintenance for those who are not economically active (that is dependent population).
2. Direct public *provision of services* (in kind), that is public goods like education, health care, housing, and other social services in order to respond to societal needs as well as demand (for example hospitals, child care, elderly homes, schooling and housing, training programmes and so on).
3. Indirect instruments of *economic policy* and protective measures with regard to the (national) economy, that is. the size and allocation of the public economy *vis-à-vis* avoiding economic misery (unemployment *and* inflation) and fiscal instability (deficits and state debt).

These instruments of the welfare state are all related to 'security' of *work and income* as well as to 'equality' in terms of access and distribution (see also: Esping-Andersen, 1990: 18–21). The various models under discussion will be explored by means of descriptive and inferential statistics. It will become clear that much of the existing explanations are either not valid *any more*, or conversely are limited as regards to our understanding of how welfare states are actually coping with both crisis and growth in the *1990s*.

In section 3.5, I shall draw together the evidence in relation to the more powerful factors that 'drive' the public programmes of the present welfare state. Instead of trying to come up with an alternative model I shall present a *systemic* overview (that is the internal working of a system), which is a combination of general trends within the universe of discourse in combination with specific features of the cases under review. This type of presentation will allow for discussing the possible future of welfare states in the 1990s, in particular how to cope with the crisis and to reshape a feasible set of policy instruments with regard to welfare statism.

3.2 MODELS OF WELFARE STATISM

Mainstream welfare state theories have modelled explanations, on the basis of the historically unique set of events that transformed free-market capitalism via the simultaneous process of nation-building and democratization, into *national* patterns of state-citizen-family-market relations. Most, if not all, theories have tailored their analytical concepts to the study of the origins, development and variations on the basis of a *cross-national* comparison (Wilensky, 1987). Below I distinguish three mainstream approaches, which all claim not only to explain the shape and size of the welfare state at present, but also – some more, others less – in what direction welfare states are likely to develop.

3.2.1 The Logic of Capitalism, Industrialism and Modernization

The common point of departure is that societal developments create a *functional* demand for social security and state intervention. The development of capitalist socio-economic relations and concomitant industrialization of the mode of production forces the state into action in order to meet the requirements of a stable social order. The logic of industrialism and the coming of 'modern' society stressed much more the correlating development of economic affluence, urbanization and demographic change than the actual diffusion of 'free market capitalism'. Yet all three logics have in common that both origin and development of the welfare state are functionally dependent on the objective problem pressure of societal integration and political order. Hence, *objective conditions* provide the explanation of welfare statism (Rimlinger, 1971; Wilensky, 1975). Wilensky, for instance, explicitly states 'However reluctant the government or affluent citizen may be, they are moved toward the welfare state by needs of political order and stable economic incentives' (Wilensky, 1975:16). In short, the welfare state is a product of the fruits of industrial capitalism which (that is economic affluence) allows for the modernization of society through state intervention.

From this functional logic two predictions follow:

1. The higher the level of economic affluence, the more social welfare can and will be provided, and conversely, the lower (or slower) the rate of economic development the lower (or: slower) the expansion, or perhaps even, the smaller the size of the welfare state over time.
2. If and when economic development and modernization coincide (and they indeed correlate strongly!), as well as this process occurring across more societies than before, then it is expected that both the size of the welfare state and policy instruments used by the state tend to become more similar. This 'convergence' thesis (Kerr, 1960; Pryor, 1968) would then imply that welfare statism is now more *identically* shaped and organized in most advanced and industrialized societies than before.

In summary: if the 'logic' of objective socio-economic conditions holds, then it may be expected that the 'crisis' correlates with socio- economic 'growth' and that this relationship can be observed throughout the OECD world of developed welfare states (see Table 3.1 for the countries that are under review here).

3.2.2 The Impact of 'Objective Conditions' on Welfare Statism

Before discussing the other mainstream theories I shall first scrutinize the functional model. The reason for this is simple: if this model (which was considered by their protagonists as exhaustive, but which should be viewed as parsimonious) is indeed 'fitting' reality, then there would be little need to explore other models in view of our research question. However, as many critics and alternative analyses have already put forward, it may well be doubted that the functional models will supply us with a complete and convincing answer (see for criticisms: Castles, 1982; Schmidt 1989; van Kersbergen, 1995). A second reason to test the impact of 'objective conditions' on the development of welfare statism will assist us in determining to what *extent* other models – which are characterized by the role of state structures (polity), politics and institutions, and parties in governments – are constrained by 'objective conditions'. Moreover, this analytical procedure protects against the fallacy of misplaced primacy of politically driven models and reduces the danger of misspecifying our systemic overview (Schmidt, 1989: 645).

The analysis of the socio-economic model will take place in three steps: firstly, I shall scrutinize the within-variation of the welfare states under review (see Table 3.1). Can one indeed discern a convergent trajectory between 1960–90? Secondly, I shall use the so-called Zöllner-equation to inspect the combined impact of economic affluence and demographic change. This may well demonstrate whether or not these factors are (still) relevant and to what extent. Thirdly, I shall inspect the separate impact of the 'objective conditions' (if proven relevant) by comparing the developments between 1960 to 1990 with those between 1975 to 1990. This will demonstrate whether or not 'objective conditions' (or: socio-economic development) in a situation of crisis are influencing welfare state developments.

Table 3.1 Expenditures of general government (% GDP)

Country	PE60	PE75	PE90	PE6090	PE7590
Australia	18.900	27.600	34.900	16.000	7.300
Austria	25.400	38.600	48.600	23.200	10.000
Belgium	27.800	41.200	53.100	25.300	11.900
Canada	26.600	36.800	46.900	20.300	10.100
Denmark	21.700	43.500	56.600	34.900	13.100
Finland	21.900	32.200	45.400	23.500	13.200
France	30.200	39.200	49.900	19.700	10.700
Germany	28.200	43.400	46.000	17.800	2.600
Greece	17.800	26.700	48.100	30.300	21.400
Ireland	24.500	42.000	41.900	17.400	−0.100
Italy	26.600	38.300	49.800	23.200	11.500
Netherlands	28.000	51.100	51.700	23.700	0.600
Norway	28.000	41.800	51.600	23.600	9.800
Portugal	15.200	27.200	39.300	24.100	12.100
Spain	13.700	21.200	36.200	22.500	15.000
Sweden	28.700	44.900	59.100	30.400	14.200
Switzerland	19.100	28.800	32.300	13.200	3.500
UK	29.300	41.000	38.000	8.800	−2.900
USA	25.000	33.600	34.600	9.600	1.000
	PE60	PE75	PE90	PE6090	PE7590
Range	16.500	29.900	26.800	26.100	24.300
Mean	24.032	36.795	45.479	21.447	8.684
Standard Deviation	5.006	7.733	7.803	6.727	6.291
Coefficient or Variation	0.208	0.210	0.172	0.314	0.724

Table 3.2 Expenditures, consumption of general government (% of GDP)

	GOVCON60	GOVCON75	GOVCON90	GC6090	GC7590
Australia	9.700	15.500	17.100	7.400	1.600
Austria	12.900	17.200	18.000	5.500	0.800
Belgium	12.600	16.400	17.500	4.900	1.300
Canada	14.300	20.000	20.100	5.800	0.100
Denmark	12.700	24.600	25.400	12.700	0.800
Finland	12.600	17.500	21.100	8.500	3.600
France	12.900	14.400	18.000	5.100	3.600
Germany	13.600	20.800	19.900	6.300	−0.900
Greece	11.400	15.200	20.300	8.900	5.100
Ireland	12.200	19.000	19.200	7.000	0.200
Italy	12.100	15.400	17.000	5.200	1.900
Netherlands	14.600	18.200	16.300	1.700	−1.900
Norway	12.700	19.300	21.000	8.300	1.700
Portugal	10.900	15.400	15.500	4.600	0.100
Spain	8.800	9.200	13.700	4.900	4.500
Sweden	17.100	23.800	27.100	10.000	3.300
Switzerland	10.200	12.600	13.300	3.100	0.700
UK	16.800	22.000	19.900	3.100	−2.100
USA	17.900	18.900	18.100	0.200	−0.800
	GOVCON60	GOVCON75	GOVCON90	GC6090	GC7590
Range	9.100	15.400	13.800	12.500	7.200
Mean	12.947	17.653	18.868	5.958	1.242
Standard Deviation	2.417	3.778	3.432	2.971	2.052
Coefficient of Variation	0.187	0.214	0.182	0.499	1.652

Table 3.3 Total expenditures of general government on transfer payments to households (% of GDP)

Country	TRANS60	TRANS75	TRANS90	TRAN6090	TRAN7590
Australia	5.500	8.800	10.800	5.300	2.000
Austria	12.900	16.900	21.000	8.100	4.100
Belgium	11.300	18.800	21.400	10.100	2.600
Canada	7.900	10.900	12.400	4.500	1.500
Denmark	7.400	13.900	16.400	9.000	2.500
Finland	5.100	9.600	11.600	6.500	2.000
France	13.500	20.600	23.300	9.800	2.700
Germany	12.000	18.400	16.600	4.600	−1.800
Greece	5.300	7.400	13.800	8.500	6.400
Ireland	5.500	14.900	17.000	11.500	2.100
Italy	9.800	16.000	17.300	7.500	1.300
Netherlands	10.300	25.600	26.400	16.100	0.800
Norway	8.300	13.600	16.400	8.100	2.800
Portugal	3.000	8.500	10.900	7.900	2.400
Spain	2.300	9.300	16.200	13.900	6.900
Sweden	8.200	15.100	18.900	10.700	3.800
Switzerland	6.200	10.100	13.600	7.400	3.500
UK	6.800	10.900	14.600	7.800	3.700
USA	5.000	11.500	11.000	6.000	−0.500
	TRANS60	TRANS75	TRANS90	TRAN6090	TRAN7590
Range	11.200	18.200	15.600	11.600	8.700
Mean	7.700	13.726	16.295	8.595	2.568
Standard Deviation	3.230	4.811	4.401	2.983	2.039
Coefficient of Variation	0.420	0.351	0.270	0.347	0.794

Notes
In Tables 3.1–3.3 the dependent variables, that is, the public expenditures on the policy instruments used to pursue welfare state goals (defined in the introduction), are presented. PE represents the size of the state intervention in relation to gross domestic product (GDP). It is an indirect measure of the weight of the public economy *vis-à-vis* the market economy (Cameron, 1978; Keman, 1993b).
GOVCON indicates the extent to which the state provides and organizes services to the public (in kind). Military expenditures and social security are excluded. Hence this variable is a proxy of the size of the public sector and state agencies (Lane *et al.*, 1991: 75).
TRANS is the extent to which social security expenditures are directly allocated to individuals and thus redistributed by the state.
Note all data are derived from various OECD publications.

Even a cursory glance at the cross-national differences, as well as the variation across time in Table 3.1, reveals that there is little ground to expect a convergent pattern of state intervention and welfare statism. The cross-national range of all variables increases over time, both in level (compare 1960–90) and in growth: the public economy grows on average from 24 per cent in 1960 to 45.5 per cent in 1990. Transfer payments double over the same period, whereas government consumption increases by one third (cross-national averages). At the same time, however, it can be observed that between 1975 and 1990 a drastic change occurs: on average the growth rates of the public economy, government consumption and transfers sink dramatically as compared to 1960–75. Hence, it appears that the growth of welfare statism has not only slowed down significantly, but it should also be noted that the cross-national variation – judging the range and standard deviation – remains quite substantial throughout the whole period.

In conclusion, between 1960 and 1990 the welfare state has grown considerably, although this development slows down after 1975. There is little room to argue that this development is of a convergent nature. Only the decrease in expenditure levels indicates to some extent that the internal variation is less than before (the coefficient of variation shows this). Yet this observation is not convincing as the growth rates appear to produce more variation over time. Notwithstanding this conclusion, it may well be that the cross-national variation over time is produced by 'objective conditions'. To this I shall now turn.

The Zöllner-model (Schmidt, 1989: 646–647) is based on the ideas of the 'functional' school discussed above. It predicts that the level of welfare provision is dependent on the growth of economic resources of a society and the proportion of the population that is dependent on nonmarket income (that is decommodified income; Esping-Andersen, 1990: 21–23).[1] The rationale behind this model is that the wider the 'gap' between more and less wealthy nations is, the larger the differences in welfare statism will become. Conversely, if the 'gap' tends to disappear the more convergent the shape and provision of social welfare may become (Lane and Ersson, 1990: 58).

Below I shall present the results of this model in two steps:

1. The model consists of economic and demographic variables only (that is. growth of GDP per capita; labour force population ratios and size of dependent population, that is. under 15 and over 65 years). This can be seen as the 'pure' model.
2. I shall extend the pure model by means of controlling for incremental effects (that is expenditures at t–1) and cyclical influences. This allows for inspecting to what extent 'structural' features are amplified by dra-

matic socio-economic developments, on the one hand, and the growth of the public sector, on the other. The 'pure' version of the Zöllner-model performed extremely poorly for our universe of discourse:

– Economic affluence and labour force population appeared only relevant for the level of government consumption (in 1990) taking into account the rate of change after 1975 (R^2 = 25 per cent).

– The same result was found for government consumption in relation to dependent population and economic affluence between 1975–90 (R^2 = 34.6 per cent).

These results can be interpreted as follows: economic development and demographic change are hardly relevant for explaining the welfare efforts of the state in the modern societies of 1990. Only the direct services rendered by state agencies are to some extent a result of national wealth and demographic changes in society. Hence, these outcomes signify that the original models of the 'functional' school are – at least in view of this evidence – not valid any more today. The only finding which to some extent fits the 'functional' model is that the level of transfer payments (1990) is related to the growth of the dependent population, if and when over 65 years and after 1975 (R^2 = 28.3 per cent). Apparently the impact of pension schemes organised through the state has produced this result over time.

The analysis by means of the Zöllner-model leads us to the conclusion that the original factors that induced welfare state cannot be considered as 'prime' movers with regard to the shaping and development of the welfare state in the 1990s. Moreover, our analysis shows that, regardless of cross-national variation in economic affluence and demographic change, the policy instruments are either continued or changed, which means that other factors are in play. Only the growth of the dependent population *after 1975* appears to influence the provision of welfare services (for example elderly homes and personnel) and the level of transfer payments (pensions) as a consequence of the ageing population (the statistical relations between these policy instruments and dependent population are (Pearson's r): 0.57 and 0.48 respectively).

Yet, there is no such trend among the OECD countries: we found a number of outliers in terms of a considerable 'underperformance' in Australia, Ireland, Italy, Portugal, Spain and Switzerland, and hardly 'overperformers'. Only in Denmark and the Netherlands the public expenditures are comparatively generous with regard to population change. Hence, a converging development cannot be observed. Although Ireland, Portugal and Spain can be seen as relative economic laggards in terms of affluence, the other countries cannot. Moreover, the Dutch level of economic affluence, for instance, is equal to or even lower than that of Italy, Switzerland and Australia, which belong to the 'underperformers'.

Let us therefore now turn to the *extended Zöllner-model* which attempts to capture the path dependence of national levels of expenditure, on the one hand, and the cyclical influence of rates of unemployment, on the other. Although the overall performance of this extended version is not strong either, and – as may be expected – the incremental effects of policy inheritance are apparent (see also: Heidenheimer *et al.*, 1990; Keman, 1993b), the direct involvement of the welfare state shows up with regard to the level of transfer payments in the 1990s. This is quite understandable: and can be attributed to, as we already surmised, the increase in the ageing population as well as the growing participation in the labour market after 1975. Yet the additional value of the extended Zöllner-model is that it demonstrates the impact of the consequences of the economic crisis (simultaneous growth of unemployment and demographic change). This is particularly visible in relation to the rate of unemployment in general as well as the rate of unemployment for women. These effects are, again, particularly noticeable *after 1975*. The model performs as follows:

1. Level of transfer payments in 1990 (Y) = constant + level in 1960 (B = 1.02) + growth of unemployment 1960–90 (B = 0.50)
   R^2 = 65.1 per cent.
2. Level of transfer payments in 1990 (Y) = constant + level in 1975 (B = 0.81) + growth of unemployment 1975–90 (B = 0.27)
   R^2 = 80.6 per cent.
3. Level of transfer payments in 1990 (Y) = constant + level in 1960 (B = 1.01) + growth of female unemployment 1960–90 (B = 0.32)
   R^2 = 62.1 per cent.
4. Level of transfer payments in 1990 (Y) = level in 1975 (B = 0.81) + growth of female unemployment 1975–90 (B = 0.72)
   R^2 = 80.9 per cent.

On the basis of the multi-variate analysis of the extended Zöllner-model it can be deduced that in general the objective, or socio-economic conditions, do not directly influence the size and type of state intervention, nor do they direct policy instruments of the welfare state. This observation is reinforced if one notes that the 'outliers' with regard to the extended model are Austria, Greece, Sweden, Germany and the USA, countries that have little similarity in economic and demographic developments.

This inspection of the 'logics' of industrialism, capitalism and modernization by means of the Zöllner-model reveals that – although economic affluence and demographic change do correlate with types of public expenditure – they have a limited impact on social policy efforts in welfare states today. As for instance Lane and Errson (1990: 142) and

Heidenheimer *et al.* (1990: 224) have correctly pointed out, size and growth of the public sector and welfare statism in particular are conditional upon a certain level of affluence and contingent upon demographic change. At the same time, however, our empirical analysis has demonstrated that, once the welfare state has been established and has grown over time other factors are becoming more important in explaining its present format and level of expenditures.The divergent pattern can be manifested by looking at the scatterplots of the relationships between the level and growth of government consumption and transfer payments (1960–90) (see Figures 3.1 and 3.2):

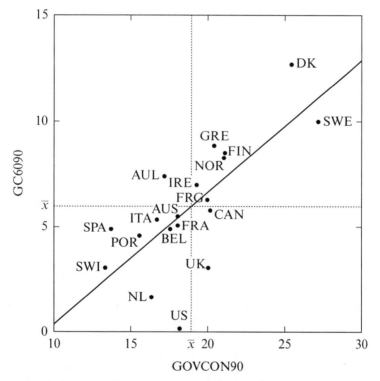

Figure 3.1 Relationship between growth and level of government services

Notes: Based on change in government consumption (percentage GDP) 1960–90.
GOVCON90: level of government consumption (percentage GDP) in 1990.
$\bar{x}$ = mean value.

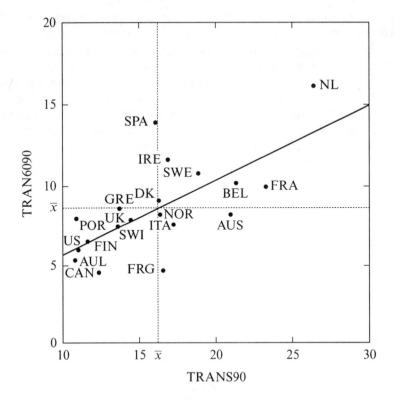

Figure 3.2 Relationship between growth and level of transfer payments

Notes: TRAN6090: Change in transfer payments to households (percentage GDP) 1960–90
TRANS90: Level at transfer line to households (percentage GDP) in 1990. $\bar{x}$ = mean value.

The countries that are located in the right-hand upper cell are those that can be considered as 'fast growing and high level' welfare states (for example. Denmark and Sweden regarding the provision of social services, see Figure 3.1; the Netherlands with respect to social security, see Figure 3.2). Conversely, countries in the left-hand lower cell belong to the opposite category (for example Switzerland and the Netherlands in Figure 3.1 and Canada and Australia in Figure 3.2). Countries in these cells have a limited unchanging level of welfare statism. Apart from the observable variation in growth and level of welfare statism, Figures 3.1 and 3.2 also demonstrate that there is a substantial variation in *types* of social welfare provision by the state: the Netherlands is a clear example of a 'social security' welfare state, whereas Denmark is much more a 'social service' welfare state (Keman, 1993b).

Again, it may be concluded that evidence for patterns of convergence is lacking, and in addition, that the influence of incremental spending *and* the cyclical impact of unemployment, in particular after 1975, only demonstrate that welfare states have developed *specific* formats and levels of welfare statism. These factors – together with the *effects* of socio-economic development – appear to determine to some extent the scope and range of the present welfare state. Yet, it is equally clear that – bearing in mind the weak performance of the simple Zöllner-model, other factors than socio-economic and demographic ones, need also to be examined to account for the way the nations under review here have coped with the problem of growth and crisis of the welfare state in a mixed economy. This brings us to the 'politics-does-matter' approach.

3.3 POLITICS, IDEOLOGY AND POLITICAL MOVEMENTS

In their contribution to Flora and Heidenheimer (1981: 58ff) that focuses on 'why and how welfare states grew' they already pointed to two key factors that may well influence welfare state development: class mobilization and constitutional factors. Much of the cross-national literature has used these concepts and elaborated them in various approaches (see, for example, Castles, 1982; Korpi, 1983; Keman, 1988; Schmidt, 1989; Esping-Andersen, 1990; Scharpf, 1992; Van Kersbergen, 1995). In this section I shall consider to what extent socio-political movements, which have (had) strong views on welfare and society, do indeed affect the development of welfare statism. In addition I shall look into the role of political parties as agencies which guide or direct welfare state developments. Let us first turn to 'politics' and 'movements'.

3.3.1 Does Politics Matter?

This debate can be seen as a reaction to the first model I discussed. The issue at hand was whether or not political factors could account for the cross-national variation in welfare state development, how they were shaped, which direct policy instrument was chosen and implemented. The consensus among most comparative studies has been that party differences and the impact of social democracy in particular was an important factor (Korpi, 1983; Keman, 1988). However, the timing and content of welfare state policies, although heavily influenced by the strength and ideology of parties, remained a topic of debate and related research. About how exactly these influences worked there has been much less consensus.

I distinguish *two types* of explanation within this 'school':

1. those researchers that adhere to the thesis of the 'social democratization of capitalism', or alternatively the impact of 'Christian democracy',
2. those who explicitly depart from the dynamics of 'party behaviour' within a national party system (see for an overview: Schmidt, 1995).

Both approaches emphasize the role of collective actors that pursue their ideological goals by means of influencing governmental policy-making choices.

The first approach heavily relies on the organization of political movements with a specific ideology concerning the shaping of society. The second approach focuses considerably on the strength of parties and the policy distances between them. As Esping-Andersen and van Kersbergen (1992) have argued, the results may well be biased towards the 'fitting' cases rather than being capable of accounting for the variation across all cases, in particular in the long run (note, for instance, the exception to the rule, that is the Dutch case; see Therborn, 1989). Of course many alternative explanations have been offered, but – however valuable they are – these were not counter-arguments, but rather offering additional variables, which were attempts to 'save' the original idea that political movements and parties are crucial actors in shaping welfare state policies and related efforts (see, for example, Cameron, 1978; Castles and Mitchell, 1991; Schmidt, 1995). For our purposes, however, it is less important to re-enter into this debate, but rather to assess the relative impact of movements and ideology on welfare statism, on the one hand, and the impact of party behaviour in democratic government on the growth and level of welfare state related policy-making, on the other. If these factors are indeed important, then they may well have a strong bearing on the future development of the size and type of welfare statism to come.

3.3.2 The Impact of Christian Democracy and Social Democracy

Several authors have stressed that, apart from social democracy, the political movement representing Christianity is a powerful collective actor with strong and coherent ideas on social welfare (Wilensky, 1981; Castles, 1994; Van Kersbergen, 1995). In fact, one could even argue that their impact would be larger because the 'natural' roots in society of this religious movement are stronger than social democracy (perhaps with the exception of the Nordic countries). In addition to that, Christian democracy is not a 'natural' enemy of Liberal or Conservative parties, which may imply that their impact can be more continuous in multi-party systems and in countries which are strongly populated by Catholics, in particular by means of coalition government (Budge and Keman, 1990).

Social democracy, on the other hand, is represented in all countries that are studied in this paper. In addition to their sizeable support in most countries, they are well organized by means of trade unions (over 40 per cent in cross-national averages, whereas the number of Catholics averages cross-nationally around 50 per cent). Social democratic governance, however, is much more volatile over time and is heavily concentrated in particular countries and periods. Hence, their impact on welfare statism is either geographically limited or of a temporary nature. It appears therefore a tenable thesis to expect that both movements will influence welfare state developments, but in a different way (Keman, 1990).

Having said this I shall conduct a test of the influence of both political movements on welfare statism by taking into account their ideological views, their relative electoral support and participation in government. In addition, I expect that both movements will have a different impact on both the *level and growth* of welfare-related policy-making *vis-à-vis* other non-socialist and secular parties. Finally, I shall also investigate whether or not the *type* of welfare provisions is different, if and when Christian democracy or social democracy is more (or less) dominant (considering the patterns that evolved from Figures 3.1 and 3.2).

Before presenting the results of the analysis I shall elaborate on the ideological differences between party families. These are derived from an international data-set composed by the Manifesto Research Group (see for details: Budge *et al.*, 1987 and Klingemann *et al.*, 1994). I have constructed three variables which indicate the extent to which Christian Democratic and Social Democratic parties emphasize the need of state intervention, the provision of social services and the urge for transfer-related expenditures. The following scores are obtained for 1960–90 period (see Table 3.4):

Table 3.4 Party families and statism

Party family	Statism	(Ranking order)	Services	(Ranking order)	Transfer	(Ranking order)	Total
Social Democrats	14.6%	(1)	8.1%	(1)	14.6%	(1)	37.3% (1)
Christian Democrats	14.2%	(2)	6.3%	(2)	10.7%	(2)	31.2% (2)
Liberals	14.1%	(3)	5.8%	(3)	11.1%	(3)	31.0% (3)
Conservatives	11.7%	(4)	4.3%	(4)	7.8%	(4)	23.8% (4)

Notes: Each score represents the N of (quasi)sentences in each party manifesto of parties belonging to the party family mentioned that stress these issues (in percentage of the whole manifesto. See, for further methodological details, Volkens, 1994).

It is clear that Conservative parties are in all respects different from other party families. It is equally obvious that other parties hardly differ with respect to the need for state intervention. Yet, the most striking result is that both Liberal and Christian Democratic parties are quite equivocal on welfare statism. Hence, if there is a differential impact from political *movements* then it should be visible and noticeable through social democracy (emphasizing welfare statism most) and Christian democracy (being a movement-cum-party, which the Liberals are not).

Therefore I shall inspect this proposition by relating both ideology and political strength of the movement to the various types of public expenditure used in this analysis. Since we know that policy patterns are strongly influenced by past spending, the focus will be on the change in levels of expenditure rather than on the levels themselves. The results of our analysis show that the actual growth of public expenditures is *not* directly related to ideological positions of political movements. Basically three factors show up from our multivariate analysis that affect the development of welfare-related expenditures:

1. The voting power of parties.
2. The degree of unionization.
3. The emphasis on welfare in social democratic programmes.

As regards to the growth of the public sector one observes that unionization plays a role, which is reinforced by the strength of left-wing parties (if available) and is enhanced if there is a strong party on the right. This outcome is concurrent with earlier findings of Korpi (1983), Keman (1988) and Castles (1994).

These models rendered an explained variance of 45.8 per cent (for the growth of the public sector between 1960–90) and 33.0 per cent (for 1975–90). It should be noted that ideological differences do not appear significantly in this equation. This is only the case (and only to some extent) with regard to the growth of government consumption and transfer payments. In both models the role of electoral support is, again, important. Unionization and ideology add significantly to the increase of government consumption (R^2 = 59.8 per cent for 1960–90; R^2 = 49.1 per cent for 1975–90). The same pattern applies to transfer payments, albeit at a lower level (R^2 = 20.9 per cent for 1960–90 and 25.2 per cent for 75–90).

All in all, it can be concluded that political movements do matter as regards to welfare statism. Yet the ideological weight appears to have been overstated and appears to fade after 1975 (which is in line with the findings regarding socio-economic circumstances and change in section 3.2). Conversely, the actual power distribution of parties (electoral strength), and the degree of working class mobilization (unionization) are more powerful in explaining the growth – and more often than not the slow-down in public expenditures (see Table 3.1) – of the public sector and the welfare-related expenditures in particular after 1975. In addition to these findings it must be noted that the impact of Catholicism and unionization does make a difference with respect to the *type* of welfare statism that comes about in the various countries under review. In Catholic countries with a strong Christian democracy the level and growth of social security expenditures is often high (see the positions of, for instance, Spain, France, Ireland and Belgium in Figure 3.2). In contrast, none of these countries appear in the right-hand upper cell of Figure 3.1 whereas all the Nordic countries do (and Greece).

The main conclusion to be drawn from the analysis of the 'political movement' model may be therefore that social democracy is an important actor in promoting state intervention and guiding the type of welfare sta-tism. At the same time, however, it can be observed that political movements, as well as their ideological views, have a less direct and imper-ative effect than has often been claimed. What does appear to matter is their power to conserve the existing welfare state after 1975, which is then more contested by other parties without a supporting movement than before that time. In other words, the actual policy-making efforts in the recent period of economic stagnation and austerity seem to be a matter that is decided by and large *within* the decision-making context of parlia-mentary democracy: party-government.

3.3.3 The Impact of Parties in Government on Welfare Statism

There is abundant literature on the role of parties in government *vis-à-vis* policy-making (Budge and Keman, 1990: ch. 5 and 10; Lane and Ersson, 1990: ch. 6; Schmidt, 1995). The overriding conclusion of this literature is that 'parties-in-government-do-matter', but the way they do varies consid-erably across nations and across time. In this section I shall confine myself predominantly to the question raised in the introduction: what is the role of party-government at this moment, and how relevant are governments *vis-à-vis* the shaping and direction of the welfare state in the 1990s?

In order to investigate this question I have made use of indicators that have been used by many researchers in this field (see, for an overview, Woldendorp *et al.*, 1993 and Schmidt, 1995). The following variables were used in the 'party-government' model:

1. Strength of the left, centre and right in government (percentage of either type of parties represented in government; Schmidt, 1995)

2. Complexion of parliament and government or: CPG (Ranking Order of degree of dominance of left, centre and right together in government and parliament; 5 = Left dominant; 3 = balance; 1 = Right dominant; Woldendorp *et al.*, 1993).

In addition the role of ideology (see Table 3.4) was controlled for. The equation used was:

$$y = a + b \,(CPG) + b \,(L\text{-}C\text{-}RGov) + b \,(\text{welfare ideology}).$$
y = public expenditures: total, government consumption and transfer payments (see Tables 3.1–3.3).

The results are quite interesting. Generally, like the impact of political movements, the role of parties in government is significant for the period *after 1975* only. Secondly, again as was the case with political movements, the centre (which is more often than not identical with Christian democracy, see Keman, 1994) is not the main actor, let alone the prime mover in this context. Thirdly, right-wing governments tend to play a strong role in slowing down or even reducing levels of expenditures, in particular in relation to transfer payments.

Finally, the more the left-wing (or in fact: social democracy) dominates party-government, the more is spent (or less is reduced) in general, but this is especially visible with regard to the direct provision of welfare services (government consumption). Conversely, transfer payments appear to be the most contested type of welfare policy, which is quite understandable since this type of welfare provision is the lowest priority of conservative, or right-wing parties (see Table 3.4). It appears to matter whether the left or right is dominant in government, on the one hand, and whether the centre is also in government with either the left or the right (as measured by the complexion of parliament and government).

The statistical results were predominantly robust ($p \leq 0.01$) for the change in expenditure levels between 1975–90 and the level of transfer payment in 1990 across our universe. The explained variance is 40 per cent for the public sector size (PE), 57 per cent for government consumption, and 37 per cent for transfer payments (between 1975–90). Looking at the cross-national distribution of the countries (by means of residual analysis), the following countries increased or decreased their level of expenditures *more* than would be expected on the basis of their government composition.

Policy	Overspending	Underspending
Public sector (= PE)	Canada	Australia
	Denmark	Germany
	Ireland	Switzerland
	Portugal	United Kingdom
Government consumption	Finland	Australia
	Greece	Austria
	Spain	Germany
		The Netherlands
Transfer payments	Greece	Australia
	Spain	Germany
	The Netherlands	USA

(Outliers are those with a residual value of $\geq 1 * SD$)

This pattern is by and large identical to the one of the previous model. This is not surprising, but what should be noted is that the majority of outliers that are underspending belong to either federal countries (for example. Australia, Germany, Switzerland and the USA), and that the 'laggards' in welfare state development (like Spain, Ireland, Portugal and Greece) are clearly overspending in order to 'catch up'. In the former case one may suspect that the state structure is a relevant additional variable to explain their consistent pattern of 'underspending'. In the latter case, it may well be that the 'objective conditions' and late(r) process of democratization make the majority of these countries perform in accordance with the factors that were relevant in the early stages of welfare state expansion elsewhere.

This short discussion on the 'outliers', however, also proves that although political actors, be it parties and political movements or parties in government, do influence patterns of welfare statism. It is also evident that these actors are, in one way or another, also constrained by other factors and produce a cross-national variation that is in need of further analysis. This conclusion brings us to the third mainstream model or 'school' of welfare statism: the institutional approach. To this I shall now turn.

3.4 POLITICAL INSTITUTIONS AS CRUCIAL MECHANISMS FOR THE WELFARE STATE?

Until now I have concentrated on the role and impact of 'objective conditions' and 'collective actors'. The first can indeed be considered as contingencies for policy-making. The second are important as being more or less effective agents of societal interests and collective preferences. Yet, what is underrepresented or, at least, not comprehensively taken into account in those analyses is the role of institutions (that is humanly devised constraints that shape behaviour and allow for specific types of actions; see Colomer, 1995). This, what I would like to label, *polity-centred* approach typically denies the simple linkage between social (aggregated) interests and societal needs, on the one hand, and the results of political actions of parties, movements and organized interests, on the other, with policy-making. Viewed in this way the polity focus is a challenge to the models outlined and analysed earlier in this paper.

The institutional approach rather focuses on the autonomous operation of political institutions and the institutional effects that often manifest themselves in path dependent policy-making (Putnam, 1993). Recall that we found, together with the cyclical effects of unemployment rates, that incremental effects also shape state-related welfare policies. In addition, it was observed that, although the collective actors representing movements and parties did add to the explanation of cross-national differences in policy expenditures, this effect was not very strong. Instead, we found that ideology and power resources play an indirect rather than a direct role. Hence, according to the institutional school (for example Steinmo *et al.*, 1992), the rules and regulative capacities of national states (see Skocpol, 1985) can be considered as crucial mechanisms determining the shape and direction of welfare state development. In fact, such a position implies that we may better understand how the various countries under review here have coped with the limits of growth as well as with the problem of reshaping the welfare state in recent times, if and when we take institutions into account (see also Flora and Heidenheimer, 1981: 337).

Below in section 3.4.1 I shall report the impact of both the 'polity-centred' model and in addition to this the influence of decentralization of government with regard to acquiring resources and autonomous policy-making on welfare statism.

3.4.1 Policy Features and Welfare Statism

Three indicators have been used to measure the impact of constitutional factors:

– *Federalism* or not, which is simply a three-point scale differentiating between fully-fledged unitarian states and federal ones. Some countries, however, cannot be considered to belong to either of these categories (for example Belgium, after 1970, Austria, and to some extent Italy and were scored in between (= 2); the data are taken from Lane *et al.*, 1991).
– *Lijpharts' indicator for centralization*, which is based on several indicators, containing, for instance, the degree of central government tax

income and controls on and opportunities for central authorities and executives (that is degree of 'Checks and Balances'; Lijphart, 1984; the data are taken from Schmidt, 1995: 15).

– *Institutional constraints* as developed by Colomer (1995: 20), in which a number of constitutional elements, as have been used by Lijphart, are reconstructed as a cumulative index of formal 'barriers' to the influence of central authorities (in particular concerning the 'executive' branch).

The latter two variables can be seen as constraints of the central powers of government. It is expected therefore (partly on the basis of the residual analysis reported in the previous sections) that public expenditures as a whole, and thus for the welfare state services too, will be lower in federal than in unitary states. Furthermore strongly centralized polities are not constrained in the exercise of their authority. In short, I expect centralized and unitary states to have more *policy-room* to manoeuvre than other states. The following 'polity-centred' model was used:

Y (= policy) = a + b (federalism) + b (institutional constraints) + b (centralization)

The results applied to the policy-related variables are shown in Table 3.5:

Table 3.5   Welfare statism and the polity model

Policy	Polity indicators (+/– is direction of impact)	$R^2 =$
PE 6090	Institutional Constraints (–)+	
	Centralization (–)	40.6%
PE 7590	Centralization (–)	18.9%
PE 90	Institutional constraints (–)	25.1%
GC 6090	Institutional constraints (–)	25.4%
GC 7590	Centralization (–)	18.7%
GC 90	Institutional constraints (–)	27.4%
TRANS 6090	Federalism (–)	41.0%
TRANS 7590	Federalism (–)+	
	Institutional constraints (–)	31.8%
TRANS 90	Federalism (–)	21.5%

Notes: The indicator mentioned is the statistically significant one ($p \leq 0.01$) and the direction is indicated by the +/– sign between brackets (hence in all cases the independent variable produces a lower increase in expenditures). Analysis based on data in Tables 3.1 and 3.2

It is immediately clear that indeed the type of state and the related institutional room for manoeuvre does matter, and it matters most regarding the long-term change in expenditures. Secondly, centralization appears to be more relevant for short-term change (that is between 1975–90). Thirdly, that the level and change in transfer payments appears to be strongly influenced by the division between federal and unitary countries. In other words, the interplay or configuration of various formal institutions do limit the level and in particular the change of public expenditures as a whole, but not those related to the formal entitlements that are part of the direct involvement of the state regarding income maintenance programmes. Federal states thus differ from others regarding their levels of expenditures on transfer payments, but it should be noted that in some of these the procedure for financing of this type of welfare statism is differently organized (in particular in the non-British Anglo-Saxon group of nations, (see Castles and Mitchell, 1991).

If one inspects the 'outliers' of this model then it is worth noting that, apart from the notorious big spenders, like Sweden and Denmark, and the small spenders, like Switzerland and the UK – the socio-economically less wealthy countries are consistently characterized by a high rate of growth of the public sector, but also having still comparatively lower levels of expenditure in 1990. This pattern is also visible in transfer payments, but not in government consumption. This finding is not too surprising, since the latter variable indicates the extent to which welfare services are organized through the central state. In terms of residuals there is a clear distinction between those countries that rely on cash-return *vis-à-vis* services-in-kind (see Flora and Heidenheimer, 1981: ch. 2; Keman, 1993b). The best example of the 'cash-return' welfare state is The Netherlands, whereas Sweden and Denmark are good examples of the state-led provisions of services-in-kind (see also Figures 3.1 and 3.2). Yet, most noticeable is the fact that, according to the statistical results, such a division can also be observed for the 'late' developers of welfare statism: Greece and Spain appear to develop in the direction of a rapid expanding public sector in combination with cash-return payments, whereas Portugal and Ireland seem to develop the opposite pattern with respect to services-in-kind (this finding is supported if one looks at the 'outliers' reported in the previous sections).

In summary, constitutional arrangements of advanced democracies have an impact on public sector growth and on the use of related expenditures. Nations that are more centrally organized and not strongly constrained in their executive powers appear to spend more than others. Yet, this effect does not show up with regard to transfer payments. Here the territorial limits of executive power tend to dampen the general redistribution of income maintenance programmes.

From this preliminary analysis it has become clear that the institutional structure of a democratic state is important for understanding both cross-national and cross-time variation of public expenditures in the welfare state. Yet, again we must emphasize that this third model only explains a part of the story of the development of the welfare state. Insum, although institutional factors, are important, they are apparently not relevant to explain in what way and to what extent have been able to cope with the economics of welfare statism crisis and growth in the 1990s, let alone, in what way this crisis has affected the securing work and income of the 1990s in the contemporary welfare states.

3.5 RATES OF WELFARE STATISM AND SECURING WORK AND INCOME

We began our 'concise contemporary quantative history' of welfare statism by asking ourselves how democratic states have coped with the apparent growth and crisis that has occurred, in particular after 1975. The question behind this question was whether or not one could (still) learn from the experiences as they have been condensed into three mainstream models that aim at explaining both the type and development of welfare statism. This quest, however, is not only a theoretical one, but also a socially relevant question: how do various rates of welfare statism affect, at the end of the day, or otherwise at present, the possibility for having work and gaining a reasonable income. This question will be addressed later on in this section. Firstly, we need to elaborate on what 'models' have taught us in terms of an explanation and also what factors may or may not produce different rates of welfare statism across democratic states as well as over time.

The analysis of the 'functional' model helped us to understand the *conditions* that directed the 'take-off' of most welfare states, but hardly directly determine its present shape and format. Yet, as we demonstrated by means of the extended Zöllner-model, demographic change and economic performance – structural and cyclical movements alike – are influencing both level and change in expenditures on welfare statism. The policy-heritage, or incremental effects, and the dramatic increase in unemployment have led to considerable variation – rather than to convergent patterns – of welfare statism. This result should not go unnoticed: highly and early developed welfare states remain among the 'leaders' and still provide more public means to cope with the loss of work, or conversely the increase in (particularly female) labour force participation. This is, for instance, reflected in the extent to which transfer payments, or cash-returns, correlate with the rate of unemployment (Pearson's r = 0.37 for total unemployment, and 0.48 for female unemployment between 1975–90). Hence, the shape and type of the original welfare state seems to be indicative for the level of income maintenance in 1990. However, as can be observed, the correlates are not extremely high. In addition, it can be observed that the present levels of employment, on the one hand, and the present proportion of the population over 65, on the other, are related to the policy-means employed in the welfare state in a rather perverse way. Both indicators, representing structural (that is ageing population) and cyclical movements (that is unemployment, in particular of women) have a dampening effect on the levels of transfer payments. Government consumption is to some extent different as it rises with the increase in elderly people.

Does this imply a 'waning of solidarity'? This question is beyond the explanatory grasp of the 'functional' school. It seems quite logical to expect the 'political movements' and 'party behaviour' approach to be able to account for this question. From our analysis it has become clear that political movements in combination with the power resources they can avail of can make a difference to the rate of welfare statism. First of all, it was observed that ideology *per se* was not a good predictor, but, if and when, social democracy was well-represented in parliament and government, it certainly makes a difference in terms of the welfare provisions that were delivered. In particular after 1975, so we found, the relative slowdown of transfer payments and services-in-kind was upheld. This appeared to be different where this movement is weaker, or, conversely the right-wing or Christian democracy becomes or is stronger (Castles, 1994).

Especially important is, after 1975 in particular, who is in government. The more left-wing, the less waning of solidarity in terms of providing public goods such as income maintenance and economic growth by means of state intervention. How important this is can be illustrated by inspecting the correlates between the development of the public sector after 1975, on the one hand, and the increase in both cash-return and service-in-kind, on the other, with the recently published data of the Luxembourg income-study (1995) concerning income inequality (here measured by the Lorenz Curve): Pearson's r : transfer *Lorenz = 0.57: government consumption *Lorenz = 0.43. Yet, at the same time this positive effect is again dampened in countries with high levels of total and female unemployment (Pearson's r is, respectively: –0.48 and –0.43). It appears plausible to suggest that in countries with a relatively high level of welfare statism income and work are better upheld than in other welfare states. At the same time it should also be noticed that, if and when unemployment rises, the overall income equality fades. Hence, although one seems to be 'better off' in an established high-level welfare state, there appears to be a negative trade-off between work and income: either mass unemployment induces income equality for all, be it active or (compulsory) inactive, or more work for many, at the cost, however, of income equality.

In sum, the higher the rate of welfare statism the better the (re)distribution of income *or* work across a society. In short political actors, who wish to maintain welfare are more or less capable of doing so by means of welfare state related policy-making in a democracy. The 'more or less' qualification, however, also refers to the matter of 'policy inheritance' or what one may label (in part) as path dependence. Path dependence however implies not only the past, but also the impact of institutions – the third mainstream model scrutinized here. I analysed the constitutional factors of the countries under review by means of their degree of centralization and existing institutional constraints to central government. In addition, we investigated the cross-national division in federal and unitary states.

The results reported showed that institutional factors add significantly to our understanding why public expenditures differ both in level and especially over time: federal states and/or states with a lower degree of centralization and/or more institutional constraints are markedly different in their patterns of spending on the welfare state. This may be good news to those who adhere to the ideas on the 'minimal state' and 'restrictive fiscalism' (see: Lane, 1985; Keman, 1993a), but it should also be realized that the effects of this type and size of welfare statism are equally different from centralized, unitarian states. Income inequality and rates of unemployment (after 1975) are negatively and significantly correlated with these institutional arrangements (institutional constraints *Lorenz = –0.45; institutional autonomy *unemployment = –0.45). Hence, the type of structure of the state is an important factor, not only for the rate of welfare statism, but also for the socio-economic redistribution of work and income.

As a final conclusion to this paper I would like to emphasize that each of the overall models for explaining welfare statism give important information for our understanding of the cross-national *differences*, rather than the similarities that are often expected. Secondly, that the patterns of development, particularly after 1975, are more directed by *systemic* features than by uniform conditions (like socio-economic change) and identical political actors (with the exception of, to some extent, social democracy under certain conditions). Thirdly, that 'objective conditions' and 'political circumstances' are more variable *over time* than is often assumed. And exactly these differences, so it appears, dictate to a large extent the different trajectories of welfare statism within a society.

The lesson may be therefore that all models presented here have delivered valuable insights into the development and maintenance of welfare statism in democratic societies. However, the extent to which each of them is capable of coping with crisis and adjusting to the limits of growth is equally dependent on how its welfare state has developed, which political movements are significant, and to what extent political action for providing work and income is feasible within the 'objective conditions' as well as the institutional features of democracies.

ENDNOTE

1. Although this model is primarily used to explain differences between 'rich' and 'poor' nations – like OECD versus Third World countries – I contend that it can also be applied to the OECD countries under review here. The cross-national and cross-time variation that can be observed in Tables 3.1–3.3 and the large variation in the independent variables warrants this.

REFERENCES

Budge, I., D. Robertson and D. Hearl (eds) (1987), *Ideology, Strategy and Party Change: Spatial Analyses of Post-War Election Programmes in 19 Democracies*, Cambridge : Cambridge University Press.

Budge, I. and H. Keman (1990), *Parties and Democracy. Government Formation and Government Functioning in Twenty States*, Oxford: Oxford University Press.

Cameron, D.R. (1978) 'The expansion of the public economy', *American Political Science Review*, **11** (22), 1243–261.

Castles, F.G. (1982), *The Impact of Parties, Politics and Policies in Democratic Capitalist States,* London: Sage.

Castles, F.G. (1989), *The Comparative History of Public Policy*, Oxford: Polity Press.

Castles, F.G.(1994) 'On religion and public policy. Does catholicism make a difference?', *European Journal of Political Research*, **25** (1) 19–40.

Castles, F. and D. Mitchell (1991), 'Three worlds of welfare capitalism or four?', *PPP Discussion paper no. 21*, Canberra: Australian National University.

Colomer, J. (1995), *Political Institutions in Europe*, London: Routledge.

Esping-Andersen, G. (1990), *The Three Worlds of Capitalism*, Cambridge: Polity Press.

Esping-Andersen, G. and K. van Kersbergen (1992), 'Contemporary research on social democracy', *Annual Review of Sociology*, 18, 187–208.

Flora, P. and A.J. Heidenheimer (1981), *The Development of Welfare States in Europe and America*, New Brunswick and London: Transaction Books.

Heidenheimer, A.J., H. Heclo and C.T. Adams (1990), *Comparative Public Policy. The Politics of Social Choice in America, Europe and Japan*, 3rd edn. New York: St. Martins Press.

Keman, H. (1988), *The Development toward Surplus Welfare. Social Democratic Politics and Policies in Advanced Capitalist Democracies (1965–1984)*, Amsterdam: CT Press.

Keman, H. (1990), 'Social democracy and welfare statism', *The Netherlands Journal of Social Sciences*, **26** (1) 17–34.

Keman, H. (1993a), 'The politics of managing the mixed economy', in H. Keman (ed.), *Comparative Politics. New Directions in Theory and Method*, Amsterdam: VU University Press.

Keman, H. (1993b), 'Proliferation of the welfare state', in K. Eliassen and J. Kooiman (eds), *Managing Public Organizations. Lessons from Contemporary European Experience*, London: Sage .

Keman, H. (1994), 'The search for the centre: pivot parties in West European party systems', *West European Politics*, **17**, 124–48.

Kerr, C. *et al.* (1960), *Industrialization and Industrial Man*, Cambridge: Harvard University Press.

Klingemann, H.-D., R.I. Hofferbert, I. Budge *et al.* (1994), *Parties, Policies, and Democracy* , Boulder: Westview.

Korpi, W. (1983), *The Democratic Class Struggle*, London: Routledge.

Lane, J.-E. and S.O. Ersson (1990), *Comparative Political Economy*, London: Pinter.

Lane, J.-E., D. Mackay and K. Newton (1991), *Political Data Handbook OECD Countries,* Oxford: Oxford University Press.

Lijphart, A. (1984), *Democracies. Patterns of Majoritarian and Consensus Government in 21 Countries*, New Haven and London: Yale University Press.

Pryor, F.L. (1968), *Public Expenditures in Communist and Capitalist Nations*, London: Allen and Unwin.

Putnam, R.D. (1993), *Making Democracy Work*, New Jersey: Princeton University Press.

Rimlinger, G.V. (1971), *Welfare Policy and Industrialization in Europe, America and Russia*, Chichester, UK and New York, USA: John Wiley and Sons.

Scharpf, F.W. (1992), *Crisis and Choice in European Social Democracy*, Ithaca, US and London UK: Cornell University Press.

Schmidt, M.G. (1989) 'Social policy in rich and poor countries: socio-economic trend and political-institutional trends', *European Journal of Political Research* **17** (6) 641–661.

Schmidt, M.G.,(1995) 'The parties-do-matter hypothesis and the case of the Federal Republic Germany', in *German Politics*, **4** (3) 1–21.

Skocpol, T., (1985) 'Bringing the state back in. Strategies of analysis in current research', in Evans, P., D. Rueschemeyer and T. Skocpol (eds), *Bringing the State Back In Cambridge*: Cambridge University Press,.

Steinmo, S., K. Thelen and F. Longstreth (eds) (1992), *Structuring Politics. Historical Institutionalism in Comparative Analysis*, Cambridge: Cambridge University Press.

Therborn, G. (1989), 'Pillarization and popular movements: two variants of welfare capitalism', in Castles F. (ed.) *The Comparative History of Public Policy*, Cambridge: Polity Press, pp. 192–241.

van Kersbergen, K. (1995), *Social Capitalism: A Study of Christian Democracy and the Welfare State*, London: Routledge.

Volkens, A. (1994), 'Dataset CMP94. Comparative Manifestos Project' Science Centre, Berlin, Research Unit Institutions and Social Change (Director H.-D. Klingemann) in *cooperation with the Manifesto Research Group* (Chairman I. Budge).

Wilensky, H.L. (1975), *The Welfare State and Equality. Structural and Ideological Roots of Public Expenditures*, Berkeley: University of California Press.

Wilensky, H.L. (1981), 'Democratic corporatism, consensus and social policy: reflections on changing values and the 'crisis' of the welfare state', in *The Welfare State in Crisis. An Account of the Conference on Social Policies in the 1980s*, Paris: OECD.

Wilensky, H.L., 1987 'Comparative social policy: theories, methods, findings', in Dierkes, M., N. Weiler, A.B. Antal (eds) *Comparative Policy Research. Learning from Experience*, Aldershot: Gower Publishers, 381–457.

Woldendorp, J.J., H. Keman and I. Budge (1993), *Handbook of Democratic Government. Party Government in 20 Democracies (1945–1990)*, Dordrecht: Kluwer.

4. Political reconstruction of the European welfare states

Stein Kuhnle

4.1 INTRODUCTION

Readjust your expectations of the 21st Century. Neither the age of superstates, nor the end of all states, is about to happen

(*The Economist*, 23 December 1995–5 January 1996)

'The welfare state is at a breaking point' (*The European,* 28 January 1994) and 'a few bold souls are even wondering if Europe should not rebuild its welfare state, creating a more modest and affordable structure before the old edifice falls into total disrepair' (*Newsweek,* 20 December 1993). These are examples of typical comments on the status of European welfare states in mass media in recent years.

The development of the 'welfare state' is so far closely linked to the development of the 'nation state'. For some, the welfare state is the crowning of the development of the nation state. What happens to the welfare state when the authoritative, 'monopolistic' economic and political competences of the nation state come under threat? Although it can be argued that (West European) states – or national governments – in some respects have steadily increased their role in society (taxes, bureaucratic controls, interference in the private sphere, public employment), they have at the same time met new challenges generated by the institutionalization of principles of more open borders for the flow of capital, goods, services, people and ideas.

The questions I shall discuss are: what is the status of European welfare states and in what direction(s) are they moving? What are their economic, political and cultural challenges? Does European integration in the form of the economic political regimes of the EU and the EEA imply a political reconstruction of European welfare states? More specifically, what are the prospects of the so-called Scandinavian or Nordic welfare model in the possible phase of reconstruction?

4.2   STATUS OF EUROPEAN WELFARE STATES

This is not the first time that the welfare state is perceived to be at 'a breaking point'.[1] Without reviewing the history of the welfare state here, let it be briefly stated that the historical origin of social security teaches us a lesson which is still relevant in the modern world: social security can be an answer both to state leaders' need for social and political stability (both in authoritarian and democratic systems) and to popular demand for social protection and security, and can also in some cases develop as a conscious reform effort by humanitarian and socially minded social-democratic, liberal and conservative politicians. Identical solutions do not imply identical causes or motives. And identical problems do not imply identical solutions: even if social insurance can be broadly interpreted as an answer to problems created by capitalist industrialization, we can only look to East Asia today to observe attempts at another cultural interpretation of welfare problems and needs, and by implication different political solutions from the European one.[2] On the other hand, some of the factors which gave rise to the European welfare states may still become manifest elsewhere in the world, such as pressures of demographic change, labour mobility and social instability, changing family patterns and relations, growing national economic wealth, democratization, and diffusion of ideas for state social action.

In the first phase of European social security development, public debate within various nation states centred around what the fundamental and constituent principles of the state's social role should be. That the state should play some kind of role, quickly gained acceptance across regimes and countries at different levels of industrialization, democratization and capitalist development. But should insurance be compulsory or voluntary? Should insurance cover only certain kinds of needs or 'all' social insurance needs? Some groups of the population or everybody? Only the most needy? Should a moral demarcation be drawn between the so-called deserving and undeserving poor? Should insurance schemes be financed by general taxation, employers and/or premiums from the insured? Means-testing or universal benefits? Organized by the state or privately – for example through trade unions and mutual benefit societies? The period 1870s–1920s has been called the period of 'experimentation' (Heclo, 1981). The period was characterized by innovation and volatility in programming, and by 'constitutional' arguments on boundary problems. The 1990s appear in many ways to reopen the old debate on boundaries: what should (and *can*) be the responsibility of the state, what are the limits of individual and family responsibilities? What are the implications of the principles of free movement of capital and labour (persons) in the EEA area? What role can or will the EU itself play? Historically, target population groups were generally the deserving poor and the (industrial) working class, although in Scandinavia the concept of a comprehensive 'people's insurance' was coined around the turn of the century, perhaps as a reflection of the strong political presence of the peasants in Scandinavian parliaments. A line can be drawn from 'people's insurance' to the post-World War II concept of 'universal coverage'. Countries differed in their specific responses to the need and problem of social security. European welfare states developed into different institutional shapes which to a large extent have persisted until this day. Institutional legacies are not easily thrown overboard in the 1990s even if state leaders who identify similar challenges across nation states would like to embark on major institutional welfare reforms.

A significant institutional difference exists between countries where claims for social transfers and services gradually came to be based on citizens' rights and countries where claims are related to employment and contribution records, and thus countries where social security schemes and health and social services are uniform and universal, and countries where schemes are differentiated among occupational groups and social classes (Flora, 1986). Most of the fundamental decisions on these institutional dimensions were taken relatively early. A major distinction can still be drawn between the Scandinavian–British system with relatively strong elements of social citizenship and relatively uniform and integrated institutions, and the continental systems with much more fragmented institutions and with a smaller citizenship component. The two major dimensions of institutional variation can also be summarized as the degree of 'stateness' (that is the degree to which the state or central government controls the various welfare institutions) and the degree of 'universalism' (that is the degree to which welfare institutions cover the whole population or specific groups only) (Flora, 1986). Both dimensions are closely related to the specific national histories of state and class formation, of nation-building and cultural heterogeneity. The state has played a more unifying ('nationalizing') and important role in Protestant Europe than in Catholic Europe, especially in the field of education, health and social services, much less so in the field of income maintenance schemes. In Scandinavia, the development of a uniform and a relatively egalitarian national system can be traced to a class compromise between industrial workers and small independent farmers, already evident to some extent at the turn of the century in the fight for political rights and influence. Class compromises, institutionalized in the 1930s in Scandinavia (Lindstrøm, 1985), made for universalism, but the major transformation of this principle into practice in most cases came as late as the 1950s and 1960s.

In the period after World War II, which is generally characterized by a vigorous and persistent growth in social expenditure in European countries – both in real terms and, until recent years, as a proportion of GDP, the development of four or five different institutional welfare models could be distinguished: the Bismarckian (or German) model with emphasis on status maintenance for gainfully employed; the Beveridgean (or British) model with emphasis on minimum security for all citizens; the Scandinavian model with emphasis on minimum security for all plus – since the 1960s – status maintenance for gainfully employed; the Communist system model (until 1990) with the principle of state responsibility for the material welfare of all members of society; and, perhaps, a Southern European model with a recently developed mixture of Bismarckian and Beveridgean traits plus the persistence of clientelism (Ferrera, 1996). Most European countries would fit into one of these models, but these models do not provide a complete perspective on the welfare system of a given country, and such model descriptions conceal developmental dynamics.[3] A typology of welfare models or regimes illustrates the fact that a differentiation of European welfare state development has taken place in the post-1945 period. With the exception of the Communist system model it is unlikely that such a differentiation will disappear rapidly. I shall take a closer look at what has happened after 1989 in countries which represent all but the Southern European model: United Kingdom, Germany, Norway and Sweden, and Poland.[4] This is one way to search for commonalities in development, to look for trends of convergence or divergence in European welfare state development, and to discern actual attempts at political reconstruction or perceived needs for reconstruction or individual or institutional adaptations to rules of action which transcend the nation state.

In 1991, the average share of social protection expenditure as a percentage of GDP in the EC[5] was 26 per cent, with the Netherlands on top with 32.4 per cent and Portugal at bottom of the list with 19. 4 per cent. The average is the same as in 1985, while the 1980 level was 24 per cent. Data for Central and East European countries for this period are not comparable, but social security expenditure as a percentage of GDP increased substantially, through a period of incipient system change, in Bulgaria, Czechoslovakia, Hungary and Poland between 1985 and 1991. Total social expenditure has grown quite dramatically in real terms also in the last decade in most of Europe (*Social Protection in Europe*, 1994). Rising public deficits and persistently high levels of unemployment are relatively common constraints on future public sector growth and have induced governments both in Eastern and Western Europe to look for ways to cut social expenditure. Changing demographic composition has also meant and will mean an increasing burden on future public budgets unless schemes and benefits are modified. But in spite of many examples of retrenchment in European welfare states in the 1980s (Alber, 1988; Cochrane, 1993), total social expenditure continued to increase in real terms, and on average also as a percentage of GDP. Partly because of rising unemployment, and partly because of a changing demographic composition with a growing proportion of old people, the number of eligible beneficiaries of social security schemes has steadily increased. Cuts in benefit levels for sickness, old age, unemployment and social assistance in many countries have not prevented the total social budget from increasing. Gross public debt as percentage of GDP has increased in all but one member states of the EC in the 1989–1995 period,[6] and all Eastern European countries are characterized by a deep fiscal crisis (Campbell, 1994), which is more profound than in Western Europe, at the same time as their welfare systems face more fundamental institutional challenges than in the West (Offe, 1993).

In the governing circles of West European countries, the beginning of the 1980s signified a marked change in the dominant thinking about the welfare state. OECD's *The Welfare State in Crisis* (1981) provided legitimacy to a change in 'mainstream' ideological thinking in governments with more emphasis on individual responsibilities for own welfare. Margaret Thatcher's first government stated in its programme declaration in 1979 that 'higher public expenditure cannot any longer be allowed to precede, and thus prevent growth in the private sector' (Walker, 1986), and the British Government was not unique in its programme. Similar statements made their way into programmes of even Social-Democratic Scandinavian Governments during the 1980s.[7] During the 1980s parties, movements and governments across the political spectrum advocated more market, less state and more decentralization, and expansion of individual and family responsibilities.

These ideological changes which imply privatization – or at least stimulation of private supplements in social insurance and health and welfare services – and individualization of welfare responsibility, may come to have significant effects for national welfare states in a context of free movement of capital and persons across national borders, and in a context where national welfare states have to extend responsibility to citizens of other nations. This marks a double challenge for the traditional European national welfare states, and I shall return to this topic below. In such a new context, tendencies to develop national policies of more targeting and means-testing of welfare, can have different socio-structural effects (more fragmentation or atomization of welfare interests in society) than in the old, nationally bounded, class-structured welfare states.

The conception of an expensive and inefficient welfare state was spread in the 1980s, and with it the idea that the public sector cannot grow any more. But in spite of new concepts such as 'third sector' and 'civil society' and a notion of the need for 'welfare pluralism' (Johnson, 1987), and in spite of all rhetoric against the welfare state or its further growth, state social expenditures continued to rise through the 1980s, and mainstream social programmes have not been substantially retrenched anywhere, not even under neo-conservative regimes in countries such as the UK and USA (Alber, 1988; Mishra 1993). Generosity of benefits and qualification criteria for benefits in some programmes have been modified everywhere, but with little effect on overall social expenditure levels. At the same time, the importance of fiscal welfare – stimulating private health and pension insurance – and occupational welfare seem to have increased in many countries (Ervik and Kuhnle, 1994). Thus, it is logically and empirically possible that all types of welfare provision increase simultaneously. The 1980s was not necessarily a decade of 'more market, less state', but perhaps rather one of 'more market, more state'. This development was possible because demographic changes and to an increasing extent high levels of unemployment in countries with well established social entitlements automatically entailed higher public social expenditure, and fiscal policies to give incentives to private insurance and occupational welfare security were effective. Many people, trade unions and firms gave priority to health and welfare security needs, and could to a greater extent than in earlier post-World War II decades afford investment in non-public welfare arrangements.

4.3 COMMON EUROPEAN WELFARE CHALLENGES

European welfare states exist in different shapes and scope, and thus face a number of specific challenges. I shall look at some of these in the following paragraph. But some challenges appear to be general, especially those related to 'Europeanization' and internationalization of trade, economic transactions and competition, to the changing composition of the population, to persistent levels of high unemployment, to changes in family structure and to high popular expectations from the welfare state.

The EU represents so far (before an eventual – and at least steadily postponed implementation of a – monetary union) no direct challenge to national welfare states within or outside of the EU, although it (and the EEA regime) represents two types of limitation on national welfare states: developments which affect the State's formal authority to take independent decisions in social welfare – its sovereignty, and developments which restrict the independence of states to act, affecting its substantive capacity to guarantee the actual flow of social benefits – its autonomy (Leibfried, 1994). European welfare states are being 'harmonized' by separate, internal, socio-economic homogenization and not by the EU. There is no vertical 'regime breaking' through the EU, but rather a horizontal 'system adaptation' (Flora, 1993a; Leibfried, 1994). Although the 'social dimension' of the EU has gained in importance and visibility over the last 10 years, the guiding principle for most social and welfare policy has been, and most likely will be, the principle of subsidiarity. Social security systems can only be harmonized through unanimity among member states, and harmonization through EU institutions must be considered very unlikely for technical, economic and political reasons. But solutions developed through subsidiarity can be highly contagious, thus leading to similar welfare policies and systems without the bureaucratic and political cost of central co-ordination and decision-making at the European level. Stronger economic integration, harmonization of indirect taxes, and moves towards a monetary union may also indirectly induce national governments to develop their social policies towards some convergence, although taxation for social and health security as well as direct personal taxation will still be a national responsibility. Calls for minimum standards of welfare within the EU may gain political strength, and thus promote welfare state growth in member states where such standards are poor or non-existent, while the more developed welfare states may come under pressure for reducing social expenditure to an average European level – or at least governments may use the EU as a handy political excuse for cutting expenditures. On the other hand, developed welfare states may also be called upon to contribute to the redistribution of welfare in Europe, but this is most likely an extremely difficult political process in a situation where national electorates are split on the role of the EU in national politics. Both the EU as such and national governments may develop a shared opinion on the recommended scope and role of social policy to make Europe competitive with North America and South-East Asia, but most likely not as a result of formal requirements to do so. The new General Agreement on Tariffs and Trade (GATT) may be one pretext for developing less expensive European welfare states. But even if governments and parliaments have ambitions to limit welfare state growth or reduce the scope of the welfare state, other factors may render this extremely difficult. As Alber (1988) showed in an analysis of welfare state change in Europe, North America and Japan in the 1975–85 period, welfare state expenditure continued to grow faster than the economic product and public revenues – despite curtailments of welfare programmes.

Why is a markedly reduced scope of national welfare states problematic or unlikely? First of all, there is the fact that European welfare states, particularly in the western part of Europe, are in a global perspective relatively well developed. People have social rights, and are entitled to benefits and services under specified circumstances. Rights and entitlements cannot be easily discarded. With the increase in the number and proportion of the elderly in European populations, social expenditure – especially pension expenditure – is bound to increase unless political steps are taken to limit the size of future benefits. In 1990 the proportion of voters over 55 in the 12 countries of the EC was 33 per cent, and the projection for 2020 is 42 per cent (Wilson, 1993:96) – with Germany on top with 45 per cent and Ireland at bottom with 31 per cent. Central and Eastern European countries will also be within this range. These facts have a number of implications for the welfare state: pension expenditure will rise, the demand for health, nursing and social services will increase, and older voters, who for the most part have experienced a career and life in developed welfare states, will make up a stronger block of voters with higher welfare demands than the present generation of old voters. On the other hand, it will also be the most affluent generation of old people ever, and we should also expect increased demand for social services from whoever is ready to supply it. Thus, we may expect a great potential for private (for non-profit or for-profit) social service suppliers who will complement and supplement public providers, and thus also soon stimulate a more dual public–private (commercial) welfare society/state than Europeans have experienced so far in the post-World War II period. A change in demographic composition means that the balance between workers and non-workers is affected, and may imply an increasing tax burden on the economically active in welfare systems which basically are based on the pay-as-you-go-principle. On the other hand, one should not rule out the possibility of gradual behavioural, institutional and political adaptations to the changing demographic structure. Old people – exposed to less hard physical work than in earlier periods – may in the future be more fit to be partially gainfully employed, thus contributing both to labour and tax revenues. The anticipation of a future generation of pensioners, who on average will be much better off economically than today's pensioners, and thus be able to pay directly for a lot more services which currently are covered by public tax revenues, may make the transformation of welfare state institutions and programmes more smooth than popularly expected. Although demographic ageing as of 2010 onwards certainly will prove a challenge for pension, health and social service systems, one should not necessarily accept a mechanistic approach to the effects on social spending (Guillemard, 1993).

The ageing of the population occurs, however, in a period with growing competition on international product markets, and rapid internationalization of monetary markets offering new profit opportunities to capital owners and thus strengthening their bargaining power both *vis-á-vis* labour and the state (Alber, 1988: 201). Although most of Europe as of 1995–96 seems to be recovering from recession and to be on the road to some economic growth – to which also the internal market within the EU may contribute – unemployment levels are on average high (approximately 11 per cent in the EU, higher in Central and Eastern Europe), and long-term unemployment is increasing. A challenge within the EU will be the potentially greater terroritorial inequality unless the economic concentration effects of the single market are met by political territorial redistributive measures at the EU level, and an all European challenge is the potential for greater inequality between countries inside and outside of the EU, unless the politically and economically system-transforming countries of Central and Eastern Europe are integrated in the EU/EEA economic system. Such territorial inequalities will most likely entail new challenges for national welfare systems – especially in the relatively less developed market economies. An EU report (Eurostat, 1994) points to the instability of the labour markets, with more frequent interruptions to working careers; the persistently high levels of unemployment; the emergence of new forms of poverty and social exclusion; and changes in the structure of families (for example growth in numbers of single mothers or one-parent families) as major current challenges for European welfare systems or societies as such.

Parallel to financial, demographic, socio-structural, and international problems, European welfare states face challenges of a socio-cultural nature. A number of studies have shown that welfare state programmes enjoy a high level of mass support (Alber, 1988). With the (temporary?) exception of France – with strikes and angry and violent demonstrations as reactions to relatively moderate curtailments of social entitlements in the autumn all of 1995 – cutbacks have not led to a legitimation crisis. Nor does one see strong indications of a welfare backlash. Citizens have on the whole tolerated curtailments of some social programmes, but popular expectations from the welfare state still run high (Ferrera, 1993). A comprehensive Eurobarometer study on these issues from spring 1992 (still the most recent study on these issues) shows overwhelming support for a strong role for the state in the field of social protection among all (at the time) 12 member countries of the EU, and Southern European populations seem in general to want and expect more from the state than Northern Europeans. In all countries more people prefer a 'maximalist' rather than a 'minimalist' approach to state social protection, even if that view may explicitly mean increasing taxes and contributions (Ferrera, 1993). A comparison of attitudes towards the welfare state in USA, UK,

(West-) Germany, The Netherlands, Italy, and Hungary in 1986[8] indicate a significant difference between the USA on the one hand and all the European countries on the other. While on average 60 per cent of the Europeans are of the opinion that the state ought to be responsible for basic income, and 68 per cent favoured the view that the state should be responsible for reducing income inequalities, the corresponding figures among Americans were 20 per cent and 27 per cent respectively (Flora, 1993a). Data on the state's role in securing work for all give a similar profile. Europeans, from North, South, West and East, are consistently more supportive of a strong state in welfare matters than Americans (and probably also other non-Europeans in industrialized countries). The high legitimacy that European welfare states enjoy may be seen as a hindrance to extensive rebuilding or reduction of welfare state responsibilities, which many governments and (economic) experts consider necessary. Welfare expectations are too high for governmental comfort. On the other hand, the data may reflect the historical uniqueness of European welfare state development, making state welfare a persistent and distinctive element of European political culture. If this is correct, is it necessarily an expression of a European drawback in the era of internationalization of money markets and global competition, or is it a European advantage? Are developed, consolidated welfare states conducive to democratic and social stability which again is conducive to future investments and productivity? Can more weakly developed welfare states provide the same degree of democratic legitimacy and social stability? Is the welfare challenge more critical in newly industrialized, and 'socially mobilized', countries of Asia, and in the more capitalist, and socially divided, America, than in European countries? There are no simple answers to these questions on the long-term implications of welfare state development, but the questions themselves are put forward to indicate that Europe is in a longer-term perspective not necessarily a loser or laggard in the global competition, and that any assessment must also to some extent be normative and value-based.

4.4   TOWARDS A EUROPEAN SOCIAL SECURITY SYSTEM?

Is it likely that European integration in terms of freedom of movement of capital, goods, services and labour (and people in general) across national boundaries will stimulate or promote the establishment of an international or transnational social security system in Europe? Social security extends beyond national borders, more now than ever in Europe, but as

Bernd Schulte (1991) has reminded us, the first transnational social security treaty was established already in 1904, between France and Italy, in order to solve problems on social security rights and obligations of migrant workers. Some of the principles and techniques of co-ordination of social rights for workers/employees moving between countries have been adopted and further developed both in the EU where a free labour market has been in force for more than 20 years, and in the Nordic countries where a free labour market has been in place for 40 years. What is or will be the welfare political effect of the EU? This is a difficult topic which has led to the production of an enormous amount of scholarly articles and books. It is difficult not least because of uncertainty as to what kind of economic, political and nation-inclusive EU will develop in coming years. Scenarios abound, from the relucytant intergrationist perspectives of Danish and British governments (although the new Labour government is more positive than the outgoing Tory government) to the more politically ambitious perspectives of (present) German and Benelux governments. If the EU survives, which is likely, as a political system of some kind, it will consist of at least two elements: European political institutions and single member states. These two elements are also likely to make up a European welfare system (Flora, 1993b). A political system with great territorial heterogeneity in cultural identities and in levels of economic development (to be dramatically greater with the eventual inclusion of Central and East European countries as members), can probably only be viable and at the same time democratic in a decentralized and federal form. If this is true for single nation states – look at Germany and Switzerland, and current trends in Belgium, Spain and Italy – then this must be even more true for Europe as a whole. And eventual decentralized and (more or less) federal Europe will reduce the likelihood of European welfare institutions and redistribution of welfare at a European level. At this stage of European integration, efforts to develop a stronger European welfare state with the EU as regisseur in a culturally and economically heterogenous Europe will probably lead to conflicts at a European level. Both the EU Commission and national authorities may fear the loss of democratic legitimacy by pressing for a centrally controlled European welfare state. If we follow a hypothesis by Peter Flora (1993b), the European welfare or social security system will in the foreseeable future consist of national welfare states plus some European welfare institutions and programmes – as are already in existence. Social policy at the EU level has so far consisted of programmes as responses to the free movement of labour (and gradually other citizens), that is. the co-ordination of social rights for transnational persons, as well as rules that do not discriminate on the basis of nation, race and gender. Another type of programme is a response to the free movement of capital, which unchecked may lead to greater regional/territorial inequalities. The importance of established social and regional funds has increased as the EU has expanded geographically. A future new element in the European welfare system may be the establishment of a European social citizenship, even if some countries (or rather governments) have reservations. On the whole, one should expect the development of future social security programmes to occur within the framework of national welfare states, and that eventual trends towards greater uniformity and harmony between national social security systems will come as a result of national decisions rather than as directives from Brussels and Strasbourg, although the EU may push the idea that minimum *national* pensions and other benefits, on a par with the directive to establish *minimum* periods of paid maternity leave from work, should exist in all member states.

4.5 WHITHER THE SCANDINAVIAN (OR NORDIC) WELFARE MODEL?

The Scandinavian welfare model is no exception to the general challenges facing European welfare states. Denmark, Finland and Sweden are now members of the EU, while Iceland and Norway are members of EFTA and the EEA. Thus, all Nordic countries participate – with all concomitant opportunities for and challenges to their national economies – in the world's most advanced system of international and interstate economic integration with few, if any, barriers to movement of capital, goods, services and people across national borders. No doubt, the Europeanization, and further internationalization, of the economy and politics represent a set of challenges to the Scandinavian welfare model. European-wide rules for companies, labour and citizens imply some constraints for national policy-making in many fields. The direct impact in the field of welfare and social policy is very limited, but the indirect impact may be significant, whether the countries maintain a formal membership of the EU or not. The tempo, scope and direction of harmonization of indirect taxes and excise duties in the EU is uncertain, and so are the consequences for public revenues. It is to be anticipated that any kind of harmonization will raise political controversy and be a slow process. As indicated above, *ideas* about economic and welfare policies have not only drifted easily across national borders, but also across the 'small divide' between EU and EFTA (EEA) members. These ideas about more emphasis on non-governmental welfare and individual responsibilities have become guiding principles for political action independently of formal EU membership.

The internationalization of the money market may strengthen capital owners and increase their strength of negotiation *vis-à-vis* both labour and government in single nation states. On the other hand, a further Europeanization of the trade union movement may bring about a balance in the system of negotiation, and offer new opportunities for more unified and solidaristic actions against transnational companies within a European space without national *state* borders. (And as the recent turmoil over welfare curtailments in France showed, even with a poor rate of trade union membership – only 9 per cent of French workers and employees are unionized – spontaneous mass action may halt or bring about changes in policies.) 'The four freedoms of movement' which are at the core of the EU single market – and also of the EEA Agreement – may encourage and accelerate tendencies towards more privatization of the welfare state – through fiscal and occupational welfare, and greater emphasis on voluntary welfare. Besides governmental fiscal constraints, the rise of a large, service-demanding, and affluent pensioners' class in Europe, may facilitate the growth of non-governmental welfare services. Organizational fragmentation, social segmentation, and greater complexity of the welfare system will likely be the result, which is not easily 'corrected' even if a political majority should wish to change this course later on. These tendencies, which have been prevalent also in Scandinavia in the last 15 years (Ervik and Kuhnle, 1994), may prove a crucial challenge to the so-called Scandinavian or Nordic welfare model. This model has empirically meant a larger element of state participation, more coherently organized welfare and social security programmes, a larger degree of tax financing of welfare, and more universal population coverage by social and welfare schemes than in other European welfare states. Compared to other European welfare models, the Scandinavian welfare model has been more state-based, enjoyed a higher degree of 'state legitimacy', has meant the largest shares of total labour force gainfully employed in the welfare, health and education sectors, and the largest shares of public employees in these sectors, has meant less social and class inequality with the interests of the well-to-do highly integrated in the relatively generous welfare state, and has – until recently – been more committed, and successful, towards the goal of full employment. The model has come under *internal* pressure for change (more occupational welfare, more individually or family-based, private welfare), but also under greater *external* pressure for change, although the Nordic countries differ among themselves as to the amount of changes and exposure to a changing international context. As to the goal of full employment, variations among Nordic countries are now as great as those among European countries in general, with unemployment levels ranging from about 7 per cent in Norway to 19 per cent in Finland, as of December 1995. The average for the EU is 11–12 per cent. The overall challenge of financing welfare varies as can be shown by different indicators of which one important one is the proportion of government budgets to be spent on interest on loans. In Sweden this percentage was 21.3 per cent in 1995, in Denmark 12.9 per cent, Finland 9.7 per cent (but rising), Iceland 5–6 per cent, and in Norway 6.4 per cent (and falling) (Veggeland, 1996). The share of the public sector in GDP varies between 55.6 per cent in Norway and 68.8 per cent in Sweden, while the OECD average is 41.5 per cent. The combination of a halt in public sector growth, a tax system which now generally encourages the well-to-do majority of tax payers to buy private pension, health and other welfare services, and the free float of capital in a big European market, may well lead to a rapid and dynamic expansion of transnational insurance, and other welfare, companies offering firms, professional groups and individuals new 'packages' of private welfare schemes. This development may relieve the pressure on politicians and the public sector, but will in its turn lead to even stronger overall social segmentation of welfare schemes. Companies, employees and individual citizens will establish ties which connect them not only to welfare schemes outside the public sector, but outside the nation state. In this way, the public share of welfare benefits and services can and may be gradually reduced, and the possibility of ever regaining complete national control of welfare policy will be reduced, whatever the desire to regain such control. The lessening of the role of the nation state in welfare provision for citizens may in the Scandinavian case make it easier to surrender political sovereignty to an international or supranational body like the EU. In this sense, membership of the EU may offer a way – perhaps the only realistic way – to regain sovereignty – or stronger national political influence on the welfare of citizens. The co-ordination of social rights across national borders in the EEA is another factor which may stimulate supranational initiatives. Leibfried (1994) has argued that 'the state may no longer limit social benefits to its citizens. Regarding 'foreigners' from within the EU [or even EEA, author's comment], the state no longer has any power to determine whether they have a right to benefits or not'. Leibfried remarks that this development is remarkable since 'citizen-making' through social benefits demarcating the 'stranger' was a watershed in the history of state-building on the Continent. But in this sense, the Nordic countries have among themselves been forerunners for this European-wide development given their free labour market and a social insurance treaty since 1955, which gave extended rights of national citizens to citizens of other Nordic countries. This instituitonal arrangement has not, however, led to harmonized labour and social policies or to a demand for supra-Nordic policies, but the situation is not completely comparable since the EU/EEA represents much stronger economic integration ('free market') and the construction of supranational political bodies. On the whole, the emergence and growth of an internal European market may remove the differences between domestic and foreign policies. As consumers – also as 'welfare consumers' – we can have more choice in a bigger space and have more political strength as a number of boycott actions across European countries have shown (such as protests against Norwegian whaling or French nuclear testing, leading consumers not to buy Norwegian fish or French wine all over Europe), and as voters we will probably gradually become more concerned with transnational problems. This development may subsequently give rise to new types of social and political communities cutting across present physical state borders. Europeanization of the economy and politics, will, if not directly through political decisions, at least indirectly through unco-ordinated decisions by companies and individuals, make it more difficult to sustain a *Sonderweg* for Scandinavian welfare states. Or as Leibfried (1994) states, 'the state may no longer mix "market and state" components of welfare at will and impose its preferred "welfare mix" of monetary transfers, benefits in kind and services. Its power to determine the make-up of the welfare state model is being relaxed'. This seems logical, and goes for all countries of the EEA area.

4.6 RESHAPING WELFARE IN DIFFERENT INSTITUTIONAL CONTEXTS[9]

Let me then move from a generalized description and interpretation of European welfare challenges to some empirical information on recent welfare politics in five nation states which cover examples of various institutional welfare models. The following paragraphs all cover only changes in public or governmental social programmes, and do not illuminate the differentiation of the welfare state into more socially segmented welfare societies with greater roles for private commercial and non-governmental welfare providers and insurers, or the growth of transnational social insurance/welfare companies and individual subscriptions to foreign welfare arrangements.

4.6.1 United Kingdom: Minimum Security with Targeted Tampering at the Margins

The British welfare model is universalist, but also characterized by basically providing low, flat-rate benefits. The system thus stimulates well-to-do groups to take out supplementary occupational and/or private insurance. A great number of studies and evaluations of welfare state development in Britain have appeared since Margaret Thatcher formed her first government in 1979. Overall expenditure continued to rise in spite of all the rhetoric against the welfare state in the 1980s. Barr and Coulter (1991) concluded their study of developments in the 1970s and 1980s that 'although social security was regarded more as a solution in the 1970s and more as a problem in the 1980s, the changes, in reality, though genuinely meeting some of the stated objectives of policy, did not come close to matching the rhetoric' (p. 333). Jonathan Bradshaw reached a similar conclusion, 'Social security is deeply impervious to change (at least from the radical right). It is ingrained in our culture, economy and system of exchange to such an extent that government can only succeed in tampering at the margins' (Bradshaw, 1993: 97–8). But some reforms have been made in the 1990s in the direction of what the government calls targeted benefits based on means-testing. The percentage of social spending absorbed by means-tested benefits has doubled between 1978–79 and 1993–94 from 17 per cent to 34 per cent (Sinfield, 1994). Several reforms aimed at curtailing expenditure have been introduced in the 1990s: benefits for child support and single parents; disability allowances and incapacity benefits; sick pay, unemployment benefits which were replaced by a much less generous 'Jobseeker's Allowance' in April 1996. The long-term effect of the 1982 decision to change the basis for indexing retirement pensions to prices only has been that the basic National Insurance pension fell from 30 per cent to 19 per cent of net average weekly earnings for men between 1980–1993 (Sinfield, 1994). According to one study poverty is widespread and poverty rates have risen substantially in the past decade to over one-fifth of the population (Millar, 1993), while inequality has become markedly greater in recent years, increasing faster than in most Western economies (Atkinson, 1993; OECD, 1993). A group particularly vulnerable to poverty have been the young, especially the homeless, people (Sinfield, 1994). The newly elected Labour government is likely to make moves towards a more benevolent welfare state than the one that the Conservative government developed and wanted to develop.

4.6.2 Germany: Status Maintenance with Minor Curtailments and Consolidated Expansion

The German model is based on employment-related coverage and benefits and the principle of status maintenance. As all other European welfare states, the German social security and welfare system is financed through contributions from employers and employees, and general taxes.

The relative importance of general taxes has increased over the last 30 years. Benefits for sickness, unemployment and old age pensions are among the most generous in Europe, but a universal (citizenship-based) pension right does not exist as in the UK, The Netherlands and the Nordic countries, although means-tested assistance is available for persons without entitlement to a pension and with no income. During the last 20 years, with high unemployment and a rising number of pensioners, reforms to reduce the cost of the income transfer system have been introduced – and the unification of East and West Germany in 1990 has naturally put the welfare system under severe pressure in recent years. Nearly all components of the income transfer system have been changed in the early 1990s, justified in the light of demographic developments, the economic situation and the unification of Germany. Due to these reforms, people (at least in West Germany) relying on social security and assistance are now worse off, although slight improvements have occurred as a consequence of decisions by the Constitutional Court (Gutberlet, 1994). Important reforms to curb expenditure growth have been made in the field of statutory health insurance[10] and in the law governing unemployment and labour market policy.[11] As of 1992, the social security system of West Germany has been extended to cover the whole of unified Germany, although levels of contributions and benefits are different in old and new *Bundesländer*, but the objective is to bring East German standards gradually in line with those of West Germany. All current pensions were changed under the new pension law in 1992.[12] As a result, pensioners also in the former German Democratic Republic (GDR) receive an earnings-related pension, which will be adjusted in line with increases in net wages in the New *Länder* (Gutberlet, 1994). The financial situation of families with children, with special rules pertaining to one-parent families, has been improved through recent reforms, while changes in the procedure for adjusting social assistance benefits will entail a fall in real income for recipients if future inflation rates increase more than standard rates (which is based on the average monthly net income of workers with low income).

A major new reform was passed in 1994 to cover the need for nursing in old age.[13] The risk of being in need of care in old age had not been covered by social insurance, and older people in need of care have had to rely on private support within the family system or to resort to the means-tested social assistance scheme in order to pay the cost of nursing home care. The need for a reform was acknowledged by all parties given the present number of persons in need of care – approximately 1.65 million people (2 per cent of the German population) (Gutberlet, 1994) – and the increase in life expectancy, reduction in birth rate, and the growing number of old people. The reform covers all members of public and private sickness insurance schemes and implies a significant new tax (or contribution) burden for employees. The nursing insurance will be financed on a pay-as-you-go basis with compulsory contributions from employees. Payment of benefits began in April 1995 for nursing care at home and in July 1996 for nursing home care for people who need constant attention (Gutberlet, 1994).

The German welfare state enjoys strong political support both at the mass (Ferrera, 1993) and elite level (an example is general support for nursing insurance). But unless Germany experiences sustained economic growth, more efforts to reduce expenditure in some programmes are likely given the cost of the new reform, and the cost incurred by the ageing of the population, by unemployment, and by German unification with its new social obligations on the state. In fact, in April 1996, the government published a comprehensive proposal for cuts in public expenditure (amounting to DM 50 billion), proposing among other things radical cuts in sickness wage compensation benefits, an increase in the pension age for women (from 60 to 63), and limitation of pre-retirement schemes.

4.6.3 Sweden: Generous Universal Welfare Model under Heavy Pressure

Sweden has long been known to have developed the most comprehensive welfare state among capitalist democracies, and together with The Netherlands, the most expensive one. It is still comprehensive and expensive, but a number of reform initiatives have been taken in recent years to curtail the growth of social expenditure – partly as an effect of too generous and costly social legislation in previous decades, partly because the recession began to affect the overall activity of the economy, partly because of the rapid increase in unemployment levels in the 1990s, partly because of the 'explosion' of public debt and budget deficits, and partly because of demographic trends as in other countries. The non-socialist government, with a Conservative Prime Minister in the 1991–94 period, also wanted less social insurance for more ideological reasons. Individual choice and family responsibilities were emphasized, as well as the view that the general level of taxation had to be lowered in order to stimulate economic growth. The Social Democrats, the main architects of the Swedish model, have reluctantly recognized the need for change and cuts in expenditure and benefits, and they won the 1994 election in spite of their pledge to cut social programmes. This says something about the crisis consciousness among Swedish voters and parties. The economic recession has been conducive to the evolution of a broad consensus – with the exception of the Left party (*Vänsterpartiet*) – on the need for change.

The first real cut came under the Social Democrats (but with the support of the non-Socialist parties) in March 1991 in the context of increasing sickness absence during the latter part of the 1980s, which made sickness cash benefits a convenient target for cutbacks (Palme, 1994). The statutory replacement rate was reduced from 90 per cent to 65 per cent for the first three days of absence, and to 80 per cent from day 4 to day 90. Another reform – with the same political constellation – was instituted in 1992, when it was decided that employers should pay benefits for the first two-week sick pay period according to maximum levels defined in the 1991 reform, which meant 75 per cent wage compensation for the first three days, 90 per cent for the rest of the two-week period, then 80 per cent until day 90, and 90 per cent from day 90 on. A further cutback came in 1993, with the same broad political agreement, when a waiting day in sick pay was introduced and an employee's contribution (tax-deductible) to sickness benefit of 0.95 per cent of gross earnings (Palme, 1994), coupled with a reduction of benefit to 80 per cent in cases exceeding 90 days. During these years there has also been downward adjustments in all types of pensions. The base amount, which is a technical parameter for the calculation of all pensions, was to be adjusted according to the consumer price index in order to control expenditure growth. The most radical changes have concerned industrial injury insurance, which is now completely co-ordinated with the sickness benefit scheme (Palme, 1994). Unemployment benefits were cut in 1993 to 80 per cent of previous earnings (which is still high by any international standard) and a five-day waiting period was (re-)introduced. Changes in industrial injury and in unemployment insurance were opposed by the Social Democrats. But the present Social Democratic Government has been prepared to cut social programmes even further. As of 1 January 1996 the Swedish Parliament decided on a number of further changes and cuts in social security benefits. As a general rule, one is now entitled to a 75 per cent wage compensation in the case of sickness (whether it is paid by the employer or national insurance) and maternity and paternity benefits. Among other cuts, mention should be made of child allowances which have been reduced (from SEK 750 to 640 per month), housing allowances to households without children which have been skipped, and the old age pension amount for married pensioners which has been reduced. The reforms enacted have reduced – and will further reduce – expenditure on several programmes, and further reforms – among other proposals, especially the one on the old-age pension – will significantly affect the level of social expenditure. The reform of the pension system is supported by the Social Democrats and the non-socialist parties.

The Swedish welfare system is doubtlessly undergoing major and profound reform work in the 1990s. Most reforms have had broad political support in parliament. How far the generous welfare state will be rolled back is dependent upon the performance of the Swedish economy. But cutbacks in social programmes have begun from a very high or generous level. The general characteristics of the Swedish welfare model are still in place, and are likely to be retained in the foreseeable future.

4.6.4 Norway: Cautious Fine-tuning of a Sustainable Model in an Oil Economy

Among the Nordic countries Sweden and Norway have developed the most similar institutional welfare models. But Sweden has in general provided more generous benefits and services, and for a long time spent relatively more on social security as a proportion of GDP: in 1981 the proportion in Sweden was 34.2 per cent, in Norway 21.8 per cent; in 1993, the proportions were 40.4 per cent and 30.8 per cent respectively (NOSOSCO, 1995). Social expenditure measured in PPP (purchasing power parities) also indicate much higher expenditure per capita in Sweden than in Norway, but the gap has narrowed significantly over the last 15 years (NOSOSCO, 1995). As indicated above, the status of the economies and government finances in the two countries differ markedly by the mid-1990s, with Sweden having to finance a huge budget deficit, and Norway being able to create a so-called 'oil fund' in a situation with a budget surplus. The anticipation of future revenues from oil and gas into the next century has not made major welfare reforms imperative – and not easily accepted by the electorate – in Norway, although there is general agreement among parliamentary political parties to curtail growth of expenditures in some programmes. The parliament and government have been concerned with the sharp increases in expenditures for old age pensions, disability pensions and sickness benefits, and in the early 1990s steps were agreed upon to make it more difficult on medical grounds to obtain a disability pension and to get sickness benefits, and the reforms have had their effect on the number of new claimants receiving disability benefits (Stokke, 1993). But in contrast to Sweden, gainfully employed persons are still paid a generous 100 per cent wage compensation (in Sweden 75 per cent) from the first day during sickness (up to an income ceiling of 6 × 'the basic amount' in the national insurance scheme, thus leaving the limited group of high-income earners with less than 100 per cent compensation). In 1992, the parliament decided to reduce future anticipated growth of old age pension expenditure by curtailing the earnings-related element in the scheme (Hatland, 1994). High-income earners stand to lose from this change (but this group has also been, and may now be more, prone to take up a private, individual tax-subsidized pension insurance scheme). It was also decided not to reduce the already high pension qualifying age (67–70 years). The unemployment benefit scheme was made more generous in the mid-1980s, the duration of benefits extended from 40 to 80 weeks, and in 1992 the 80-week rule ceased to be applied automatically, thus transforming the scheme in practice into a pension scheme for long-term unemployed (Lødemel, 1994). The child allowance scheme has been steadily made more generous, and there has been a steady, gradual extension of paid maternity leave – from 18 weeks in 1977 to a maximum of 52 weeks by 1993 (42 weeks with full pay or 52 weeks with 80 per cent pay). The entitlements to benefits of parents with sick children were improved through three reforms between 1991 and 1993, so that, for example, a single parent with more than one child is now granted 30 days of sick leave with full wage compensation for a year (Lødemel, 1994).

On the whole, cuts in social security schemes only pertain to the future accumulation of earnings-related benefits and reforms have only affected the high-income earners. Changes in entitlement rules for disability and sickness benefits have been very modest, and consolidation and expansion of important welfare state elements have also taken place in the 1990s. The government, partly mediated through a White Paper to parliament (St.meld. nr 35, 1994–95) is concerned about cautious reorganization of the welfare state by trying (among other things) to strengthen the 'work orientation' of social security as opposed to 'passive support'; to target more effectively with benefits those in greatest need; to consider increased taxation of pensioners' income; to introduce higher levels of user payments in health and social services; and to propose a more flexible wage structure to encourage employers to take on young, unemployed persons. In a European context, the problems and concerns of Norwegian welfare political authorities are small. The strongest representative of the 'Scandinavian welfare model' is currently Norway, but with 5–7 per cent unemployment, and the growth of private and occupational pensions and other welfare services and benefits as supplements to public, national universal schemes, the model appears to be slowly shifting towards a more general 'European' mixed public–private welfare model.

4.6.5 Poland: in Search of a New Concept of Social Protection

Poland is here taken as one example of the countries which laid the Communist system model to rest in 1989. Some of the trends described are valid for several of the countries, such as restructuring of industry, financial problems, inflation and high unemployment (with the exception of the Czech Republic), but developments of specific reform efforts diverge. It is too early to assess and characterize the kind of welfare model which will emerge and sustain itself during and after the period of transition in Central and Eastern Europe.

Under the system prevailing from 1945 until 1989, social objectives were pursued through a policy of low prices for basic products such as food, items for children and youth, and housing, as well as a policy of employment-based social insurance and service provision. The change of the political and economic system into a democratic, market-type economy since 1989 meant that a major transformation of the welfare model has (had) to be undertaken (Golinowska and Ochocki, 1994). Developments since 1989 are marked by a restructuring of industry, a rapid increase in unemployment – reaching a level of 15–16 per cent in 1994, a high rate of inflation in the early 1990s (over 600 per cent in 1990), public debt and financial problems, and an increasing number of old-age pensioners. Unemployment benefits were introduced in 1989, and can now be paid for a maximum period of one year. Social assistance, which played an insignificant role under the previous system, has increased in importance. The health care system had problems before the change, but the financial situation has deteriorated, leading to spontaneous privatization of health services which are out of reach for wide sectors of the population (Florek, 1994).[14] Several new laws have been adopted concerning old-age and disability pensions. 'These are the topic of endless social and political debates leading to proposals of fundamental reforms within the system' (Golinowska and Ochocki, 1994: 7). Fundamental changes in the regulatory regime governing pensions were adopted in a law in October 1991, which secured the insurance-related right to old-age and disability pension benefits, by introducing criteria relating to the length of time for which social security contributions have been paid and to the amount of earlier earnings. The formula for calculating old-age pension benefits also takes into account a social component which is equal for everybody (Golinowska and Ochocki, 1994). Benefits were constrained through parliamentary and presidential decisions in 1992 and 1993. Work on changing the system of pensions is being continued with the objective of adding an additional pension scheme to the existing one. The rapidly growing private sector (comprising about 40 per cent of the working population) cannot compensate for the decline in contributions from the state sector, thus the potential for financing social insurance is presently weak. Social expenditures financed through budgetary means in the years 1989–1992 diminished in real terms, but their share in the national income increased from 15.3 per cent to 22 per cent. This implies that the decline in real value of budgetary social expenditures was lower than the national income. Thus one may say that social objectives were protected by the state policy (Golinowska and Ochocki, 1994: 10).

The establishment of new types of institutions, which would implement social policy functions and relieve the state budget of the need to fund social objectives directly, has proved difficult due to the political situation with a 'myriad' of political groupings (Golinowska and Ochocki, 1994). The economic situation in Poland has improved since 1992 with an increase in real GNP every year between 1992–94. Industrial output increased by 5 per cent from March 1994 to March 1995.[15] Unemployment has risen continuously, and there is a widening gap in the distribution of wealth. A survey of family budgets indicates that in 1992 some 34 per cent of people in Poland lived below the officially defined subsistence level – the so-called social minimum (adjusted for the OECD equivalency scale) (Golinowska and Ochocki, 1994: 20).

The difficulties of the Polish system of social insurance and welfare imply that there exists at the moment no clear concept for (re-)designing it. Social policies pursued during recent years have been dominated by short-term activities as a result of deep-rooted economic recession and the crisis in state financing accompanying it (Florek, 1994). Trends so far seem to point in the direction of 'the German model', but possibly with less organizational fragmentation of the social insurance system.

4.7 THE FUTURE EUROPEAN WELFARE STATE: (AGAIN) A MODEL FOR THE WORLD?

Governments across Europe are concerned about the current and future developments of their national welfare states. Europeanization and globalization of economic competition and money markets, ageing of the population and rising entitlements, persistent high levels of unemployment, and financial constraints represent pan-European challenges. Curtailments of expenditure are attempted everywhere, but there are also examples of improvements of social programmes and the creation of new ones. Developments are thus not entirely uniform, and it must also be taken into account that expenditure reductions and programme developments occur in diversified institutional contexts. Tampering with Swedish or German programmes has less dramatic consequences than tampering with British and Polish programmes for the populations which shall live with the consequences of policy changes. European welfare states enjoy high political legitimacy, perhaps creating voter expectations which are higher than governments can cope with (cf. recent mass protests in France). The idea and support for state welfare is relatively strong all over Europe. European past and recent welfare history is distinctive in the world. National European welfare states have not been dismantled, and are not likely candidates for dismantlement. Successful European monetary and political integration may prove conducive to convergence of total social expenditure and taxation levels, but institutional convergence is a much more complicated and long-term prospect – if it is likely – or wanted – at all. The 'four freedoms' of the EEA area will offer an incentive to market forces, to established and new providers of welfare insurance and services, and to individuals and companies who increasingly may cross national borders to take out insurance against various future welfare needs. National states have lost welfare monopolies in two ways: by having to adjust to rights and entitlements of non-citizens ('foreigners') and by having to allow people to go beyond the nation state to seek better welfare contracts. Welfare politics have become much more invidualized than before, and developments towards more means-testing and targeting of national social programs will make welfare politics even more individualized. It will become more difficult for national political parties to rally common interests (by class or group) in the welfare field. One cannot rule out the possibility that the effects of the 'four freedoms' of the EU and EEA area may, after a period of probable accelerated privatization of welfare and social security and increasing social inequalities, lead to a re-politicization of welfare issues, but it is not obvious to what extent this will be possible at the level of the nation state given the simultaneous internationalization and individualization of welfare rights. Re-politicization is probably more likely within the framework of – or at least parallel to efforts of – a supranational EU. Already, political initiatives to fight social exclusion and poverty, to develop basic citizen income programmes, to agree on a common policy to encourage more employment, are being discussed at the same time as the big challenge (for every country concerned) of extension of the EU to incorporate as members the poorer Central and East European countries.

There are some observable tendencies in Europe today, that the universalist, Scandinavian welfare states are becoming less uniform, with more space for private pension and health insurance, as well as occupational insurance schemes as supplements to the national public schemes. The principle of universality will most likely prevail, but the public system may provide less generous benefits. On the other hand, continental social security systems in Europe are moving in a universalist direction. Health insurance is universal or near universal all over Western Europe, and The Netherlands in addition to Britan and Scandinavia has a universal old-age pension scheme, and other countries contemplate the introduction of a universal basic pension as a matter of citizen right. Perhaps one can discern a trend towards a European model in which all citizens are guaranteed basic social rights – health services, pensions and so on – on top of which citizens are free to take on (more or less tax-subsidized) private insurance, thus creating social security and welfare systems which to a greater extent than today are dual, socially segmented or structurated.

We shall probably enter a period of more intense struggle on the interpretation of what the problem of our social security systems and welfare states is: is it a problem (only) of cost? inefficiency? bureaucracy? overregulation? moral decay? or how to survive global competition? Or is it a problem of increasing inequality? marginalization? non-participation? increasing social and political divisions? poverty? lack of solidarity? This prospective political struggle will again – as 100 years ago – centre around questions such as the boundary between public (but at which level?) and private welfare responsibility, about morality and norms, about work incentives. How do changes in family and social structures affect the debates and their outcomes in terms of policies? Will extensive targeting, means-testing, and individualization of welfare security destroy the potential for political realignments in favour of (national) state welfare? Can the EU replace the traditional historical role of the national welfare state? Probably not, given the different social structure of Europe today compared to the period when national welfare states were built.

We may enter a new period of experimentation, but in a very different context: European states have developed mature national welfare states. Europe was and still is 'number one' in terms of welfare stateness in the world. Not everybody thinks this is worth a medal, but this is meant as a descriptive characteristic. The international economic and political context is different from 100 years ago: today Europe is challenged by powerful and growing economies of a continent – Asia – in which about 60 per cent of the world population live, while only 6 per cent live in Europe. Both economically and politically, Europe will almost surely become relatively less important. European social security solutions, considered expensive by many politicians and by economists – who are often advisers to governments – may come under increased pressure. But, will 'globalization' only represent a threat to European welfare states, or can Europe (again) become a model for other developing regions of the world for the social role and responsibility of the state in society? But what model? Perhaps a model in which national (or even supranational) political authorities guarantee basic, universal social rights and individuals (and/or families, employers) are 'encouraged' to ensure supplemental welfare services and benefits for various risks? Without considering the risks and effects of actual war and ecological disasters, one may ponder if it is not possible that European voters and governments are inclined to think that in the longer run the combination of market-oriented, democratic, and mature welfare states is a better guarantee of social, labour market and political stability, and thus of a productive work force and attractive investment context, than the combination of (more capitalist) market-oriented, democratic or authoritarian and less developed welfare states.

ENDNOTES

1. Alber (1988) claims that ever since the end of the last century the welfare state has been accused of surpassing its reasonable limits and of producing undesired side effects. In Germany, for example, a heated debate over the excessive economic burdens entailed by Bismarck's social legislation already opened shortly after the turn of the century. At that time the social insurance schemes spent 1.4 per cent of the GDP. Lowe (1993) has registered that in 1952 *The Times* inaugurated the first of many debates on 'The Crisis in the Welfare State'. In that year, 15.6 per cent of the British GDP was spent on social security and services. In 1991 the average social protection expenditure as percentage of GDP in the 12 countries of the EC was 26.0 per cent (Eurostat, *Social Protection in Europe 1993*, 1994).

2. For example, Singapore passed in 1994 a law on 'Maintenance of Parents', through which families rather than the state or community are given care responsibilities for their old and sick.

3. There are many, and a growing number of, attempts in the welfare literature to make ideal-typical welfare models or to classify welfare systems or regimes. Titmuss (1974) distinguished between the residual, industrial achievement, and the institutional model, to which Great Britain, Germany and Sweden would more or less fit as empirical examples. Esping-Andersen (1990) elaborated a classification of welfare states into liberal, conservative-corporatist and social democratic welfare state 'regimes', where again the three mentioned countries would fit into the categories in the order listed above. The liberal welfare state is characterized by means-tested, modest universal transfers and modest social insurance schemes; the corporatist welfare state regime is characterized by social security schemes which preserve status differentials; the social democratic welfare regime is composed of countries in which the principles of universalism and equality and market-independent rights are extensive. Castles and Mitchell (1990) make a four-fold typology which corresponds to the Esping-Andersen's, but split up the liberal welfare state category into two through which USA remains as an example of a liberal welfare state and the UK becomes a 'Labourite' welfare state. Ginsburg (1992) likewise presents a four-fold typology of welfare regimes: corporate market economy (for example USA), liberal collectivist (for example UK) social market economy (for example Germany), and social democratic (for example Sweden). Jones (1985) distinguishes between low and high-spending welfare *capitalist* states, and between *welfare* capitalist and welfare capitalist states, thus also arriving at four categories. Leibfried (1993) uses a typology reminiscent of Esping-Andersen's, but adds a fourth category – 'the Latin rim countries', or 'rudimentary' welfare states – basically characterized by being weakly developed welfare states. Ferrera (1996) suggests some other specific characteristics of the Southern European countries, and put the label 'Southern model' on these welfare states. An attempt to include East European and communist welfare systems into these typological exercises has been done by Deacon (1992) who calls those systems 'bureaucratic-collectivist'. The various typologies represent summary answers to questions and dimensions which vary from one 'typologist' to another, dependent upon what each author puts into the concept of the welfare state.

4. Germany, the UK and Sweden are frequently taken as prototypes of three of the models distinguished between, and Poland is selected to represent countries moving out of the Communist system model. It is too early to tell what kind of welfare system will develop in former Communist countries in Central and Eastern Europe, but the evolution of social security prior to 1989 was designed to a great extent according to the Soviet model throughout Central and Eastern Europe (Zacher, 1982).

5. According to Eurostat (1994). Average for 11 member states: Greece not included, because of lack of data.
6. According to *The European*, 28 January–3 February 1994, with reference to OECD statistics.
7. For example in the Long Term – Governmental Programme of the Labour government of Gro Harlem Brundtland in 1989 for the period 1990–93 (Kuhnle and Solheim, 1991).
8. Data from 1992 (source) confirm the differences, but they are less marked. (1992, data to be inserted in text).
9. This paragraph is primarily based on overview publications from the Danish National Institute of Social Research in Copenhagen: Ploug and Kvist (eds) (vols. 1, 2 and 4, 1994).
10. *Gesundheitsstrukturgesetz*, in effect from 1 January 1993.
11. *Arbeitsförderungsgesetz*, in effect from January 1994.
12. *Rentenreformgesetz*, passed in 1992.
13. *Pflege-Versicherungsgesetz*, in effect from January 1995.
14. A law on private health care was passed in 1989 (Golinowska and Ochocki, 1994).
15. *The European*, 17–23 March 1995.

REFERENCES

Alber, Jens (1982), *Vom Armenhaus zum Wohlfahrtsstaat*, Frankfurt: Campus.

Alber, Jens (1988), 'Is there a crisis of the welfare state? Cross-national evidence from Europe, North America, and Japan', *European Sociological Review*, **4**, (3) 181–207

Atkinson, A.B. (1993), 'What is happening to the distribution of income in the UK?', *Discussion Paper 87*, London: LSE, STICERD Welfare State Programme

Barr, N. and Coulter, F. (1991), 'Social security', in J. Hills, (ed.), *The State of Welfare: The Welfare State in Britain Since 1974*, Oxford: Clarendon Press 274–337.

Bradshaw, J. (1993), 'Social security', in D. Marsh and R.A.W. Rhodes, (eds.), *Implementing Thatcherite Policies : Audit of an Era*, Milton Keynes, Open University Press: 81–100

Campbell, J. (1994), 'The fiscal crisis of the post-socialist countries', in K. Nielsen, Jessop, B. and Hausner, J (eds.), *Strategic Choice and Path Dependency in Post-Socialism*, Aldershot: Edward Elgar.

Castles, F. and Mitchell D. (1990), 'Three worlds of welfare capitalism or four?', *Public Policy Discussion Paper No. 21*, Canberra: Australian National University.

Cochrane, Allan (1993), 'Looking for a European welfare state', in A. Cochrane and J. Clarke (eds.), *Comparing Welfare States. Britain in International Context*, London: Sage, 239–68.

Deacon, Bob (1992), 'East European welfare: past, present and future in comparative context', in Bob Deacon *et al.* (eds.), *The New Eastern Europe. Social Policy Past, Present and the Future*, London: Sage, 1–30.

Ervik, Rune and Kuhnle, Stein (1994), 'The Nordic welfare model and the European Union', *Mimeo.*, University of Bergen.

Esping-Andersen, Gösta (1990), *The Three Worlds of Welfare Capitalism*, Cambridge: Polity Press.

Eurostat (1994), *Social Protection in Europe 1993*, Luxembourg: Commission of the European Communities.

Ferrera, Maurizio (1993), *EC Citizens and Social Protection. Main results from a Eurobarometer Study*, Brussels: EC Commission, Division V/E/2.

Ferrera, Maurizio (1996), 'The 'southern model' of welfare in social Europe', *Journal of European Social Policy*, **6** (1) 17–37.

Flora, Peter (1986) 'Introduction', in P. Flora (ed.), *Growth to Limits. The Western European Welfare States Since World War II*, Vols 1 and 2, Berlin. xi–xxxvi Walter de Gruyter.

Flora, Peter (1986, 1987) *Growth to Limits. The Western European Welfare States Since World War II*, Vols. 1and 2 (1986), Vol. 4 (1987) Berlin: Walter de Gruyter.

Flora, Peter (1993a), 'Europa als Sozialstaat?' in B. Schäfers (ed.) *Lebensverhält-nisse und soziale Konflikte im neuen Europa*, Frankfurt a.M: Campus.

Flora, Peter (1993b) 'The national welfare states and European integration', in L. Moreno (ed.), *Social Exchange and Welfare Development*, Madrid: Consejo Superior de Investigaciones Cientificas. 11–22.

Florek, Ludwik (1994), 'Evolution of social security in Poland', in Maydell, B. von and Hohnerlein, E.M. (eds), *The Transformations of Social Security Systems in Central and Eastern Europe*, Leuven: Peeters Press, 35–46.

Ginsburg, N. (1992), *Divisions of Welfare*, London: Sage.

Golinowska, Stanislawa and Ochocki, Andrzej (1994), 'Social policy and social conditions in Poland: 1989–1993', *Occasional Paper No 4* Warsaw: Institute of Labour and Social Studies.

Guillemard, Anne-Marie (1993), 'European perspectives on ageing policies', in L. Moreno, (ed.), *Social Exchange and Welfare Development*, Madrid: Consejo Superior de Investigaciones Cientificas, 37–66.

Gutberlet, Gabi (1994) 'Social security in Germany – recent trends in cash benefits', in Niels Ploug and Kvist, Jon (eds.), *Recent Trends in Cash Benefits in Europe*, Social Security in Europe, Copenhagen: The Danish National Institute of Social Research, vol. 4, 85–102.

Hatland, Aksel (1994), 'Alderspensjonene', in A. Hatland, S. Kuhnle, T. I. Romøren, *Den norske velferdsstaten*, Oslo: Ad Notam, Gyldendal.

Heclo, Hugh (1981), 'Towards a new welfare state?', in P. Flora and Heidenheimer, A.J. (eds), *The Development of Welfare States in Europe and America*, New Brunswick, US and London, UK: Transaction Books, 383–406.

Johnson, Norman (1987), *The Welfare State in Transition: The Theory and Practise of Welfare Pluralism*, Brighton: Wheatsheaf Books.

Jones, Catherine (1985), *Patterns of Social policy: An Introduction to Comparative Analysis*, London: Tavistock.

Kuhnle, Stein and Solheim, Liv (1991), *Velferdsstaten: Vekst og omstilling*, 2nd rev. ed. Oslo: TANO.

Leibfried, Stephan (1993) 'Towards a European welfare state?', in Catherine Jones (ed.), *New Perspectives on the Welfare State in Europe*, London: Routledge, 133–56.

Leibfried, Stephan (1994) 'The social dimension of the European Union: *en route* to positively joint sovereignty?', *Journal of European Social Policy*, **4** (4), 239–262.

Lindstrøm, Ulf (1985), *Fascism in Scandinavia 1920–1940*, Oslo: Norwegian University Press.

Lødemel, Ivar (1994), 'Recent trends in cash benefits: Norway', in N. Ploug, and Kvist, J. (eds), *Recent Trends in Cash Benefits in Norway,* Copenhagen: The Danish National Institute of Social Research, 61–72.

Lowe, Rodney (1993), *The Welfare State in Britain since 1945,* Basingstoke and London: Macmillan.

Millar, J. (1993), 'The continuing trend of rising poverty', in A. Sinfield, (ed.), *Poverty, Inequality and Justice*, New Waverly Papers 6, Edinburgh: Department of Social Policy and Social Work, University of Edinburgh.

Mishra, Ramesh (1993), 'Social policy in a postmodern world', in Catherine Jones (ed.), *New Perspectives on the Welfare State in Europe*, London: Routledge, 18–42.

NOSOSCO (1995), *Social Security in the Nordic Countries*, Copenhagen: Nordic Social Statistical Committee (2: 1995).

OECD (1981), *The Welfare State in Crisis*, Paris.

OECD (1993), 'Earnings inequality: changes in the 1980s', *Employment Outlook*, Paris.

Offe, Claus (1993), 'The politics of social policy in east european transition: antecedents, agents, and agenda of reform', *Seminar Papers No. 12*, Cracow: Cracow Academy of Sciences.

Palme, Joachim (1994) 'Recent developments in income transfer systems in Sweden', in Niels Ploug and Kvist, Jon (eds.), *Recent Trends in Cash Benefits in Europe*, Vol. 4, Copenhagen: The Danish National Institute of Social Research Social Security in Europe, 39–60.

Roebroek, Joop M. (1991), 'Social policy diversities in Europe', in Danny Pieters (ed.), *Social Security in Europe*, Brussels: Bruylant, Antwerpen: Maklu Uitgevers, 61–96.

Schulte, Bernd (1991) 'Social security legislation in the European communities: coordination, harmonization, and convergence', in *Social Security in Europe*, Antwerpen: Maklu Uitgevers, Brussels: Bruylant, 153–75.

Sinfield, Adrian (1994) 'The latest trends in social security in the United Kingdom', in Niels Ploug and Kvist, Jon (eds.), *Recent Trends in Cash Benefits in Europe*, Social Security in Europe, Vol. 4, Copenhagen: The Danish National Institute of Social Research, 123–48.

Social Protection in Europe 1993 (1994), Eurostat, Luxembourg.

St. meld. nr 35 (1994–95) (Norwegian Government White Paper to parliament on welfare).

Stokke, Liv J. (1993), *Uførepensjonistar i offentleg sektor*, Oslo: FAFO.

Titmuss, Richard H. (1974), *Social Policy. An Introduction*, London: Allen and Unwin.

Veggeland, Noralv (1996), 'Den nordiske modellen smuldrer bort', *Aftenposten*, 20 January.

Walker, Alan (1986) 'The future of the British welfare state: privatization or socialization?', in Adalbert, Evers *et al.* (eds.), *The Changing Face of Welfare*, Aldershot: Gower, 184–205.

Wilson, Gail (1993), 'The challenge of an ageing electorate: changes in the formation of social policy in Europe?', *Journal of European Social Policy*, 3 (2), 91–105.

Zacher, Hans F. (1982), 'Sozialrecht in sozialistischen Ländern Osteuropas', *Jahrbuch für Ostrecht*, 33.

5. Welfare state and welfare mix in a new labour market

Peter Scherer[1]

This brief paper addresses three interrelated issues:

- changes in the distribution of employment;
- the relation of these changes to changes in the demand for labour;
- trends in family formation, and how these interact with labour market changes to influence the incidence of low incomes across households.

It concludes with some remarks on social insurance institutions and arrangements.

5.1 EMPLOYMENT DISTRIBUTION

Over the past 25 years, labour markets in OECD countries have changed their structure profoundly. The broad outlines of these changes are summarized in Table 5.1. This shows employment growth over the 21 years more than kept pace with population growth in OECD countries. In fact as far as total number of people in employment is concerned, if the OECD was characterized by 'full employment' in 1972, then it still is. The proportion of the population in remunerated employment of all types is essentially the same as in 1972: a little higher for the OECD as a whole; a little less for Europe (Table 5.2).

This overall stability is, of course, the result of significant changes in the composition of employment. Firstly, the share of young people in total employment has fallen: this would have been expected because the fall in the birth-rate has stabilized the size of this sector of the population, but in fact the fall in employment has been even greater, particularly for young men: the fall for young women has been less pronounced. Employment of adult men has grown, but not kept pace with population growth, so that while their share of employment has remained stable, the proportion of adult men not in employment has increased from 5 to 12.5 per cent of the age group (and to 15 per cent in Europe). Employment has also failed to keep pace with population change for older men.

Table 5.1 Employment, unemployment and population, 1972–95: 12 OECD countries[a]

	Employment				Unemployment				Population			
	1972	1979	1989	1995	1972	1979	1989	1995	1972	1979	1989	1995
					Millions							
Men 15–24	27.6	27.5	25.1	22.3	2.2	3.2	3.5	3.8	45.9	48.8	48.1	46.4
Men 25–54	99.4	109.9	122.2	130.4	2.0	3.2	5.5	7.8	105.5	118.5	135.2	148.9
Men 55–64	20.4	20.1	21.4	21.0	0.5	0.7	1.1	1.3	26.4	28.1	33.9	34.6
Women 15–24	21.9	23.0	22.0	19.5	1.7	3.2	3.5	3.5	46.3	48.5	47.2	45.0
Women 25–54	50.8	65.3	86.5	97.7	1.5	3.1	5.8	7.5	109.7	121.0	136.7	150.1
Women 55–64	10.2	11.4	12.7	13.6	0.2	0.4	0.5	0.7	30.5	32.9	36.9	37.0
Persons 15–24	49.4	50.5	47.2	41.9	3.9	6.5	7.0	7.2	92.2	97.3	95.4	91.4
Persons 25–54	150.2	175.2	208.7	228.1	3.5	6.3	11.4	15.3	215.2	239.5	272.0	299.0
Persons 55–64	30.5	31.5	34.1	34.6	0.7	1.1	1.6	2.0	57.0	61.0	70.7	71.6
Persons 15–65	230.2	257.2	289.9	304.6	8.1	13.8	20.0	24.5	364.4	397.7	438.1	462.0
					% distribution							
Men 15–24	12.0	10.7	8.7	7.3	27.2	23.3	17.4	15.4	12.6	12.3	11.0	10.0
Men 25–54	43.2	42.7	42.1	42.8	24.5	23.4	27.7	31.9	28.9	29.8	30.9	32.2
Men 55–64	8.9	7.8	7.4	6.9	6.4	5.0	5.3	5.2	7.2	7.1	7.7	7.5
Women 15–24	9.5	8.9	7.6	6.4	20.8	23.5	17.7	14.1	12.7	12.2	10.8	9.7
Women 25–54	22.1	25.4	29.8	32.1	18.4	22.1	29.2	30.6	30.1	30.4	31.2	32.5
Women 55–64	4.4	4.4	4.4	4.5	2.7	2.8	2.7	2.8	8.4	8.3	8.4	8.0

79

Table 5.1 Continued...

	Employment				Unemployment				Population			
	1972	1979	1989	1995	1972	1979	1989	1995	1972	1979	1989	1995
Persons 15–24	21.5	19.6	16.3	13.7	48.4	46.7	35.1	29.5	25.3	24.5	21.8	19.8
Persons 25–54	65.3	68.1	72.0	74.9	42.8	45.5	56.9	62.5	59.1	60.2	62.1	64.7
Persons 55–64	13.3	12.3	11.7	11.4	9.1	7.8	8.0	8.0	15.6	15.3	16.1	15.5
Persons 15–65	100.0	100.0	100.0	100.0	100.0	100.0	100.0	100.0	100.0	100.0	100.0	100.0

	Ratio to population (%)								Unemployment rate (%)			
	1972	1979	1989	1995	1972	1979	1989	1995	1972	1979	1989	1995
Men 15–24	60.0	56.3	52.3	48.2	4.8	6.6	7.2	8.1	7.4	10.5	12.1	14.4
Men 25–64	94.2	92.8	90.4	87.5	1.9	2.7	4.1	5.2	2.0	2.9	4.3	5.7
Men 55–64	77.2	71.7	63.2	60.6	2.0	2.5	3.1	3.6	2.5	3.3	4.7	5.7
Women 15–24	47.3	47.4	46.6	43.4	3.7	6.7	7.5	7.7	7.2	12.4	13.8	15.1
Women 25–54	46.3	54.0	63.2	65.1	1.4	2.5	4.3	5.0	2.9	4.5	6.3	7.1
Women 55–64	33.2	34.6	34.3	36.8	0.7	1.2	1.5	1.9	2.1	3.2	4.1	4.8
Persons 15–24	53.6	51.9	49.5	45.8	4.2	6.6	7.3	7.9	7.3	11.4	12.9	14.8
Persons 25–54	69.8	73.2	76.7	76.3	1.6	2.6	4.2	5.1	2.3	3.5	5.2	6.3
Persons 55–64	53.6	51.7	48.1	48.3	1.3	1.8	2.3	2.7	2.4	3.3	4.5	5.4
Persons 15–65	63.2	64.7	66.2	65.9	2.2	3.5	4.6	5.3	3.4	5.1	6.4	7.5

Note: ^a USA, Japan, West Germany, France, Italy, Canada, Spain, Australia, Sweden, Netherlands, Norway, Finland.

Table 5.2 Employment, unemployment and population, 1972–95: eight European OECD countries[a]

	Employment				Unemployment				Population			
	1972	1979	1989	1995	1972	1979	1989	1995	1972	1979	1989	1995
						Millions						
Men 15–24	10.3	9.6	8.8	6.2	0.5	1.2	1.7	1.7	17.3	18.8	19.2	17.3
Men 25–54	40.0	41.5	43.1	47.1	0.5	1.2	2.7	4.2	42.2	44.7	48.7	55.7
Men 55–64	9.0	8.5	8.3	7.6	0.2	0.3	0.5	0.6	12.2	12.3	15.1	15.3
Women 15–24	7.8	7.4	6.7	4.8	0.4	1.4	2.0	1.7	16.8	18.2	18.4	16.5
Women 25–54	17.8	21.8	26.8	32.0	0.3	1.1	3.3	4.4	42.8	44.7	48.2	55.1
Women 55–64	3.6	3.9	3.9	4.1	0.1	0.2	0.3	0.4	14.4	14.4	16.3	16.2
Persons 15–24	18.1	17.0	15.5	11.0	0.9	2.6	3.7	3.5	34.1	37.0	37.6	33.8
Persons 25–54	57.8	63.3	69.8	79.1	0.8	2.4	6.1	8.7	85.0	89.4	96.9	110.8
Persons 55–64	12.7	12.4	12.2	11.7	0.2	0.5	0.8	1.0	26.6	26.7	31.4	31.6
Persons 15–65	88.5	92.6	97.5	101.8	2.0	5.4	10.6	13.1	145.7	153.1	166.0	176.2
						% distribution						
Men 15–24	11.6	10.4	9.0	6.1	26.5	22.1	15.8	13.0	11.9	12.3	11.6	9.8
Men 25–54	45.2	44.8	44.2	46.3	26.2	22.7	25.8	32.3	28.9	29.2	29.4	31.6
Men 55–64	10.2	9.2	8.5	7.5	9.0	5.3	5.0	4.7	8.4	8.0	9.1	8.7
Women 15–24	8.8	8.0	6.9	4.7	19.0	25.9	19.2	13.3	11.5	11.9	11.1	9.4
Women 25–54	20.1	23.5	27.4	31.4	16.4	20.6	31.2	33.7	29.4	29.2	29.0	31.3
Women 55–64	4.1	4.2	4.0	4.0	2.8	3.3	2.9	2.9	9.9	9.4	9.8	9.2

Table 5.2 Continued...

	Employment				Unemployment				Population			
	1972	1979	1989	1995	1972	1979	1989	1995	1972	1979	1989	1995
Persons 15–24	20.4	18.3	15.9	10.8	45.5	48.0	35.0	26.4	23.4	24.2	22.7	19.2
Persons 25–54	65.3	68.3	71.6	77.7	42.6	43.3	57.1	66.0	58.4	58.4	58.4	62.9
Persons 55–64	14.3	13.4	12.5	11.5	11.9	8.7	7.9	7.6	18.3	17.4	18.9	17.9
Persons 15–65	100.0	100.0	100.0	100.0	100.0	100.0	100.0	100.0	100.0	100.0	100.0	100.0

	Ratio to population (%)				Unemployment rate (%)			
	1972	1979	1989	1995	1972	1979	1989	1995
Men 15–24	59.2	51.0	45.6	35.8	4.9	11.2	16.0	21.7
Men 25–64	94.9	92.8	88.4	84.5	1.3	2.9	6.0	8.3
Men 55–64	73.9	69.1	55.1	49.8	1.9	3.3	6.1	7.5
Women 15–24	46.5	40.5	36.5	29.1	4.6	16.1	23.3	26.6
Women 25–54	41.4	48.7	55.5	58.0	1.8	4.9	11.0	12.2
Women 55–64	25.3	27.0	23.6	25.2	1.5	4.5	7.3	8.4
Persons 15–24	53.0	45.9	41.2	32.6	4.8	13.4	19.3	23.9
Persons 25–54	68.0	70.8	72.1	71.3	1.4	3.6	8.0	9.9
Persons 55–64	47.6	46.4	38.7	37.1	1.8	3.7	6.5	7.8
Persons 15–65	60.7	60.5	58.7	57.8	2.2	5.5	9.8	11.4

Note: [a] West Germany, France, Italy, Spain, Sweden, Netherlands, Norway, Finland.

The overall stability in the ratio of employment to the population has been due to the strong increase in the proportion of adult women in employment: it rose by 18.5 percentage points in the OECD as a whole, and by 17.5 per cent in Europe. This increase, and a smaller related increase in employment among older women, was enough to counterbalance the fall in male employment in the OECD as a whole, and almost counterbalanced its stronger fall in Europe.

This stability in overall employment has been accompanied by an increase in unemployment, both in absolute and in relative terms, so that the proportion of the population not at work, looking for work and available to work, has increased from 2.2 to 5.6 per cent of the population, and from 3.4 to 7.8 per cent of the labour force. This increase in unemployment has usually been explained by an increase in participation. As employment has, overall, kept pace with population growth, this is a tautology rather than an explanation: the labour force comprises the employed plus the unemployed, and so an increase in unemployment is by definition an increase in the labour force for a given level of employment. The stability in overall employment does not mean that unemployment can be dismissed as 'merely' the consequence of higher participation. Only by looking more closely at the way in which unemployment has grown can its real significance be assessed.

5.1.1 Adults

It turns out that the relationship is very different for the two sexes. Firstly, among adult men, the rise in unemployment has nothing to do with an increase in participation. Figure 5.1 shows that there is a clear and strong relation across countries between employment and unemployment: the growth in unemployment is not due to any rise in participation (which is in any case over 90 per cent). For this sector of the population, it is true that that the growth in unemployment has been the consequence of the fall in employment and *vice versa*: in countries (such as the USA) where adult male employment has fluctuated, unemployment has done so in sympathy (Figure 5.2). Where adult male employment has fallen steadily, unemployment has risen (as is the case for France), but no more than would be expected by a movement down the slope in Figure 5.1.

Unemployment has risen among adult women too, as much as for men, and now accounts for as much of the total as does unemployment among adult men. But in this case the growth in unemployment has been accompanied by a *growth* in employment. There is in fact no clear relation at all between unemployment among adult women and the proportion of adult women who are employed: neither when comparison is across countries (Figure 5.3) nor when looking at trends over time (Figure 5.4).

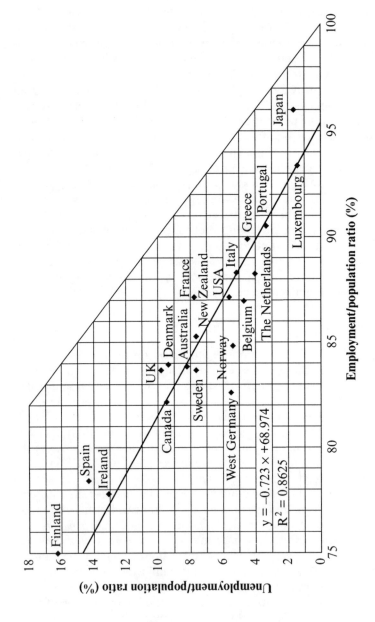

Figure 5.1 Employment and unemployment, men aged 25–54, 1993: OECD countries

Source: OECD labour force statistics database.

84

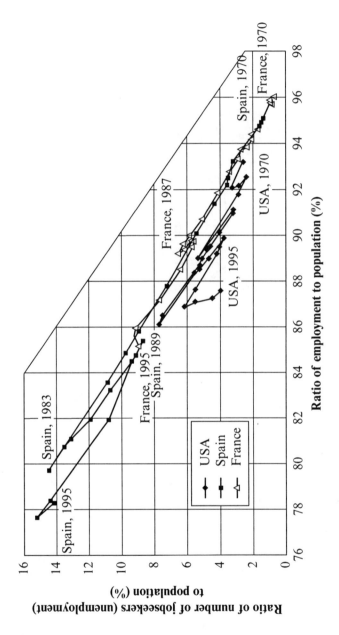

Figure 5.2 Relation between employment and unemployment, men aged 25–54, 1970–95: France, Spain and the USA

Source: OECD labour force statistics: database.

85

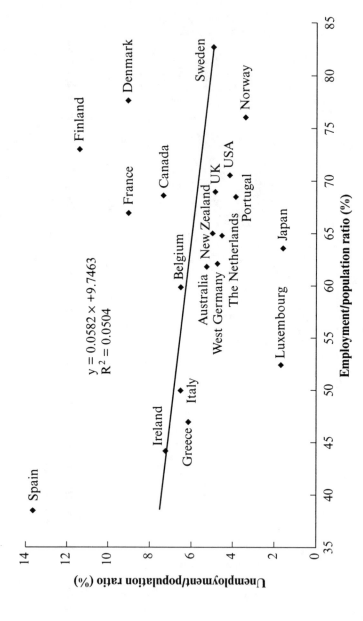

Figure 5.3 Employment and unemployment, women aged 25–54, 1993: OECD countries

Source: OECD labour force statistics database.

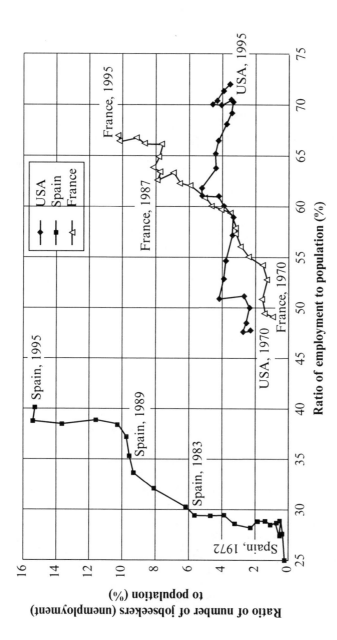

Figure 5.4 Relation between employment and unemployment, women aged 25–54, 1970–95: France, Spain and the USA

Source: OECD labour force statistics database.

The differences between countries are not due to part-time employment. Although part time employment has grown among men in recent years (Table 5.3), it remains a minor part of employment, and the fluctuations of employment that have occurred over the last two decades are largely fluctuations in full-time employment. Among women, part-time employment has also grown, but remains (in all but a minority of OECD countries) much less important than full-time employment.

Table 5.3 Number of persons in total and part-time employment in 15 OECD countries[a] in 1975 and 1995, in millions

	Employment classified as						Proportion part-time %	
	Total			Part-time[b]			1975	1995
	1975	1995	change	1975	1995	change		
Males	162.6	186.3	23.7	9.9	16.4	6.5	6.1	8.8
Females	96.2	142.6	46.4	25.7	45.2	19.5	26.7	31.7
Persons	258.8	328.9	70.1	35.6	61.6	26.0	13.8	18.7

Notes:
[a] Australia, Austria, Belgium, Canada, Denmark, France, West Germany, Italy, Japan, Luxembourg, The Netherlands, New Zealand, Norway, UK, USA.
[b] Definitions of part-time work differ across countries.

Source: OECD full-time/part-time database.

5.1.2 Youth

The strong growth in employment among adult women in OECD countries would have meant a strong rise in overall employment rates if it had not been for the other change which stands out in Table 5.1 – the collapse in employment among young people. As a result of the fall in the birthrate from the mid-1960s onwards, young people now comprise a smaller proportion of the working age population, but employment has fallen even faster, so that the employment rate among them, and their share in total employment, has fallen even faster. Unemployment in this group has also risen – by no means as much as the fall in employment, and the gap between youth and adult unemployment (when expressed as a proportion of the respective populations and labour forces) has fallen in relative terms, although it has increased in absolute terms.

The difference between the fall in employment and the (smaller) rise in unemployment is largely – though not completely – accounted for by the increase in participation in full-time education. The fall in demand for unskilled labour has been most pronounced for young people, among

Table 5.4 *Labour force status and school attendance of persons aged 15–24: France, Germany, Spain, UK, USA*

		At work			At school			Jobseeking			Neither at school nor at work			Total in age cohort		
Country	Year	At work only	Total at work	At school and at work	Total at school	At school only	Job seeking while at school	Total job seeking	Looking for work	Not looking for work	Total	%	Thousands	Labour force participation rate	Unemployment rate	School attendance rate
France	1984	36.1	39.7	3.5	41.7	37.9	0.2	12.9	12.7	9.5	22.2	100.0	7 510.0	52.6	24.6	41.7
	1989	33.1	37.1	4.0	50.2	46.0	0.2	9.1	8.9	7.8	16.7	100.0	7 330.6	46.2	19.7	50.2
	1994	21.0	26.1	5.1	65.4	59.3	1.0	10.6	9.6	4.0	13.6	100.0	7 412.6	36.7	28.8	65.4
Germany	1984	34.3	51.3	17.0	56.5	38.1	1.3	5.9	4.6	4.7	9.2	100.0	9 721.3	57.2	10.3	56.5
	1989	37.0	56.2	19.2	53.6	34.1	0.3	3.3	3.0	6.5	9.5	100.0	8 495.2	59.5	5.5	53.6
	1994	28.5	48.5	20.0	63.7	43.3	0.5	4.5	4.0	3.8	7.8	100.0	8 398.0	53.0	8.5	63.7
Spain	1989	29.2	31.3	2.1	49.7	44.9	2.6	16.3	13.7	7.4	21.1	100.0	6 409.1	47.6	34.3	49.7
	1994	21.1	23.6	2.4	58.1	51.5	4.2	19.4	15.2	5.6	20.8	100.0	6 425.9	43.0	45.1	58.1
UK	1984	40.6	53.6	12.9	38.0	23.8	1.2	12.6	11.4	9.9	21.4	100.0	9 073.3	66.2	19.1	28.0
	1989	46.5	65.1	18.6	40.2	20.5	1.1	7.5	6.4	6.9	13.3	100.0	8 541.2	72.7	10.3	40.2
	1994	39.1	54.6	15.5	39.7	22.8	1.4	10.6	9.2	12.0	21.3	100.0	7 272.3	65.2	16.3	39.7
USA	1973	46.0	55.6	9.6	35.4	23.8	2.0	6.2	4.2	14.5	18.6	100.0	36 377.6	61.7	10.0	35.4
	1978	46.6	57.2	10.6	35.1	22.0	2.6	8.5	5.9	12.3	18.3	100.0	39 328.5	65.7	13.0	35.1
	1983	44.0	53.5	9.5	35.6	23.0	3.0	12.0	9.0	11.4	20.4	100.0	40 346.7	65.6	18.4	35.6
	1988	47.9	59.5	11.6	36.6	22.8	2.3	7.6	5.4	10.1	15.5	100.0	37 488.6	67.1	11.4	36.6
	1993	45.4	56.6	11.2	38.0	24.2	2.5	8.6	6.1	10.5	16.6	100.0	34 479.6	65.2	13.2	38.0

% of age cohort

whom on-the-job experience is least likely to compensate for poor formal qualifications. In most OECD countries, the last decade has seen a strong rise in participation in school and in higher education. This has meant that while the number in employment has fallen, the number of unemployed has not necessarily risen – most young people in school are not recorded as looking for work, even if school participation has occurred as a substitute for full-time education In fact, unemployment (which at least indicates a formal attachment to the labour market) is, in my view, overused as an indicator of social distress among young people.

This is illustrated by Table 5.4, which shows, for the USA, the UK, France Spain and Germany how participation in schooling and labour force participation interact. It will be seen that there much of the fall in employment in Europe for this age group has been accompanied by a rise in school participation (including higher education). The proportion of young people neither in school nor at work has little relation to the unemployment rate.

Interpreting these data is difficult, since some of the school participation is clearly 'forced': young people may well remain at school in the absence of job opportunities, and so some unemployment has been converted into unwilling school attendance. Minimum wages (and – in some countries – the availability of basic income support) put a floor on the wages payable to young people, which in turn restricts employment opportunities for those with low educational attainment. However, allowing wages to fall does not solve the problem: technological change is in any case reducing the demand for poorly educated workers, making it unlikely that downward wage flexibility will ensure adequate employment opportunities. This can be seen most clearly in the UK, which has eliminated all minimum wage regulations, and yet has seen employment fall among young people since 1989, while school participation by teenagers has remained static.

5.1.3 Older workers

Among older people, employment growth has also failed to keep pace with population growth, and employment has fallen absolutely in Europe. However, the growth in this sector of the population has meant that older workers have maintained their share of total employment.

In summary, then, the big change in the labour market has been a rise in female adult employment accompanied by a simultaneous rise in unemployment, with a fall in youth employment being the main offset. Overall employment rates have not changed significantly. The growth in productivity has been accommodated, not by a fall in employment, but by a reduction in average working time – largely through the growth in part time employment.

5.2 DEMAND FOR LABOUR

Underlying these changes in employment patterns have been changes in the structure of labour demand – changes which are not understood fully. The clearest evidence is from the USA, where census and survey data for a number of decades are available in unit record form. Average hourly earnings for men have been stagnant in the USA for at least two decades now. At the same time, the variance between income deciles has increased steadily, so that the real earnings of those in the lower deciles have fallen. Earned incomes in the lowest decile have fallen even more than hourly earnings, as employment has become more interrupted (USA, 1995).

Over the same period, earned incomes among women have increased steadily largely because of the strong increase in female participation. Looked at from the aggregate level, it would appear that this was a response to the stagnation or fall in male incomes. However, studies of the joint participation of married couples (Juhn and Murphy, 1996) show that the strongest increases in earnings and in participation have occurred among the spouses of high male earners: the increase in female incomes has largely been a response to the demand for new skills which this educated (and previously unmarketed) sector of the population can offer. In the bottom deciles, participation by women has increased also, and where this has been done successfully it has prevented absolute falls in real household incomes.

In Europe the basic story is similar. However because of the existence of a *de facto* floor on earnings (due to the availability of subsistence income transfers) and the influence of minimum wages on the demand for low-skilled labour, real hourly earnings for those at the bottom of the distribution have not fallen (even, on the whole, in the UK) or have generally risen in line with earnings (OECD, 1996). Partly as a result, entry level jobs are hard to find, and employment for young people has fallen more than in the USA. Employment levels for adults have not diverged from those outside Europe to a significant extent.

When countries are compared (Figure 5.5), and when changes over time are observed within countries (Figure 5.6), there is in fact a stronger relationship between *male* employment and female unemployment than there is between female employment and unemployment. This would appear to be the result of the complexities of the labour market, a complexity which has important implications for social policy. Fluctuations in male employment largely represent fluctuations in the demand for unskilled labour, and these fluctuations affect women as much as men (although where – as in Spain – female employment is very low, rises in male employment do not appear to be associated with pauses in the rise in female unemployment).

5.3 HOUSEHOLD EMPLOYMENT PATTERNS

The result of these changes has been a significant shift in the incidence of employment among households. The entry of women into the labour force has meant a significant increase in the proportion of households with two or more income earners. The proportion of households with no income earner has not fallen: if anything it has risen (although on this point the evidence is not decisive) (Gregg and Wadsworth, 1996b). The decline in youth employment has been accompanied by a compensating rise in adult employment. There has been no noticeable change overall in the proportion of households without an income earner: the main shift has been from one- to two-earner households.

This growth in the proportion of households with two incomes has not been purely a purely coincidental response to labour market changes, however. It has also in part been a dynamic response to changes in market opportunities. The point is illustrated in a path-breaking study by Picot and Myles (1995) of trends in Canada over the past two decades. They consider the impact of the tax transfer system on the proportion of the population with a low income, as measured by the proportion for whom income per head (after adjustment for economy of scale within households) is less than half the median. The results for three age groups and the total population are shown in Table 5.5.

It will be seen that the tax transfer system can be credited with averting a high incidence of low income among many age groups – the low incomes being due to the fall in earned incomes among families at the bottom of the income distribution. This is the conventional story of the success of tax transfer systems. However, Picot and Myles go on the show that this is only part of the story:

> Among children aged 0–6, the actual proportion with low incomes rose slightly, by 0.9 percent. But this small change masked two larger changes: a 4.7 percent-age point *increase* because the likelihood of being in a low income group rose *within* the family types, and a 3.8 percent age points *decline* because the mix of children among family types changed. More children were in households with two earners, they had fewer siblings.
>
> At first glance this finding seems contrary to popularly held beliefs, as it is well known that the proportion of children in single parent families has been increasing, and this would tend to increase the incidence of low income. But other changes in family structure have been taking place which tend to swamp the effect of rising numbers of single parent families They include in particular the trend towards more dual earner families and the decreasing number of children per family. The effect of the increase in the number of single parent families is small relative to other changes in the household composition of children.

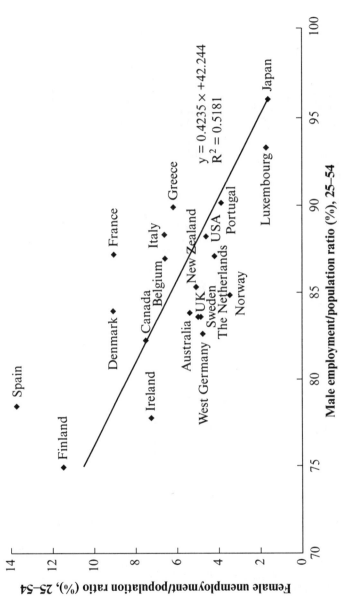

Figure 5.5 Relation between unemployment among women aged 25–54 and employment of men aged 25–54, 1993: OECD countries

Source: OECD labour force statistics database.

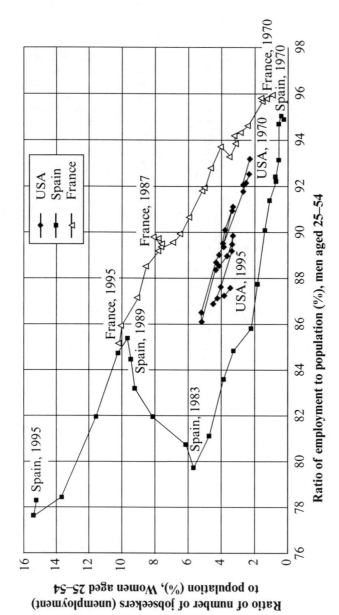

Figure 5.6 Relation between unemployment among women aged 25–54, 1970–95: France, Spain and the USA

Source: OECD labour force statistics database.

Table 5.5 Changing economic status of Canadians aged 0–6, 25–34, 65–74 and all ages combined, 1973–91

Age group	Characteristics	1973	1981	1986	1988	1991
0–6	Number of persons ('000)	2 452	2 442	2 497	2 519	2 643
	Pre-tax pre-transfer income					
	Median income (1991 $000's)	16.9	20.2	20.1	20.8	19.5
	Index (base year = 1973)	100	120	119	123	115
	Relative median income	0.93	0.90	0.90	0.89	0.88
	% Below 0.5 median income	19.9	20.2	24.0	23.7	28.0
	Post-tax post-transfer income					
	Median income (1991 $000's)	15.4	18.3	18.2	18.7	18.0
	Index (base year = 1973)	100	119	118	121	117
	Relative median income	0.91	0.88	0.88	0.87	0.87
	% Below 0.5 median income	15.6	14.8	16.3	16.0	16.5
25–34	Number of persons ('000)	3 053	4 169	4 478	4 581	4 624
	Pre-tax pre-transfer income					
	Median income (1991 $000's)	21.7	25.1	24.6	25.6	23.6
	Index (base year = 1973)	100	115	113	118	109
	Relative median income	1.19	1.12	1.09	1.09	1.07
	% Below 0.5 median income	11.9	14.0	18.0	16.9	20.1
	Post-tax post-transfer income					
	Median income (1991 $000's)	19.2	22.2	21.7	22.2	21.1
	Index (base year = 1973)	100	116	113	116	110
	Relative median income	1.13	1.07	1.05	1.04	1.03
	% Below 0.5 median income	8.7	9.3	11.7	10.3	11.0
65–74	Number of persons ('000)	1 109	1 438	1 607	1 726	1 837
	Pre-tax pre-transfer income					
	Median income (1991 $000's)	6.7	8.7	7.7	8.2	8.8
	Index (base year = 1973)	100	115	113	118	109
	Relative median income	0.37	0.39	0.34	0.35	0.40
	% Below 0.5 median income	56.4	56.2	60.1	59.7	56.3
	Post-tax post-transfer income					
	Median income (1991 $000's)	13.0	16.2	16.8	17.4	18.1
	Index (base year = 1973)	100	125	129	134	139
	Relative median income	0.77	0.78	0.81	0.81	0.88
	% below 0.5 median income	23.1	16.6	8.5	9.3	4.7
All ages	Number of persons ('000)	20 805	23 814	24 807	25 347	26 495
	Pre-tax pre-transfer income					
	Median income (1991 $000's)	18.2	22.4	22.4	23.4	22.1
	Index (base year = 1973)	100	123	123	129	121
	Relative median income	1.00	1.00	1.00	1.00	1.00
	% Below 0.5 median income	21.5	21.1	24.4	23.8	25.6
	Post-tax post-transfer income					
	Median income (1991 $000's)	16.9	20.8	20.7	21.4	20.6
	Index (base year = 1973)	100	123	122	126	122
	Relative median income	1.00	1.00	1.00	1.00	1.00
	% Below 0.5 median income	14.3	12.3	12.1	11.5	11.5

Source: Picot and Myles (1995).

This result points to a crucial social consequence of the change in labour market demand structures. People are reacting to the change in labour demand by lengthening schooling, deferring childbirth, jointly participating in the labour force and having fewer children. They are thus taking the initiative and providing their own protection against social changes and the risks they entail by changing their family formation patterns. These tendencies are even more pronounced in European countries.

5.4 SOCIAL POLICY IMPLICATIONS

Social policy systems in OECD countries are generally based on securing families against fluctuations in their income, whose base is regular earnings from a 'regular' job. Interruptions to regular earnings – from unemployment, illness, family responsibilities or invalidity – are regarded as 'risks' against which insurance is necessary. This idea is behind the international conventions on social security (including those sponsored by the ILO and the Council of Europe).

To the extent that the industrialized societies are adjusting to the changing patterns of labour demand in the ways described above, the social basis of this system is eroding. If most households have a single earner, then the risk to that household of the loss of income from interruption of employment is considerable, and the conjunctural nature of the events make private insurance impractical. Social insurance provides income security which cash-constrained households cannot obtain otherwise.

However once employment shifts from the young to two earner families, the system is eroded at both ends. Two-earner families are better able to accumulate cash reserves and other resources which provide a cushion against income fluctuations. Hence, to the extent that social insurance is funded by specific levies (rather than from the general tax system), they will find themselves paying two premiums for a coverage neither of them really needs[3]. At the same time, those trying to enter the labour market with low qualifications or few marketable skills can find that the cost of social insurance charges payable by the employer makes job opportunities hard to find – or where (as in the UK) these are relatively low, the low rates of wage on offer can make income in work lower than income support payments, particularly for part time work. Hence the system provides an insurance which they do not really need for those who fund it, while failing to provide employment opportunities to those who desperately need them. The problem is not a lack of capacity to fund the transfers, it is a growing divergence of economic interests between those who fund them and those who receive them.

This is not the result of any 'failure' in the labour market. The labour market is changing its nature in response to technological change – and in response to the feedback from these processes themselves: twin income households have different patterns of demand to single earner ones. Nor, in my view, is there any evidence of 'moral' failure on the part of those who have been excluded: the growth in the number of jobseekers is a sign of the desire to participate economically: social pathology is starting to show elsewhere, in groups who are neither at work, nor in school, nor seeking work, nor responsible for dependants.

ENDNOTES

1. Head, Social Policy Division, OECD. Revised version of a paper prepared for the symposium on Challenges to the Welfare State: Internal and External Dynamics for Change, Universidad de Navarra, 23–25 May 1996. The views expressed are the author's own and do not engage the OECD.
2. To adjust for family size, composition and economies of scale, family income is adjusted using a family income scale, which converts family income to a form of per capita income, where the income is per adult equivalent in the family. In the scale used to derive Table 5.5, the first adult is given a weight of 1, other adults and the first child in single parent families a weight of 0.4, and other children a weight of 0.3.
3. As a result, in Spain and other countries with relaxed administrative controls, families try to arrange matters so that only one member is recorded as being in the formal economy and liable to social insurance taxes.

REFERENCES

Greg, P. and Wadsworth, J. (1996b), 'It takes two: employment polarisation in the OECD', *Centre for Economic Performance Discussion Paper No. 304*, London: CEPR, London School of Economics.

Juhn, C. and Murphy, K.M. (1996), 'Wage inequality and family labor supply', NBER *Working Paper No. 5459*, Cambridge: MA.

OECD (1996), 'Earnings and equality, low-paid employment and earnings mobility', Ch. 3 of the *Employment Outlook*, Paris.

Picot, G. and Myles, J. (1995), 'Social transfers, changing family structure, and low income amongst children', *Research Paper Series, No. 82* Analytic Studies Branch, Statistics Canada, Ottawa.

United States of America. Department of Labor (1995), *Report on the American Workforce,* Washington: USGPO.

6. The welfare state backlash and the tax revolt[1]

Kenneth Newton

In large part, the growth of the state in twentieth-century Western Europe is the growth of the welfare state. Indeed, among the nations in the world, the welfare state is particularly associated with the wealthiest, and among the wealthiest it is particularly associated with Western Europe. Other OECD nations, such as the USA, Canada, New Zealand, and Japan, are not particularly outstanding in this respect, although they too have expanded the scope of the public sector and the range of welfare services.

Although the European experience seems to confirm Wagner's law (the public sector share of the economy grows faster than the economy as a whole), the law appeared to have lost its universal and timeless qualities by the mid-1980s and 1990s. The first oil shock of 1971–2 brought the long boom of the 1950s and 1960s towards its close. Lower economic growth and rising unemployment created social problems and greater need for public expenditure. At the same time inflation and higher taxes started to cut into take-home pay so that citizens began to feel the economic squeeze acutely. Consequently, it was said, the post-war mood of active support for public and welfare services, and perhaps the passive acceptance of the tax levels they incurred, seemed to be replaced by a tax revolt and welfare state backlash.

The new public mood was reflected by parties and political movements. In Denmark, the Glistrup 'anti-tax party' took 16 per cent of the poll in 1973 to become, almost overnight, the second largest party in the Danish Parliament. In Britain, local tax increases provoked civil disturbances – the ratepayer revolts of the 1970s. In Sweden in 1976 the Social Democrats were voted from office for the first time since the 1930s and high taxes were a major election issue. A German anti-tax party was formed in 1978, though it was unsuccessful and short-lived. Anti-tax parties were also formed in Norway and Finland, though with little more success.

The new climate of public opinion in the 1980s encouraged many governments in Western Europe to rethink their welfare state, restructure their public sectors, and cut public spending. Kohl in Germany, Schluter in Denmark, and above all Thatcher in Britain, best exemplify the new politics, but equivalents and imitations are to be found all over western Europe. Most notably the majority of Western states remodelled their tax regimes. In fact, the scale, speed and radical nature of the changes in many Western countries in the 1980s were quite remarkable (see, for example, Peters 1991a: 271–99 and Pechman, 1988). In a relatively short time many of the OECD countries had restructured their tax regimes, and it is notable they all did so in similar ways.

The 45 years from 1945 to 1990 in Europe seems to divide into two periods. From 1945 to about 1975 the public and welfare sector expanded rapidly, and public opinion seems to have favoured state activity as a solution to social and economic problems. By the end of the 1970s the scope and pervasiveness of state activity were at their maximum in many countries. From about 1975 the expansion seems to have been halted, if not reversed. As Claus Offe (1984: 157) put it, perhaps with some exaggeration, 'Nowhere is the welfare state believed any longer to be the promising and permanently valid answer to the problems of the socio-political order of advanced capitalist economies.' Doubts were raised about the efficiency and effectiveness of public solutions to social and economic problems, politicians favoured rolling back the state, privatization became the watchword, and individualism, self-sufficiency and the market began to replace collectivism, public welfare and the state. It was not just welfare state's taxing and spending that was called into question, but the entire role of the state in modern society (Peters, 1991b: 116–17). Government action was increasingly presented not as a solution to public problems, but as a cause of them (Hadenius 1986; Douglas 1989).

This paper examines survey evidence of declining support for government welfare services. Is there a growing belief that the scope of government should contract? If so, what sort of people are leading the trend? Is there a welfare state backlash and tax revolt, and if so has it been lead by the middle mass, or by the young, well-educated, and affluent post-materialists? Or perhaps slow economic growth and disillusionment with overloaded government and high taxes is so widespread that the new mood pervades the whole of society, encouraging people to think in terms of individual reliance, rather than public provision of welfare services? Perhaps post-materialism has undermined mass beliefs in the welfare state and set the public agenda flowing in a quite different direction? Perhaps public opinion has turned against public services, and the age of the welfare state is over?

The empirical evidence on which this chapter is based is drawn from volume 3 of the 'Beliefs in Government' volumes, *The Scope of Government*, edited by Ole Borre and Elinor Scarbrough and from Max Kaase and K. Newton, *Beliefs in Government*, both published by Oxford University Press, 1995. This paper does not go into great research details, which are presented in full in volume 3. Rather it provides a few statistical tables to illustrate the argument, and leaves volume 3 to lay out the detailed argument and evidence.

6.1   A TAX REVOLT AND WELFARE STATE BACKLASH OF THE MIDDLE MASS?

Many of the theories of the 1960s and 1970s, which explain the contraction of the state, assume that public opinion was a driving force behind the trend. The first, and in many ways the most prescient, theory on the scene, was Wilensky's theory of 'the middle mass' (Wilensky 1975: 116–19). Wilensky argues that fundamental social change in modern society generates a complex division of labour, high rates of social and geographical mobility, a diffuse 'success ideology' and economic individualism. These changes will produce a growing middle mass of lower-middle class and skilled workers who are detached from the old social class groupings and the values of industrial society. Looking upwards in the social hierarchy the middle mass sees the upper-middle class – libertarian, privileged, educated, living well but apparently paying little in taxes, and allowing its children to run wild at university, often at public expense. Looking down, the middle mass sees the lazy, amoral, often criminal and undeserving poor living off welfare.

The middle mass's reaction to this alliance of immoral poor and upper class liberals is to reaffirm the virtues of hard work, law, order and self-discipline. Taxes and the welfare state serve as symbols for its grievances, expressed as an anti-state feeling covering not just welfare and taxes, but also the issues of public morality, law and order, liberalism and a 'sick society'. According to Wilensky, the movement will be led by the middle mass initially, but as public service costs rise and the tax burden grows, it will be joined by the upper-middle class. Together they will form a political alliance against the working class to turn the welfare backlash into a powerful political force.

Looking back, we can see that Wilensky's book anticipated some recent writing on post-modern individualism, but we can can also see that he exaggerated some local events and over-interpreted a short-lived though quite widespread shift of mood. This, in itself, might lead us to be at least a little bit sceptical about some of the large claims of contemporary post-modernism. The evidence about public opinion towards taxes, public services and public policy shows that there was no fundamental or sustained shift of public opinion in the 1970s or 1980s. On the contrary, support for the state and its services has remained surprisingly and consistently strong, as a comparison of figures for 1974, 1985 and 1990 show (see Tables 6.1 and 6.2). By 1990, no less than in 1985, very large majorities (usually over 70 per cent) in seven West European nations continued to believe that it was government's responsibility to provide health care, services for the elderly and the unemployed, to provide jobs, control prices, assist industry and reduce income differences (see Table 6.2).

Table 6.1 Attitudes towards government responsibility, 1974

	GE	GB	NL	AU	IT	SW	FI	Mean
Elderly	93	88	93	89	92	90	96	92
Medial care	94	95	93	94	96	86	95	94
Education	93	92	98	90	93	89	88	92
Housing	88	85	94	81	92	71	77	84
Equalization of wealth	71	52	82	68	72	75	58	68
Job security	94	85	90	94	94	89	94	91
Low prices	96	–	94	92	95	–	94	94
Minority rights	66	59	73	53	–	68	61	63
Equal rights for sexes	76	49	75	63	64	72	63	66
Pollution control	93	85	92	85	89	92	87	89
Crime prevention	97	87	90	94	95	82	96	92
Energy supply	96	–	95	94	91	–	96	94
Mean	88	78	89	83	88	81	84	85
N	1.483	1.483	1.201	1.585	1.779	1.290	1.224	

Notes: Entries are percentages who think it is essential or important that government take responsibility in the policy field stated. Question: 'Now we would like to know how you feel about some of the particular issues and problems that people often talk about these days. We would like to know (a) how important these issues and problems are in your view. and (b) How far you feel (the) government has reponsibility for them.' Codes: Is it something that you feel (1) is essential for government to do; (2) something that governement has an important responsibility to do; (3) some responsibility to do; (4) no responsibility at all to do? Entries in the table are category (1) and (2) from question (b).

Source: Political Action (1973–6), as presented in vol. 3, *The Scope of Government*, Table 4.1.

Table 6.2 Attitudes towards government responsibility, 1985 and 1990

	GE	GB	IT	AU	IR	SV	NO	Mean
Provide health care								
1985	98	99	100	98			99	
1990	95	100	99	99	97	99	98	
Provide for elderly								
1985	97	98	100	99			99	
1990	95	99	99		98	97	99	98
Provide for the unemployed								
1985	85	86	85	68			81	
1990	78	80	78		91	90	91	85
Provide jobs								
1985	82	72	89	84			82	
1990	74	63	85		71	75	84	75
Control prices								
1985	76	93	98	93			90	
1990	70	89	96		92	86	92	88
Assist growth of industry								
1985	54	95	84	75			77	
1990	52	94	82		90		67	77
Reduce income differences								
1985	67	75	84	78			76	
1990	64	74	78		82	74	72	74
Mean								
1985	80	88	91	85			86	
1990	75	85	88		89	87	86	85
N								
1985	1.048	1.530	1.580	987	–	–	–	
1990	2.812	1.197	983	–	1.005	1.320	1.517	

Notes: Entries are percentages who think it is probably or definitely the government's responsibility. Question: 'On the whole, do you think it should be or should not be the government's responsibility to ...?' Response codes: definitely should be = 1; probably should be = 2; probably should be = 3; definitely should not be 4.

Source: Data for Germany, Britain, Austria, Italy, Ireland, and Norway are from ISSP 1985 and 1990. Data for Sweden are from Research Programme on Comparative Political Culture, G. Gustafsson and O. Johnsson, Umea University. The table appears in vol 3, *The Scope of Government*, Table 4.2.

Nor is there much evidence to indicate a backlash of the middle mass or the liberal, educated, upper class – what might more generally be thought of as the 'yuppy' generation of the Thatcher and Reagan eras in Britain and the USA. On the contrary, social variables such as class and education are not generally or strongly associated with attitudes towards tax, the welfare state, or the scope of government (see the chapters by Huseby, Newton and Confalonieri, Pettersen and Roller in *The Scope of Government*). The extensive mass survey figures presented by these authors do not confirm the middle mass hypothesis. Rather they suggest a simple, linear relationship in which support for the public sector tends to decline, though only marginally, as one goes up the education, income and socio-economic ladder.

The flaw in the middle mass, backlash theory seems to be the assumption that post-industrial changes in the division of labour will result in individualism and a new success ideology which would automatically translate into opposition to taxes and the welfare state. The survey evidence of the 1980s and 1990s makes it clear that there has been no conspicuous shift towards a success ideology based upon economic individualism. On the contrary, traditional attitudes towards social and economic equality and towards the core services of the welfare state seem to have held quite firm. Perhaps it will take another generation or two before social structural change percolates through to mass opinion, but meanwhile there is little evidence to suggest a tax revolt or welfare state backlash among the middle mass, or sustained revolt or backlash on the part of any other social group in Western Europe, for that matter.

6.2 GOVERNMENT OVERLOAD?

Like the theory of the middle mass, the theory of ungovernability or government overload also emphasizes the importance of public opinion as a political force undermining the expansion of the modern state. Unlike middle mass theory, however, it claims that opposition to the state and its activities will come not from particular groups or social strata, but from all quarters of public opinion.

According to overload theory, modern society generates an ever expanding range of special groups and interests each of which urgently presses its case for benefits and services on government. The public is all the more demanding because the revolution of rising expectations makes today's luxuries tomorrow's necessities. Experience of satisfactory government services may also fuel the demand for still more services. As a result claims on government services both proliferate and escalate. At the same time, pluralist democracies are also becoming more sensitive and account-able to public opinion. Politicians promise more and more at election time, but the more demands they recognize, and the more 'false expecta-tions they encourage' (Brittan 1975) the less they are likely to deliver. As Crozier *et al.* wrote: The demands on democratic government grow, while the capacity of democratic government stagnates' (Crozier *et al.,* 1975: 9). Government becomes overloaded and society becomes ungovernable. As a result, public opinion becomes increasingly cynical and disillusioned. Ultimately, it withdraws its support from the state, so undermining the system of government.

Once again the mass survey evidence fails to confirm this diagnosis. While overload theory suggests the most active states with the highest public expenditures will come under the greatest pressure, the evidence suggests the reverse. Although there are too few cases to allow confident generalization, the heaviest demand for public services seems to be found in the least economically developed countries, which also show the weakest support for their governments. The highest levels of demand for services are found in the less well-developed societies because they have the greatest social and economic problems (Huseby, 1995). At the same time, high levels of unsatisfied demand for public services tend to undermine support for government. In contrast, the more developed states are best placed to satisfy demand, and their recent histories of stability and security have allowed them to build up a bank of political trust and allegiance which helps them survive short- to medium-term crises. As a result, the most developed states seem to have the lowest levels of overload and are best equipped to deal with them (Borre, 1995). The evidence suggests that over-load theories are right to suggest a link between excess or unsatisfied demand upon government and dissatisfaction with that government. They are wrong to suggest that this problem is to be found in an acute form in the most advanced capitalist economies of the West. On the contrary these societies seem to suffer less from overload and unsatisfied demand than the less economically developed countries of West Europe.

There are three possible reasons for the failure of overload theory so far as mass attitudes are concerned. Firstly, the theory tends to assume that citizens are insatiable consumers of public goods and that, under normal circumstances, demands upon the state will rise indefinitely. Demand for services is assumed to be irreversible (see, for example, Eichenberger 1977: 107) – it will ratchet up, but will not go down. In con-trast, survey data suggests that public opinion is not irreversible. For example, Borre and Viegas (1995) show that belief in government man-agement of the economy appears to decline with increasing economic development. Support for government economic intervention is highest in

Greece, Ireland and Italy, lowest in Denmark and Germany. In the same way, demands for government spending on some services seem to level off in wealthier nations compared with poorer ones. In short, the spiral of rising expectations of the public sector has been replaced – to some extent at any rate – by a spiral of falling expectations.

Secondly, the public agenda does not expand indefinitely. The public seems to constrain its agenda to a fairly constant number of matters. As new issues enter the agenda so other issues fall off (Roller, 1995a). Perhaps the general public is capable of holding only a few issues in its mind at any one time. Perhaps it is sensible enough to realize that there can only be a few priorities. Whatever the reason, the number of issues on the public agenda does not keep on expanding as new issues present themselves, but appears to be limited to a fairly constant number.

Thirdly, overload and ungovernability theory argues that as modern pluralist societies tend to fragment into special groups and interests, so public opinion splinters into many issue publics which then bombard government with their incompatible demands. Theorists of post modernism make much the same claim. In fact, there is little evidence of fragmentation of opinion and interest so far as state policy is concerned. As the figures in Table 6.3 show, opinion on eight major policy areas tends to cluster neatly into three general groups, one concerned with the welfare state, one with the environment and culture, and one with defence and law and order.

Table 6.3 Attitudes towards government spending in eight policy fields: Germany, Britain and Italy, 1985

The government should spend more on:	Factor 1	Factor 2	Factor 3
Old-age pensions	0.79	−0.08	0.04
Health	0.72	0.07	0.14
Unemployment benefits	0.68	0.12	−0.13
Education	0.64	0.26	0.17
Environment	0.08	0.77	−0.14
Culture and arts	0.12	0.77	0.06
Law enforcement	0.05	0.16	0.84
Military and defence	0.08	−0.30	0.72

Notes: Entries are loadings on rotated factors (varimax rotation). Question: 'Listed below are various areas of government spending. Please show whether you wold like to see more or less government spending in each area. Remember that if you say 'much more', it might require a tax increase to pay for it.' Categories: spend much more; spend more; spend the same as now; spend less; spend much less.

Source: ISSP (1985), as presented in vol 3, *The Scope of Government*, Table 4.5.

Other evidence confirms this conclusion. Roller (1995a) uses factor analysis on opinion about 12 important problem areas and, again, finds three clear and distinct opinion clusters (see *The Scope of Government*, Table 3.2). Whatever the trends in post-industrial or post-modern social structure, these do not seem to have caused a decomposition, splintering, or a fragmentation of public opinion. On the contrary, opinion remains organized into a few main camps, each organized around a general policy position.

6.3 A LEGITIMACY CRISIS?

Although it originates in a different political tradition, legitimacy crisis theory arrives at much the same sort of conclusion as overload theory. There are different forms of legitimacy crisis theory but basically the argument is that the modern state is faced with contradictory demands. It must create the conditions for profitable business by investing heavily in infrastructure, while keeping taxes down. It must also legitimize itself and maintain the conditions of social order by providing welfare services (O'Connor, 1973; Habermas, 1975; Offe, 1984). It cannot possibly meet these contradictory demands and so it increasingly alienates both its capitalists and its workers. As a result, public opinion turns against the state, and legitimacy crisis results.

Notwithstanding the political protests of the 1968 generation, which provided the inspiration for the theory, mountains of survey data presented in *The Scope of Government* show little evidence of a widespread or growing disillusionment with the state and its services in the 1970s, 1980s or early 1990s. Nor is there much evidence to support Offe's hypothesis of 'rational' opposition on the part of the higher and the lower income groups because of the difference between what they pay and what they get in the welfare state. On the contrary mass survey evidence collected by the World Values study and the Eurobarometer shows that opposition to taxation is surprisingly low in most West European nations, and that so far as there is much variation between social and income groups, resistance rises slowly as income increases (Confalonieri and Newton, 1995).

A basic problem of legitimacy crisis theory seems to be that it underestimates the rather subtle yet hard-headed nature of public opinion. Citizens understand that a scarcity of resources is a basic condition of life, as Confalonieri and Newton show in their chapters on attitudes towards taxation in *The Scope of Government*. Consequently, public demands and expectations are tempered by realism. The public also understand that circumstances change. For example, had writers in the 1960s been able to foresee unemployment levels of the 1980s and 1990s, they would in all likelihood have predicted widespread and pretty massive crisis and cata-strophe. Such expectations would have been entirely understandable in the low unemployment era of 1950–1975. But things have changed, and with them public opinion about unemployment. The goal of full employment, once thought essential for modern governments, is not currently regarded as realistic.

The public also realizes that governments, whatever they may promise, are limited in what they can deliver. Whether best described as 'cynical' or as 'realistic', modern public opinion is not necessarily disillusioned by the failures of politicians and governments. On the contrary, it has often (usu-ally?) treated their rhetoric and promises with scepticism and a pinch of salt. Legitimacy crisis theorists may take the promises of politicians at their face value, but the general public is far more hard-headed and realis-tic, and far less discomfited by political failure – it never expected much else. Similarly, public opinion recognizes that some political goals may be incompatible and that there is a trade-off between them. The trade-off between unemployment and inflation is an example.

More fundamentally, the citizens of Western Europe have long believed that there is an incompatibility between freedom and equality, and have tended to divide themselves according to their preference for one or the other. The balance of opinion may well shift over time, as Roller (1965b: Chapter 7) and Thomassen (in Citizens and the State, 1995) argue. But the public mood does not slide towards disillusionment, as legitimacy crisis theory seems to assume, because it cannot have everything it wants and has to sacrifice something for a higher priority.

Last, the general public is able to distinguish between the limitations of democratic systems and of particular parties or governments. The failings of the latter do not necessarily contaminate faith in the former, at least in the short- to medium-term. Legitimacy crisis theory fails to distinguish between the failure of politicians and of parties and governments, and the failure of the political system. In the short run, at last, these are different. In the long run they may amount to pretty much the same thing. In this respect public opinion seems to be both more subtle and flexible, and at the same time more hard-headed, realistic and sensible than theories of the legitimacy crisis assume. It is a curious fact that this left-wing theory seems to have seriously underestimated public opinion.

6.4 A RATIONAL CHOICE REVOLT?

According to some versions of rational choice theory (see, for example, Alt 1983 and Pelzman 1980), as the welfare state develops so it increases the tax burden on all while spreading its serves increasingly thinly. As different social strata pay more but seem to get less, opposition to taxes and public services strengthens. In the early days of the welfare state relatively few people paid tax, and marginal tax rates were relatively low. Benefits, in contrast, were believed to be concentrated among the bulk of the lower income groups. As a result the majority of voters benefited from public services and low taxes, and for self-interested reasons they supported the free-rider welfare state and its taxes. As more people were brought into the tax net and higher tax brackets, so they were inclined to calculate the balance of costs and benefits and change their mind. Informed by a rational, self-interested calculation, the majority mood shifted from support for an expansionist state towards a contractionist view favouring lower taxes and fewer services. According to this theory, criticism of the state, taxes, and of the welfare system is likely to be strongest among those with the highest incomes and the best education, because they will pay the highest taxes and understand what is going on. At the same time the higher taxes are, and the more thinly benefits are spread, the more public opinion in general is likely to favour the contraction of the state.

By and large the evidence does not confirm these rational-choice expectations. There is a clear but relatively slight tendency for the best educated and highest income groups to support the welfare state less strongly, although more noticeable is the relatively strong support across all income, education and social groups. Nor do citizens seem to behave entirely in the rational, self-interested and calculating way posited by rational choice models. Their attitudes seem to be informed, at least in part, by other considerations related to social justice, fairness, a wish to guarantee minimum standards for all and a desire for a degree of greater social and economic equality (see *The Scope of Government*, Chapters 3–7).

Perhaps the clearest single example in the recent past is the fate of the Thatcher government's poll tax in Britain. As a per capita, flat-rate, and regressive charge the poll tax was widely criticized and opposed for its unfairness, a view shared as much by those who benefited from it as those who did not (Crewe 1988: 41–3). No doubt individuals, social groups and nations vary in this respect, but survey evidence suggests that west European publics are not motivated only or even primarily by hard-headed economic self-interest. This is mixed to some degree by a sense of the public interest and the public good.

6.5 A NEW POLITICAL AGENDA?

Theories of welfare state backlash, government overload, legitimacy crisis and rational-choice revolt all argue that public opinion will change its expansionist mood to a contractionist one. A fifth approach argues not that public opinion will become contractionist, but that the nature of the public agenda will change. According to Inglehart (1990: 249–88) the law of diminishing returns means that the closer people get to material satisfaction, the less importance they attach to them, and the more they turn to the non-material benefits of quality of life and self-expression. These include such things as work satisfaction, self-realization, participation and environmental protection. According to this theory, the very success of the welfare state has undermined itself – having solved many social problems of capitalism, support for the material goals of the welfare state is slowly draining away. Individualism, freedom and self-fulfilment begin to replace collectivism, economic growth and security as priorities. Younger, more affluent and better educated people lead the way to post-materialist politics.

From this there follows two possibilities. Either the old, materialist agenda is being replaced by the new, post-materialist one, or the new has been added to, or fused with the old to create a different agenda. The first theory of replacement has been called the 'proximity model', and the second the 'dominance model' (Baker *et al.*, 1981). Either way, the result is that the old collectivist, welfare state agenda of the first half of the twentieth century is now giving way to a new individualist and post-material public agenda. There is already some evidence in favour of the dominance model. In the first place, it seems that some of the new social movements, which are strongly associated with the new politics, have managed to combine items from the old and new agendas (Dalton and Küchler, 1990). Secondly, some of the European Green parties have emphasized both environmental issues and the old themes of social and economic equality (Goodin 1992: 197). Thirdly, as Offe (1985) has pointed out, the 'new' issues are firmly rooted in Western political theory of the last two hundred years and are integrated in the traditional and predominantly materialist agendas of established parties and interest groups. Fourthly, as Budge *et al.* have shown, some of the 'new' issues have been built into old party manifestos (Budge *et al.*, 1987). In short, a lot that was thought to be new about the new social movements in the 1970s and 1980s turns out to be not so new, and what there is that is new has sometimes been incorporated by the 'old' parties and interest groups. Not only have the 'new' movements gradually accommodated to the world, but the 'old' organizations have managed to steal some of their new clothes.

The Eurobarometer surveys which cover all the member states of the EU enable us to test the proximity and dominance models, and trace the changes in public opinion with respect to the old and new agendas.

The results show that, with one significant exception, the old policy agenda coexisted with the new from 1976 to 1991. Throughout the EU in this period over 90 per cent of respondents said that the issues of wealth, unemployment and environmental protection were important or very important. Between 70–80 per cent said the same of social and economic equality, and of defending their national interests against the superpowers. About 60 per cent rated military defence as important or very important.

The exception concerns international security and co-operation. On the one hand, there is a gradual decline in the importance attached to military defence and to defending interests against the superpowers. This is not surprising given the decline of the cold war and the eventual collapse of the Communist threat. On the other hand, there is also a gradual increase in the importance of giving aid to less developed countries. In this sense, one item of the old agenda fades, and one item of the new grows stronger. The pattern applies at the national level when individual responses are aggregated by country, and at the individual level within each country. In sum, the public agenda across Western Europe is not so much a new post-materialist one, but a combined and modified new-and-old materialist and post-materialist one. Public attitudes, beliefs and values are evolving slowly, not suddenly changing or transforming themselves (Roller, 1995). The conclusions seems to be that the welfare state has not lost its early popularity, but it may well be in the process of evolving in the public mind – as indeed it most probably has since it was first a gleam in the eyes of nineteenth-century reformers.

6.6 SUBTLETY AND SOPHISTICATION: CITIZENS ARE NOT FOOLS

The citizens of Western Europe also seem to be rather more sophisticated than many theories allow. They distinguish and discriminate between different kinds of public policies and programmes, choosing to support some strongly, others less strongly, and some not at all. For example, there seems to be robust support across most of Western Europe for a greater degree of income equalization. Many think their societies are not yet equal enough, but this does not mean strong support for radical or total equalization. Rather, the public seems to want a narrowing of existing income differences and greater equality of opportunity, not the complete equalization of society (Roller 1995b: Chapter 7).

Similarly the public picks and chooses between services which it wants cut or protected. As we have just seen, in 1985 and 1990 there was a strong preference for spending tax money on welfare policies, less pronounced support for culture and the environment, and less still for law and order and defence (Table 6.4). Those who want more spent on one set of services are less keen on spending on other sets (Table 6.3). This reinforces the earlier suggestion that mass attitudes tend towards internal consistency, though it does not, of course, suggest that they are always so.

Individuals do not either support or oppose the welfare state; they discriminate between different parts of it, and between different policy instruments. For example, strong and consistent support for social security programmes, including those for the unemployed, does not necessarily spill over into support for a guaranteed income (see Table 6.5). Perhaps the idea of a guaranteed income conflicts with other popular principles, such as the idea that people should work where possible, and that there should be differences of income based upon differences of ability and effort. At any rate, the general public distinguishes between different unemployment policies, strongly supporting some, weakly supporting or rejecting others.

It does not follow that the general public does not sometimes have contradictory values and sometimes want contradictory things. After all, the established methods for analysing the most intelligent and subtle ideologies of the great political theorists and philosophers of world history is to show some inconsistencies and contradictions. If Aristotle, Machiavelli, Hobbes, Mill and Marx can suffer from these human frailties, why not the general public too? The point made here is not that public opinion is perfectly rational and consistent, nor that it is no more irrational than the great thinkers, but that it is fundamentally no more irrational and inconsistent than the opinions of those who tend to criticize it for its irrationalities and inconsistencies.

6.7 A TAX REVOLT?

It is abundantly clear from the survey data that the great majority of citizens in almost all West European nations support the welfare state. They do not like all welfare policies, but the great majority believe that their government should maintain minimum social and economic standards for all. They also seem to believe (or say that they believe, which is not the same thing) that they should pay their fair share of tax towards the costs of these services.

Most citizens also believe that the state should ensure a degree of economic equality. West European publics not believe in absolute equality, but belief in equality of opportunity is widespread across the whole of the sub-continent, and most think that the distribution of wealth in their country is not as fair as it should be (Figures 6.1, 6.2 and 6.3). The point is made again in Table 6.6.

Table 6.4 Attitudes towards government spending in five countries, 1985 and 1990

	Germany		Britain		Italy		Austria		Norway		Mean	
	1985	1990	1985	1990	1985	1990	1985	1990	1985	1990	1985	1990
Welfare policies												
Spend more	50	69	83	85	76	81	43			71	70	78
Spend same	45	29	16	14	20	18	52			28	27	20
Spend less	5	2	1	1	4	2	5			1	3	2
N	966	2.635	1.427	1.115	1.462	950	864			1.360		
Order policies												
Spend more	8	6	16	11	13	13	9			8	12	10
Spend same	66	59	71	79	67	68	69			80	68	69
Spend less	26	35	12	10	20	19	22			12	20	21
N	979	2.664	1.436	1.128	1.477	961	862			1.431		
Culture policies												
Spend more	36	50	9	18	26	48	25			17	27	39
Spend same	61	48	74	74	59	49	70			74	65	57
Spend less	3	2	17	8	5	3	5			9	8	4
N	983	2.629	1.345	1.070	1.465	956	868			1.398		

Notes: Entries are percentages. Question: 'Listed below are various areas of government spendig. Please show whether you would like to see more or gess government spendig in each area. Remembers that if you say "much more", it might require a tax increase to pay for it.' 1 = spend much more1 2 = spend more; 3 = spend the same as now; 4 = spend less; 5 = spend much less. The variables are: (1) the environment; (2) health; (3) law enforcement; (4) education; (5) defence; (6) retirement; (7) unemployment benefit; (8) culture and arts. Variables (1) and (8) have been added together to form the additive index 'culture policies' and the categories recorded: 2–4 = spend more, 5–7 = spend same, 8–10 = spend less. Variables (2), (4), (6) and (7) form the additive index 'Welfare policies', and recorded: 4–8 = same, 15–20 spend less. Variables (3) and (5) form the additive index 'Order policies' and recoded: 2–4 = spend more; 5–7 = same; 8–10 = spend less. The mean in each case includes only those countries surveyed in both 1985 and 1990 (Germany, Britain and Italy).

Table 6.5 Support for different socio-economic equality policies, 1987

Dimension	Item	AU	GB	GE	NL	SW	IT	Average
Equality of opportunity	The government should provide more chances for children from poor families to go to university	80	84	87	85	81	90	85
Equality of result National minima	The government should provide a job for everyone who wants one	80	59	77	75	50	82	71
	The government should provide everyone with a guaranteed basic income	57	61	56	50	43	67	5
Redistribution	The government should reduce the differences in income between people with high incomes and those with low incomes	81	64	61	65	43	82	66
	People with high incomes should pay a larger proportion of their earnings in taxes than those who earn low incomes	86	77	80	73	82	79	80
Means index		77	65	71	66	51	83	69
N		972	1.212	1.397	1.638	987	1.027	

Notes: Entries for 'The government should ...' items are percentages of respondents who agree strongly or agree. Entries for the second taxes items are percentages of respondents who say much larger proportion or larger proportion.

Source: ISSP (1987), as presented in vol 3, *The Scope of Government*, Table 7.2.

Table 6.6 Attitudes towards issues of tax fairness

(a) Government's responsibility to reduce income differences between rich and poor

	GE 1985	GE 1990	GB 1985	GB 1990	IT 1985	IT 1990	NO 1990	IR 1990
Should be	67	64	75	74	84	78	72	82
Should not be	33	36	25	26	16	22	28	18
N	1.048	2.812	1.530	1.197	1.580	983	1.517	1.005

(b) Government's responsibility to reduce income differences between those with high and low incomes

	GE 1987	GE 1990	GB 1987	GB 1990	IT 1987	IT 1990	AU 1987	SW 1987	NO 1990	IR 1990	NL 1990
Agree	61	56	64	57	82	70	81	43	56	69	65
Disagree	24	20	23	24	9	15	11	40	25	18	24
N	1.397	2.812	1.212	1.197	1.027	983	972	987	1.517	1.005	1.638

(c) People with high incomes should pay a larger share of their income taxes than those with low incomes

	GE 1987	GE 1990	GB 1987	GB 1990	IT 1987	IT 1990	AU 1987	SW 1987	NO 1990	IR 1990	NL 1990
Larger	80	87	77	85	79	84	86	82	75	82	73
Smaller	19	12	22	14	20	15	13	17	24	17	22
Smaller	1	1	1	1	1	1	1	1	1	1	4
N	1.397	2.812	1.212	1.197	1.027	983	972	987	1.517	1.005	1.638

Notes: Entries are percentages.

Source: ISSP (1985, 1987, 1990), as presented in vol 3, The Scope of Government, Table 5.1.

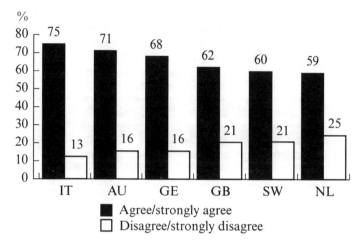

Figure 6.1 Inequality continues to exist because it benefits the rich and powerful?

Source: ISSP (1987).

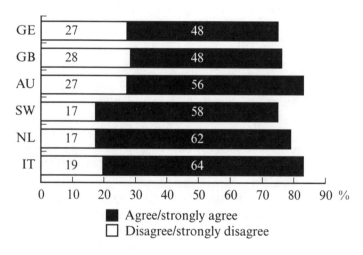

Figure 6.2 Large differences in income are necessary for (respondent's country's) prosperity?

Source: ISSP (1987).

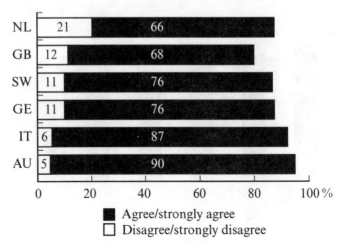

Agree/strongly agree
Disagree/strongly disagree

Figure 6.3 Differences in income in (respondent's country) are too large?

Source: ISSP (1987).

Although it is difficult to draw firm conclusions, most citizens seem to be prepared to pay taxes, or more taxes, in order to fund what they think are important public services. This view is contrary to the 'something for nothing' interpretation of mass opinion (see, for example, Sears and Citrin 1985). The difficulty here is that some surveys ask 'unpriced' questions of tax payers: asked if taxes are too high, most say they are; asked if they want more or better public services, most say they do. Neither response is the slightest surprising, and put the two together and it seems the general public wants 'something for nothing'. More sensible questions ask respondents to say which, if any, services they would cut in return for lower taxes, or which if any services they would like to see improved and at what increase to their own tax bill. These sorts of priced question elicit more sensible responses (see, for example, Peters 1991a). Moreover, as we have already said, there is a rough match between the services people believe are important, and the services they say they are prepared to pay more taxes for (Table 6.7). Reviewing the literature with these qualifications in mind, Peters (1991a: 160) writes that 'citizens have demonstrated that they are not really as naive about public finance as is sometimes assumed. Most citizens appear to recognise that if they want more services they will have to pay for them through taxes.'

The figures in Table 6.6 and Figures 6.1–6.3 are interesting in this respect. If survey data is to be believed at all, they show that the great majority of citizens across West Europe believe that it is their govern-

Table 6.7 Percentage favouring more government spending (by service), 1985 and 1990

	Germany		Britain		Italy		Austria	Norway
	1985	1990	1985	1990	1985	1990	1985	1990
Health								
Much more	19	36	36	36	32	39	22	25
More	52	73	88	90	79	85	60	83
Old age pension								
Much more	11	16	25	29	22	26	13	16
More	46	55	75	82	75	81	51	72
Environment								
Much more	43	61	6	15	17	26	34	24
More	83	90	37	63	63	76	73	74
Education								
Much more	10	20	23	27	17	23	9	11
More	40	59	75	79	64	66	36	56
Law enforcement								
Much more	9	12	9	11	12	17	5	13
More	30	43	40	50	49	57	23	62
Unemployment benefit								
Much more	8	9	12	8	15	15	3	4
More	35	37	41	36	56	52	15	19
Culture, theatre								
Much more	2	5	1	2	8	10	3	2
More	14	22	10	13	36	45	12	10
Culture, theatre								
Much more	2	2	5	2	3	2	3	7
More	4	5	18	9	12	12	12	4
N	1.048	2.812	1.530	1.197	1.580	983	987	1.517

Source: ISSP (1985, 1990).

ment's responsibility to reduce income differences between the rich and the poor – not to make everybody equal in income, but to reduce the inequality that currently exists. The same conclusions emerge in all countries whether the questions ask about the 'rich and poor', or about those with 'high and low incomes'.

The last of the three questions in Table 6.6 also shows that the great majority of people believe that the rich should pay higher taxes. If we were to produce the rest of the figures for middle- and low-income groups (not laid out here for reasons of space, but see Confalonieri and Newton, 1995) they would show no less conclusively that most West Europeans (irrrespective of country, or of income group) believe that middle-income groups pay too much tax. An overwhelming majority believe that the poor pay too much tax. It is evident that European publics are not opposed to taxation as such, not even to paying higher taxes themselves in return for better public services of certain kinds. What they object to is the unfairness of the tax system. A large majority believe that the rich pay too little tax. A smaller majority believe that middle-income groups pay too much. And the overwhelming majority believe that the poor pay too much. The general public does not want something for nothing. On the contrary, it believes that the rich are getting something for nothing, and that the tax burden between income groups should be redistributed. Under a fair tax system, most would be prepared to pay more tax if this guaranteed better services of the kind they value.

It would be foolish to conclude from this patchy and circumstantial evidence that citizens only and always follow their notion of the public good and the general interest, even less that their actual behaviour is determined by high-minded principles. At the same time, the evidence suggests that they do not always express selfish opinions, or always behave in ways which maximize their own economic interests.

6.8   THE WEST EUROPEAN PATTERN

There is a surprisingly large measure of agreement among the citizens of different West European nations about the proper scope of modern government, and the priorities that should be set for it. National variations are relatively minor; far more striking is the strong family resemblance in the national profiles of attitudes towards the scope of government, its responsibilities, its public services priorities and towards issues of taxing and spending. There is a consistency of views across Western Europe on a wide range of other matters, including: ratings for important public issues; government responsibilities; issues of equality and redistribution; issues of social security; economic intervention; and government control of communications.

At the same time, there are also indications of some differences between social democratic and Christian democratic welfare states. In the Protestant and Anglo-Scandinavian nations of the north, where social democratic parties are strong, attitudes towards the scope of government are quite strongly correlated with the left–right variable and with party identification. In the southern, Catholic countries where Christian democratic ideology is strong, attitudes are less strongly correlated with political indicators such as voting and party identification.

What makes this consistency of attitudes all the more striking is that the same pattern is not found with such things as trust in government, political participation, beliefs in democracy, the efficacy of the citizen or measures of political alienation (see Klingemann and Fuchs, 1995) On such matters there is no consistent pattern stretching across Western Europe, but rather a varied set of trends which seem to be specific to particular nations at particular times. In this respect the findings of two 'Beliefs in Government' volumes, *The Scope of Government* and *Citizens and the State* stand in sharp contrast.

In spite of different forms of government, different forms of state services and provisions, different histories, economies and cultures, there is a general West European view about public services and the welfare state. It is not too much to speak of a West European view, something which is relevant to the EU in its attempts to form a common European welfare policy.

6.9 CONCLUSIONS

In 1980 one of the few systematic and comparative studies of public opinion about welfare (Coughlin 1980, 153-4) argued that:

> It is fair to conclude that despite the presumed fiscal crisis of the welfare state, the taxpayers revolt, runaway inflation, and other scenarios of doom and gloom, the American people, like their west European counterparts, are not quite ready to abandon the commitments of providing the benefits and services of the welfare state...As we have seen repeatedly throughout this study, some types of social welfare are deeply entrenched in popular attitudes, and are likely to survive whatever the developments over the next few years.

The present study amply confirms this conclusion, not just so far as welfare is concerned but also on a wide range of other government services and activities. The core services of the welfare state – health, education, housing, and provision for the old, the ill and the unemployed – are almost universally (usually more than 90 per cent) regarded as government responsibilities. A rather lower percentage – but still a large majority of around 65 per cent – believe this to be the case for minority rights, gender equality, economic equality, and assistance for industry. There is little evidence that support for public services is crumbling; on the contrary, it seems to be resilient.

To be accurate, what most of the statistical material shows is that support for public services and the welfare state in the late 1980s and early 1990s remained at a high level. The data for this period are relatively good and plentiful. Information about earlier decades is thin and patchy. Therefore, we cannot show that support has not declined, although it was so high in the 1980s and 1990s that it is difficult to see how it could have fallen appreciably from even higher levels in the 1960s and 1970s.

To this extent the predictions about government overload, legitimacy crisis, and rational-choice revolt are not borne out by the data we have. There is little sign of a welfare state backlash, tax revolt, legitimacy crisis, or general disillusionment with public services. That is not to say there has been no change, but change is not necessarily decline. The public agenda has not remained constant over the decades. West European publics now place less importance on defence than during the cold war, and they believe in less government regulation of the economy. Equally, environmental matters have increased in importance in the public mind.

It is important to distinguish between fluctuations and trends in mass opinion. Fluctuations are relatively short term, lasting from a few months to a few years They may be quite sudden and steep, but iron themselves out in the long run. Trends last for decades or generations and show long-term continuity. Theorists have been tempted to generalize – or rather to over-generalize and over-interpret – fluctuations in order to anticipate trends. This tries to sort out the trends from the fluctuations and draw the appropriate conclusions about long-term change.

Changes in mass attitudes have been slow and limited in the 1970s and 1980s. There have been shifts in public priorities but these have not resulted in a widespread rejection of the old attitudes and agendas. Rather the old has been modified and the new has been incorporated. The result has been stability, continuity and adaption, rather than fundamental or wholesale change.

Perhaps the general conclusion is that theories of change might concentrate less exclusively on what are undoubtedly enormous pressures for change in modern society, and look also at the enormous pressures for continuity and stability. If there is merit in this suggestion, then the paradox is that theories of change have concentrated too much on change, and too little on obstacles to change.

ENDNOTES

1. This paper is a small part of a project on 'Beliefs in Government' which was financed by the European Science Foundation, Strasbourg. The final draft of the paper was completed while the author was a Visiting Professor at the Wissenschatszentrum Berlin fur Sozialforschung. I gratefully acknowledge the support of the Foundation and of WZB. In particular I would like to thank Frau Yu and Frau Hohne for their essential help in producing the paper.

REFERENCES

Alt, J.E. (1983) 'The evolution of tax structures', *Public Choice,* 41, 181–222.

Baker, K.L., Dalton, R., and Hildebrandt, K. (1981), *Germany Transformed: Political Culture and the New Politics*, Cambridge, Mass.: Harvard University Press.

Borre, O. (1995), 'Scope-of-government beliefs and political support', in O. Borre and E. Scarbrough (eds), (Beliefs in Government, vol. 3) *The Scope of Government*, Oxford: Oxford University Press: 343–66.

Borre, O. and Scarbrough, E., (eds), (1995) (Beliefs in Government, vol. 3), *The Scope of Government*, Oxford: Oxford University Press.

Borre, O. and Viegas, J.M. (1995), 'Government intervention in the economy', in O. Borre and E. Scarbrough (eds), (Beliefs in Government, vol. 3) *The Scope of Government*, Oxford: Oxford University Press.

Brittan, S. (1975) 'The economic contradiction of democracy', *British Journal of Political Science*, 5: 129–59.

Budge I., Robertson, D., and Hearl, D. (1987), *Ideology, Strategy and Party Change*, Cambridge: Cambridge University Press.

Coughlin, R.M. (1980), *Ideology, Public Opinion, and Welfare Policy*, Berkeley, Calif.: Institute of International Studies, University of California.

Crewe, I. (1988) 'Has the electorate become Thatcherite?', in R. Skidelsky (ed.), *Thatcherism*, Oxford: Oxford University Press: 112–37.

Confalonieri M., and Newton, K. (1995), 'Taxing and spending: tax revolt of tax protest,' in O. Borre and E. Scarbrough (eds.), (Beliefs in Government, vol. 3), *The Scope of Government*, Oxford: Oxford University Press: 121–480.

Crozier, M.J., Huntington, S.P., and Watanuki, J. (1975), *The Crisis of Democracy*, New York: New York University Press.

Dalton, R.J. , and Küchler, M. (eds)., (1990), *Challenging the Political Order: New Social and Political Movements in Western Democracies*, Cambridge: Polity Press.

Douglas, J.D. (1989), *The Myth of the Welfare State*, New Brunswick, NJ: Transaction Press.

Eichenberger, K. (1977), 'Der geforderte Staat', in I. Brand et al.(eds.), *Regierbarkeit*: Studien zu ihrer Problematisierung, Stuttgart: Ernst Klett: 42–61.

Goodin, R. (1988), *Reasons for the Welfare State*, Princeton, NJ: Princeton University Press.

Goodin, R.E. (1992), Green Political Theory, Cambridge: Polity Press.

Habermas, J. (1975), *Legitimation Crisis*, Boston: Beacon Press.

Hadenius, A. (1986), *A Crisis of the Welfare State*, Stockholm: Almqvuist and Wicksell.

Huseby, B. M. (1995), 'Attitudes towards the size of government', in O. Borre and E. Scarbrough (eds.), (Beliefs in Government, vol. 3), *The Scope of Government*. Oxford: Oxford University Press: 87–118.

Inglehart, R. (1990), *Culture Shift in the Advanced Industrial Societies*, Princeton, NJ: Princeton University Press.

Kaase, M. and Newton, K. (1995), *Beliefs in Government*, Oxford: Oxford University Press.

Klingemann, H-D, and Fuchs, D. (eds), (1995), (Beliefs in Government, vol. 1), *Citizens and the State*, Oxford: Oxford University Press.

Newton, K. and Confalonieri, M. (1995), 'Politics, economics, class, and taxation', in O. Borre and E. Scarbrough, (eds). (Beliefs in Government, vol. 3), *The Scope of Government*, Oxford: Oxford University Press: 149–64.

O'Connor, J. (1973), *The Fiscal Crisis of the State*, New York: St. Martin's Press.

Offe, C. (1984), *Contradictions of the Welfare* State. London: Hutchinson.

Offe, C. (1985) 'New social movements: challenging the boundaries of institutional politics', *Social Research* 52, 817–68

Pechman, J.A. (1988), *World Tax Reform: A Progress Report*, Washington, DC: Brookings Institute.

Peltzman, S. (1980), 'The growth of government', *Journal of Law and Economics* 23, 285–7.

Peters. B.G. (1991a), *The Politics of Taxation,* Oxford: Basil Blackwell.

Peters. B.G. (1991b), *European Politics Reconsidered*, New York: Holmes and Meir.

Pettersen, P.A. (1995), 'The welfare state: the security domension', in O. Borre and E. Scarbrough (eds.), (Beliefs in Government, vol. 3), *The Scope of Government*. Oxford: Oxford University Press: 198–233.

Roller, E. (1995a), 'Political agendas and beliefs about the scope of government' in O. Borre and E. Scarbrough (eds.), (Beliefs in Government, vol. 3), *The Scope of Government*, Oxford: Oxford University Press: 55–86.

Roller, E. (1995b) 'The welfare state: The security dimension' in O. Borre and E. Scarbrough, (eds.) Beliefs in Government, vol. 3, *The Scope of Government*, Oxford: Oxford University Press: 165–97.

Sears and Citrin, J. (1985), *Tax Revolt: Something for Nothing in California*. Cambridge, Mass.: Harvard University Press.

Thomassen, J. (1995), 'Support for democratic values', in H.-D. Klingemann and D. Fuchs (eds), (Beliefs in Government, vol. 1) *Citizens and the State*, Oxford: Oxford University Press: 383–416.

Wilensky, H.L. (1975), *The Welfare State and Inequality: Structural and Ideological Roots of Public Expenditures*, Berkeley, Calif.: University of California Press.

7. Welfare reform in Southern Europe: institutional constraints and opportunities

Maurizio Ferrera

7.1 A DISTINCT MODEL? SOME COMMON TRAITS OF THE SOUTH EUROPEAN WELFARE STATES

Until very recently, comparative social policy literature has largely neglected the study of the welfare states of Southern Europe. At most, it has tended to treat them more or less explicitly as belonging to the 'industrial achievement' (*à la* Titmuss) or 'conservative corporatist' (*à la* Esping Andersen) model of welfare. In the last few years however the idea has started to emerge that the Portuguese, Spanish, Italian and Greek cases may constitute a separate cluster in the universe of welfare states: a 'family of nations' characterized by common social policy traits. Leibfried (1992) has for instance suggested the idea of a 'Latin-rim' model of welfare, displaying a wide gap between ambitious legislative promises and only rudimentary policy instruments and outputs. More recently authors such as Castles (1994, 1995), Van Kersbergen (1995) or Gough (1996) have added new elements to this characterization, underlining the strong role of Catholicism, of traditional family and social solidarities in the protection systems of southern Europe. Other authors (for example Saraceno, 1994) have in their turn stressed the peculiarity of gender relations in the south, which have obvious implications for social policy.

I suggest that a comprehensive characterization of the Southern model of welfare should include at least seven major distinctive traits.[1]

The first of these traits is the high relevance of transfer payments and especially the internal polarization of South European income maintenance systems. Cash benefits play a very prominent role in the countries of this area: indeed the South European welfare states constitute an extreme version of the 'transfer-centred model' typical of Continental Europe. As in the other Bismarckian countries, South European income maintenance is based on occupational status and its degree of institutional fragmentation is very marked. The most distinctive peculiarity of these systems is however the dualistic, almost polarized character of the protection which is offered. On the one hand the schemes of these countries provide generous protection to the core sectors of the labour force, located within the regular or institutional labour market; on the other hand they only provide weak subsidization to workers located in the so-called irregular or non-institutional market. Spain, Portugal, Italy and Greece are also the only member states of the EU where there is no national, right-based minimum income scheme for individuals and families with insufficient resources.

The second distinctive trait is an unbalanced distribution of protection across the standard risks, and more generally the various functions of social policy. This imbalance is especially revealed by three interrelated elements:

(a) The overprotection of the risk of old age and of the aged as a social group. This is manifested by the larger share of pension expenditure, with respect to other types of expenditures (especially in Italy and Greece) and by expenditure data which break down total social expenditure by type of beneficiary: the aged and the non-aged. According to recent calculations of the OECD (1994), for instance, in 1989 the ratio between social protection expenditure for the aged and expenditure for the non-aged was above the EU average in all four countries, remarkably so in Italy and Greece (EU average: 1.27; Portugal: 1.40; Spain: 1.30; Italy: 4.14; Greece: 3.2).

(b) The underdevelopment of family benefits and services. According to Eurostat calculations, in 1993 'family' expenditures in cash and in kind averaged 3.5 per cent of GDP in the EU, but amounted to a modest 0.8 per cent in Portugal, 0.2 per cent in Spain, 0.8 per cent in Italy and 0.1 per cent in Greece (the four lowest figures of the 12 states) (CEC, 1995).

(c) The underdevelopment of public housing and of housing subsidies, coupled with an especially tight regulation of the private rental market. Partly as a consequence of this element, South European countries (especially Spain, Italy and Greece) display the highest rates of home ownership in Europe. They are also virtually the only countries in the advanced world where the elderly (at least typical elderly) enjoy both generous pensions and own their homes, thus defying the logic of the 'home ownership/age pension' trade-off, which seems to hold almost everywhere in the OECD (Castles and Ferrera, 1996). Housing policies are not normally regarded as a central component of the welfare state (though Eurostat does include 'housing' as a function of social protection). This is unfortunate as the distribution of housing resources – as shaped by specific governmental policies – does play an important role in determining the outcomes of the welfare state as a whole. These three interrelated elements (overprotection of the risk of old age, underdevelopment of family benefits and services, underdevelopment of public housing) work to activate a demographic bias in the Southern European welfare systems, which, as will be shown later on, has very serious consequences for their overall performance and stability.

The third distinctive trait has to do with health care. While displaying high institutional fragmentation along occupational lines in their income maintenance systems, the South European welfare states are characterized by a universalistic approach in their health care systems. All four countries have legislated into existence a National Health Service inspired by the British model – though only Italy has fully implemented its reform. The mix between income maintenance occupationalism and health care universalism is a trait quite peculiar of the welfare states of this area of Europe, which distinguishes them further from the other continental European systems.

The fourth trait is constituted by a low degree of state penetration of the welfare sphere and a highly collusive mix between public and non-public actors and institutions.[2] This trait is particularly evident in the field of health care and social services. In Britain and Scandinavia, the establishment of a NHS has not only implied a universalization of coverage and a standardization of norms and structures, but also a crowding out of private providers from the health sector. The public/private mix has evolved differently in Southern Europe. Here the establishment of NHS (Italian or Iberian and especially Greek style) has not promoted a strengthening of the public sphere and the crowding out of private provision, but quite to the contrary a peculiar collusion of public and private, often with great advantages for the latter.

The fifth important trait has less to do with the formal or tangible architecture of the welfare state and has more to do instead with its concrete mode of functioning. We refer to the persistence of 'institutional particularism', if not outright clientelism and in some cases the formation of fairly elaborate 'patronage' machines for the distribution of cash subsidies. The Mediterranean welfare states are characterized by a double deficit of 'stateness'. On the one hand they display a low degree of state penetration of welfare institutions – especially in the field of health care and social services, as just mentioned. On the other hand they also display a low degree of state power proper: public institutions in these countries tend to be highly vulnerable to particularistic and partisan pressures. This is especially true of Italy and Greece, although also in the Iberian countries examples of partisan manipulations of certain sectors of the welfare state can be found. It is certainly true that some degree of institutional particularism characterizes all developed systems of social protection. But when particularistic ties or networks play a prominent and in some cases decisive role in granting access to important benefits or services, when they even display some sort of formal institutionalization (as is the case in Italy in the sector of invalidity benefits or as has been the case in Spain in the sector of unemployment benefits for the agricultural unemployed), then particularistic norms and clientelistic circuits do make a difference in systemic terms (Ferrera, 1996).

The sixth trait of the South European welfare state has also to do with its functioning and is constituted by the low efficiency of its services. A full treatment of this aspect would lead us astray from the main theme of this paper. Let me just point out that all available surveys do indicate that South European users display much higher rates of dissatisfaction with respect to the functioning of welfare services (for example health care services: see Ferrera, 1993) and that there is an extensive literature on the peculiarly low productivity of civil servants in these countries, partly connected in turn with their low degree of professionalism and with the prevailing methods of recruitment and work organization of the administrative apparatus (see Dente, 1995).

Finally, the seventh trait has to do with the financing of welfare. Here the major problem is constituted by the highly uneven distribution of burdens across the various occupational groups due to normative disparities but especially due to the high incidence of the black economy and therefore of tax evasion. The black economy is estimated to produce between 15 and 30 per cent of total GDP in the countries of this area and its presence has serious implications for the welfare state and its financing. According to some recent calculations, for instance, without a black economy and the ensuing tax evasion, Italy would now have a public debt of 60 per cent instead of more than 120 per cent – *ceteris paribus* (Alesina and Marré, 1996).

These seven traits do not exhaust the list of social policy peculiarities of Southern Europe. Taken together, however, they do add up to a rather coherent set of elements which can be treated as a single institutional configuration, with a somewhat autonomous internal logic.

We have elsewhere discussed the various socio-economic and political-cultural factors which have historically promoted the emergence of this configuration (Ferrera, 1996). In the remainder of this paper, we will therefore concentrate on its structural consequences and discuss the 'institutional predicament' in which the South European welfare states (and particularly the Italian one) currently find themselves.

7.2 THE INSTITUTIONAL PREDICAMENT OF THE SOUTHERN MODEL

In recent years the configuration which has just been illustrated has started to generate increasing problems and contradictions, which risk entangling Southern welfare in a true vicious circle.

The root of the problem lies, arguably, with the polarized and demographically biased character of social protection. This state of affairs has in fact become largely incongruent with respect to the external socio-economic context. At the same time its internal logic works to block adaptive changes, in a process which shows clear signs of 'institutional entrapment'. This argument can be best explained in an evolutionary perspective.

In its early phases of development a polarized and demographically skewed pattern of social distribution did not pose particular problems to other institutional spheres (especially the family and the labour market) and it was indeed perfectly compatible with:

(a) the traditional 'Southern family', with its extended network of solidarities and its intense flow of intergenerational transfers and
(b) with the traditional 'fordist' labour market, capable of offering a growing number of stable jobs providing a family wage to the younger generations. As is known, despite their late industrialization and the persistence of a large informal sector, the South European economies have created in the past highly rigid labour markets, offering tenured jobs and relatively good wages to all regular employees. There is a systematic link between the existence of strong family ties, a rigid institutional labour market and an emphasis on pensions. Only the availability of secure jobs during active life and of high intra-familial transfers (material and immaterial) in the crucial phases of the life cycle can in fact sustain a concentration of benefits for the aged, which in turn crowds out resources for welfare benefits and services to the young and/or to active workers and their families. In other words, in the past decades the South European configuration was based on the following 'circle' (maybe not a virtuous circle, but at least a relatively coherent one):

- active workers in the regular labour market would finance the generous benefits of their parents (more generous benefits than in other Continental countries);

- high pension contributions would crowd out the possibility of other welfare benefits such as family allowances and services or public housing;
- the family and housing needs of active workers could be catered for both through the relatively generous wages drawn from tenured jobs in the regular labour market and through intra-familial transfers at the time of marriage or childbearing and so on.

The persistence of the informal economy also contributed to absorb the adverse effect of a demographically skewed social distribution to the extent to which it allowed working families to earn additional incomes through marginal activities or to avoid taxes on the second income.

Things still work this way to a large extent. But the transformation of the external socio-economic context on the one hand, and the very maturation of generous pension systems on the other hand, absorbing an increasing share of resources, has turned this relatively coherent institutional mechanism into a vicious circle, which is gradually eroding its very material foundations.

Let us in fact consider the effects of the configuration on the family. The lack of external supports and opportunities as regards housing, transfers and services has started to restrict the range of choices for young people and to act as a clear obstacle to family formation (marriages) and family expansion (children). There is evidence of a gradual delay in the age of first marriage and childbearing throughout Southern Europe, which partly explains the remarkable decline of fertility witnessed by the countries of this area (Jurado Guerrero and Naldini, 1996). Housing and welfare are not the only factors which influence marriage and reproductive decisions, but the current distributive *status quo* certainly works to aggravate the bleak demographic prospects of the Southern European populations, which seriously undermine the financial stability of this area's pension systems.

The consequences of the demographic bias of the South European welfare states are equally serious with respect to the labour market. In the new globalizing context, insisting on contribution heavy and highly rigid regular jobs means only one thing: accelerating their decline. The absence of public services for working parents and of flexible rental markets hinders in its turn that mobility which is increasingly becoming a prerequisite for processes of post-industrial or neo-industrial economic restructuring. Despite their long historical record of foreign migrations, South European workers are today among the least mobile of Europe. And one fundamental reason for their unreadiness to move is the cost of relocation or its sheer impossibility – for instance for a lack of affordable housing.

Also the other elements of the institutional configuration which has been outlined above are producing many perverse effects. The extent of insecurity and exclusion produced by the dualism of the income maintenance system, the absence of a minimum safety net and the crisis of the labour market has reached the level of a real social emergency in certain areas (for example the Italian Mezzogiorno: see Negri and Saraceno, 1996). Budgetary constraints and the recent pressures towards political 'moralization' (also in the wake of corruption scandals) have put severe limitations on the old particularistic–clientelistic forms of subsidization, destabilizing the traditional patterns of welfare-mediated social integration. The half-hearted universalism in health care – especially on the financial side – has created increasing equity dilemmas, especially with the introduction of costly forms of co-payments at the point of service utilization. The waste associated with collusive practices between the public and the private sector in health and social services is no longer compatible with the new climate of austerity, while the level of user dissatisfaction has reached impressive levels, as illustrated by opinion polls. In other words, in the new demographic and socio-economic context the institutional configuration of the South European welfare states works particularly badly and appears to be almost trapped in contradictions which are partly an effect of its own functioning.

Even if the predicament of the South European welfare state has primarily internal origins, external challenges in the last few years and certainly in the years to come are working to exacerbate it. These external challenges mainly stem from the process of European integration and the increasing pressure to meet the Maastricht convergence criteria as early as possible, hopefully by 1998. This is a virtually implausible scenario for Greece, but it is not an implausible one for Portugal, Spain and Italy – though joining the EMU will severely intensify the pressures for budgetary discipline, bureaucratic rationalization and the containment of non-wage labour costs to maintain competitiveness. All this is directly affecting the welfare state, which is the object of heated debates and rather controversial policy measures in all these countries. Unfortunately the external challenge can only be met through a continued process of rebalancing the public budgets involving further containment of welfare expenditures. There may perhaps be some room for further tax increases in Spain and Portugal. But it must be considered that public revenues have already been increasing very rapidly during the last decade; moreover due to the size of the informal sector the tax pressure on the formal share of GDP is more intense in these countries. The rapid increase of taxation, its concentration on certain occupational categories and territorial areas, the uneven distribution of the tax burden, the widespread perceptions of patronage links and frauds, the low efficiency of services: all these elements offer an extremely fertile ground for the explosion of a real tax-welfare backlash should there be further tax increases. As a matter of fact, the explosion of a tax–welfare backlash could be the natural conclusion of the process of 'entrapment' which is created by the institutional configuration of Southern social policies: an entrapment which not only works to erode its socio-economic basis for institutional reproduction, but also its politico-ideological basis. This is at least what seems to be happening in Italy, the national case to which we now turn for closer inspection.

7.3 REFORM OR DISINTEGRATION? THE UNCERTAIN PROSPECTS OF THE ITALIAN WELFARE STATE

As is well known, in the last two decades the comparative debate has been paying increasing attention to the 'tax–welfare backlash' syndrome, that is the possible emergence of social coalitions interested in lower taxes and a containment of social spending. In the early phases of the debate, the main empirical referents were the Scandinavian countries (where anti-tax parties suddenly made their appearance at the beginning of the 1970s), the Reaganite USA and Thatcherite Britain. Until the early 1980s few would have bet on the plausibility of a 'backlash' scenario for the Italian case. Indeed, in the first comparative investigations of this issue, Italy displayed the lowest scores of 'tax–welfare backlash potential'.[3] But things have been changing very rapidly in the last 15 years. Public opinion surveys show that support for the welfare state has been declining quite sharply, while the protest against the incidence and distribution of taxes has been rising even more sharply. On the centre-right of the political spectrum a new formation has emerged (Freedom Alliance) which overtly speaks in favour of a substantial retrenchment of the state from social welfare, while the Lega Nord has made the tax issue a major target of its strategy: it overtly denounces 'wasteful' social spending in the South and vocally advocates a substantial curbing of inter-regional solidarity and a drastic shedding of public employees. All these symptoms are clearly associated with the structural traits and functional developments illustrated in the previous sections. But how exactly has this nexus worked?

Despite all its imbalances and defects, at least until the early 1980s, the Italian model of welfare was indeed surrounded by a highly consensual politics. All those categories in need of social protection (and even some groups who did not need it) could get at least some form of subsidy, not infrequently through the clientelist circuits. The high degree of evasion tolerated by the tax system and the massive recourse to deficit spending contributed in their turn to keep explicit costs as low as possible. Both the 'patronage system' and the 'plague of evasion' were periodically the object of public reprobations; but neither politicians nor voters had any real interest in putting an end to them. The policy of *risanamento* (that is the restoring to health of public accounts), inaugurated since the mid-1980s, gradually altered, however, this constellation of interests. The first cuts and the sharp tax increases started to make the welfare costs much more explicit and painful for a number of categories, in particular active workers. Despite its failures, the fight against frauds and abuses contributed in its turn to undermine the legitimacy of the social transfer system, especially among the so-called *tartassati*.[4] Thus the 'grand coalition' of social groups supporting the traditional tax-welfare *status quo* started to grow thinner, with a 'backlash' constituency gaining increasing ground.

This process is neatly revealed by survey data. As Table 7.1 shows, in 1986 almost two-thirds of citizens were in favour of the traditional model of the welfare state. Already in 1992 things had clearly changed.[5] In 1996, the situation appears to be dramatically opposed to that of 1986: the supporters of a 'lean' welfare, limited to only essential benefits and services, have reached the impressive percentage of 67 per cent of the total sample. The degree of welfare minimalism is more widespread among the central age groups, the self-employed (75.3 per cent), centre-right (78.6 per cent) and right-wingers (75.6 per cent) as well as people living in the North-eastern regions of the country (71.9 per cent). As Table 7.2 shows,

Table 7.1 The role of the state in the welfare sphere

	1	2
1986	61.1	38.8
1992	54.7	45.2
1996	33.0	67.0

Percentage of agreement with the following statements:
1 'The government must continue to provide everyone with a broad range of social security benefits even if it means increasing taxes and contributions'.
2 'The government should provide everyone only with a limited number of essential benefits and encourage people to provide for themselves in other respects'.

Sources: DOXA (1985): EUROBAROMETER (1992): ISPO (1996):

popular dissatisfaction with respect to the level and fairness of taxation is also impressively high – 47.4 per cent of the respondents to the 1996 survey (the absolute majority, excluding non responses) declared that taxes are too high with respect to the benefits received. If we include also those respondents who have declared that taxes are 'rather high', the percentage of dissatisfied taxpayers reaches the peak of 85.4 per cent. In 1986 the corresponding figure was 'only' of 73.3 per cent: in 10 years there has been an increase of 12 percentage points. And it must be noted that the increase is due essentially to the first response category (taxes are too high): the tax protest has been increasing not only in terms of level, but also in terms of intensity. Again, this protest is more marked in the central age groups, among the occupied and among the medium-high income strata that is. those categories which have actually suffered the above-mentioned 'tax harassment' in the past decade. In particular, tax protest is very closely associated with self-employment, residence in the North-Eastern regions and support for the Lega Nord. Table 7.2 also indicates that there is a widespread perception of tax unfairness: 85.2 per cent of the 1996 respondents think that taxes are unjustly distributed. In this case

Table 7.2 Attitudes towards taxation (% of agreement)

Considering all the advantages you receive (healthcare, pensions, education etc.) do you think that taxes are:

	1985	1996
Too high	30.4	47.4
Rather high	42.9	38.0
Neither high nor low	24.5	6.0
Rather low	1.6	0.4
Very low	0.2	1.0
Don't know	0.4	7.3

Do you think that in Italy taxes are justly or unjustly distributed among the citizens?

	1967	1985	1996
Justly	7.0	8.2	2.7
Unjustly	65.0	87.0	85.2
Don't know	28.0	5.0	12.1

Source: ISPO (1996): DOXA (1985), Daviter (1967):

it is possible to make a comparison with 1967. Already at that time the perception of unfairness was quite high (65 per cent): there was however also a high number of 'Don't knows'. The massive decrease of this type of response in 1986 and 1996 shows that the visibility of the tax question has been significantly increasing in the last three decades.[6]

If it is true that austerity measures bear the largest responsibility for the activation of anti-tax, anti-welfare and, more generally anti-bureaucratic sentiments, it must not be forgotten that since the late 1980s the impact of these measures has been clearly exacerbated by a second factor: European integration. The completion of the internal market has in fact posed two additional challenges to all those categories whose wealth hinges upon foreign exports: stronger competitive pressures and higher costs (for example owing to more stringent health and safety or environmental regulations on businesses). The 1992 devaluation of the lira greatly helped to attenuate both challenges. But the establishment of EMU will soon rule out a similar option for the future. These categories (mainly concentrated in the North) thus have an interest in demanding lower taxes and better public services. And some of them have come to believe that this can be achieved only by 'dumping the South', even at the price of outright secession.

It would be obviously too simplistic to interpret the Lega Nord phenomenon in socio-economic terms alone: there is more to it than just a 'tax–welfare backlash'. However, the relevance of the overall configuration, which has been just described (austerity measures, rapid tax increases, stronger foreign competition and so on), cannot be neglected in the explanation of the emergence and the persisting success of this new political formation. More importantly, it would be a terrible mistake to underestimate the weight which the Lega Nord and its underlying social coalition is exerting and will continue to exert on the evolution of Italy's welfare state. A new, powerful territorial cleavage has emerged in the country's social politics, which is destined to condition most of the future policy choices.

Again, the gravity of the situation may be captured with the help of attitudinal evidence. The above mentioned 1996 survey asked its sample whether they agreed on the desirability of more regional autonomy as regards taxes and public services. As Table 7.3 shows, the vast majority of respondents (especially in the North) express a high degree of consensus on this option. The most alarming indications stem however from Table 7.4. To all respondents who were in favour of more regional autonomy, the survey asked whether poorer regions should continue to get financial aids from the government or from the more prosperous regions in order to develop: 36.6 per cent of Northern 'autonomists' (that is 28.7

Table 7.3 Attitudes towards regional autonomy (% of agreement)

Today people often speak about attributing to the regions greater autonomy also as regards taxes and public services. Do you agree?

	Italy	North-west	North-east	Centre	South
Strongly agrees	24.2	30.1	35.4	18.4	16.7
Agrees	42.1	48.2	44.5	40.9	36.6
Disagrees	13.1	9.9	10.3	11.8	18.0
Strongly disagrees	4.6	2.4	1.6	6.4	6.8
Don't know	16.0	9.4	8.2	22.5	21.9

Source: ISPO, 1996

Table 7.4 Attitudes towards territorial solidarity (% of agreement)

In your opinion, should poorer regions continue to receive financial aids
from the government or from more prosperous regions in order to develop?

	Italy	North-west	North-east	Centre	South
Yes	54.6	44.3	35.1	52.1	84.0
No	27.0	32.3	42.0	27.9	8.2
Don't know	18.3	23.3	22.9	20.0	7.8

Notes: This question was posed only to those respondents who had declared themselves in
favour of more regional autonomy (see Table 7.3).

Source: ISPO, 1996.

per cent of the whole Northern sample) answered *negatively*. In the
North-east a relative majority of 42 per cent of the autonomists (33.6 per
cent of the whole sample for this area) gave a negative answer. Within the
supporters of the Lega Nord almost two-thirds of respondents (63 per
cent) declared themselves against territorial redistribution. Not all these
'anti-solidaristic autonomists' would be prepared to subscribe to
Umberto Bossi's recent proposals for a secession of the *Padania* (that is,
basically, Northern Italy). But, certainly, these data do signal that the new
North–South conflict around the public budget has far-reaching roots in
Italy's new political culture of the 1990s and that the issue of tax and welfare federalism – largely transversal with respect to the more traditional
distributive issues – has acquired a structural prominence which is not
likely to subside until major institutional reforms will be able to defuse it.

It will not be easy for the new olive-tree government elected in April
1996 to effectively respond to the many challenges which are currently

confronting the Italian welfare model. The debt legacy, external economic and monetary constraints as well as in-built growth pressures (such as ageing, health care prices, system maturation and so on) will keep cost containment as a top policy priority for many years to come. Given the high potential of a tax revolt, there is very little room for new revenue-raising measures. Between 1992–1995 a number of important measures were taken to reform the health care system and in particular the pension system:[7] further structural changes are bound to meet the firm resistance of entrenched interests and expectations, while in its turn the fight against frauds and abuses finds objective limits in the persistent absence of an efficient tax system and administration. Thus the distributional rebalancing of the model and the correction of its historical defects does not appear within easy reach. All European countries are facing hard times these days in paying their welfare bills in an increasingly unified European economy and in the wider context of globalization. In Italy, two additional problems make this task even more difficult. In the first place, there is still an outstanding debt for all the 'free meals' of the past; secondly, Mr Prodi and his team have to convince their Northern and richer voters (and not only the Lega hard-liners) that this debt repayment must remain a collective business of the entire nation, with no viable (or permissible) separatist short cut.

In Southern Europe olive trees are known to grow ripe fruits even on impervious terrain. It remains to be seen whether the first left government of Italy will be capable of keeping the good promises of the symbol which it wisely chose for its electoral campaign.

ENDNOTES

1. A less comprehensive, but more detailed characterization was presented in Ferrera, 1996.
2. For a discussion of the notions of 'state penetration' and 'welfare stateness', see Flora, 1986.
3. See,. for instance, the pioneering researches by Wilensky, 1976 and Coughlin, 1980.
4. *Tartassati* is a popular metaphor which started to circulate during the 1980s and which can be translated as 'the tax harassed'. It refers to all those categories which, for various reasons (including the technical impossibility of evading taxes on their incomes), the tax burden is especially heavy.
5. The data for 1992 are drawn from a comprehensive Eurobarometer survey on social protection. According to this survey, the degree of welfare 'minimalism' tended to be significantly higher in Italy than in the other EU countries (Ferrera, 1993). With respect to the original source, the data included in Table 7.1 are slightly different: some statistical corrections have been made to neutralize differences in definitions.
6. For a more detailed illustration of the data mentioned in this section, see Ferrera and Piazzini, 1996.

7. In 1992–93 a reform introduced more competition within the NHS and other changes aimed at improving efficiency. The pension system was in its turn thoroughly reformed in 1995. According to the new rules the basis of calculation of benefits will no longer be related to earnings but to past contributions. The total amount of contributions paid during working life will be divided by a 'conversion coefficient' ranging from 4.719 (at the age of 57) to 6.13 per cent (at 65). This coefficient will be reviewed every 10 years and potentially adjusted in line with demographic and economic development. The rate of contribution payable will be reviewed annually on the basis of changes in GDP. The pension itself will be inflation-proofed and a state-financed social allowance will continue to be paid to those not eligible for a contributory benefit. The system will remain pay-as-you-go but actuarial criteria will in the future govern the determination of benefits. For a critical review of the effects of the 1995 pension reform see Padoa Schioppa Kostoris (1996).

REFERENCES

Alesina, A. and M. Marré (1996), 'Evasione e debito', in A. Monorchio (ed) *La finanza pubblica italiana dopo la svolta del 1992*, Bologna: Il Mulino, 325–93.

Castles, F. (1994), 'On religion and public policy', *European Journal of Political Research*, **25** (1), 19–39.

Castles, F. (1995), 'Welfare state development in Southern Europe', *West European Politics*, **18** (2), 291–313.

Castles, F. and M. Ferrera (1996), 'Home ownership and the welfare state: is Southern Europe Different?', *Southern European Society and Politics*, **1** (2), 163–85.

Commission of the European Communities (1995), *Social Protection in Europe*, Luxembourg.

Coughlin, R.M. (1980), *Ideology, Public Opinion and Welfare Policy*, Berkeley: Institute of International Studies.

Dente, B. (1995), *In un diverso stato*, Bologna: Il Mulino.

Ferrera, M. (1993), *EC Citizens and Social Protection*, Brussels: Commission of the European Communities.

Ferrera, M. (1996), 'The Southern model of welfare in Social Europe', *Journal of European Social Policy*, **6**, (1), 17–37.

Ferrera, M. (1997), 'The uncertain future of the Italian welfare state', *West European Politics*, **20**, January, 231–49.

Ferrera M. and A. Piazzini (1996), 'Una rivolta fiscale alle porte?, *Political Trend*, 6 April, 15–25 .

Flora, P. (1986), 'Introduction', in P. Flora (ed), *Growth to Limits. The West European Welfare States Since World War II*, Berlin and New York: De Gruyter.

Gough, I. (1996), 'Social assistance in Southern Europe', *South European Society and Politics*, **1** (1), 1–23.

Jurado Guerrero, T. and M. Naldini (1996), 'Is the South so different? Italian and Spanish families in comparative perspective', Working Paper of the MZES, Mannheim, January.

Leibfried, S. (1992), 'Towards a European welfare state', in S. Ferge and J. Kolberg (eds), *Social Policy in a Changing Europe*, Boulder: Westview Press, 279–345.

Negri. N. and Saraceno, C. (1996), *La lotta contro la povertà*, Bologna: Il Mulino.

OECD (1994), *New orientations in social policy*, Paris.

Padoa Schioppa Kostoris, F. (1996), *Pensioni e risanamento della finanza pubblica*, Bologna: Il Mulino.

Saraceno, C. (1994), 'The ambivalent familism of the Italian welfare state', in *Social Politics*, 1, 60–82.

Wilensky, H. (1976), *The New Corporatism, Centralization and The Welfare State*, London: Sage.

Van Kersbergen, K. (1995), *Social Capitalism*, London: Routledge.

8. From the Communist welfare state to social benefits of market economy: the determinants of the transition process in Central Europe

Vladimir Rys

8.1 SUMMARY

Looking back at the developments which have taken place since the fall of Communism, the article reviews the general trends in the orientation of social security reform in some key countries of Central Europe. The lessons learnt during this process reveal a number of original myths, such as the mistaken belief that the social reform has to intervene from the very outset of the economic transformation.

After the initial predominance of ideological thinking in the orientation of the reform, a 'normalization process' has taken place, in the sense of governments following closely the interplay of social security fundamentals, and above all the political and economic imperatives of the moment, which determine the shape of social security legislation.

This evolution has brought the situation in Central Europe close enough to that prevailing in Western countries, so as to justify the question whether some guidelines can be derived from the process of dismantlement of the Communist welfare state for the ongoing effort regarding the question of scaling down the benefits of the Western welfare state. Two areas of concern are singled out as a result of this reflection. One refers to the extreme brutality of the impact of the economic factor, once the available financial resources fall below a certain level. The other draws attention to the relative instability of the basic value judgements on which the welfare state has been built.

8.2 INTRODUCTION

Six years after the fall of Communism in Europe, any attempt to establish a clear pattern of the social security reforms currently taking place in the countries concerned is becoming increasingly difficult.[1] We note a growing differentiation in the prevailing economic and political conditions in each country and tend to conclude that post-communist societies are now developing each in their own way.

One thing seems certain: the well-meaning economic advisers preaching a complete abandonment of a 100-year-old tradition in social protection and a return to basic social assistance are no longer listened to.[2] After many years of hesitation and experimentation, governments have come to the conclusion that the policy of overall priority to economic development at the expense of social development is doomed to failure. However, no particular welfare state model seems to stand a chance of being followed. We are witnessing what may be described as a return to reality (Rys, 1995) in the sense of governments following closely the changeable interplay of social security fundamentals (that is the various components of demographic, economic, social and political factors in society) which broadly determine – as they have always done – the shape of a country's social security institutions.

In spite of the growing differentiation, there is one feature all the countries concerned have in common: the rhythm of transformation of basic societal structures. While political institutions have been transformed rapidly to meet the requirements of a democratic system (which does not necessarily mean that they are animated by democrats), the establishment of economic institutions has been more laborious and their progress often hesitant. As for social protection institutions, apart from partial adaptations to the needs of the market economy, no major or global reform of the system had taken place in any country before 1995.[3] Several factors explain this striking delay. At the beginning, there is a general lack of knowledge regarding concepts and techniques of social insurance on the part of both experts and members of the legislative bodies. And even when the techniques are mastered, in times of total economic instability any financial planning of new social security schemes is extremely hazardous. Furthermore, and this is no doubt the most important reason, given the excessive volume of social expenditure under the Communist regime and the need for gradual adaptation of the level of benefits to available financial resources, any social reform is bound to be restrictive and have a negative impact on the population. It was hence the political risk involved in such an operation which made the governments hesitant and inclined to delay their decisions. Among the contributing factors we should also include the process of gradual crystallization of political, ideological and nationalistic attitudes which led to the changes in the orientation of governments, and even to the collapse of old and the creation of new states.

8.3 EARLY ORIENTATIONS IN SOCIAL REFORM

After the fall of Communism, social security reform was considered an indispensable measure destined to cushion the adverse social impact of economic transformation; it was not an objective in itself but rather a means for ensuring the success of the transformation. The starting point of a new social security concept in all countries of the region was a strong reaction against state paternalism, accompanied by declarations exhorting citizens to take over the responsibility for securing their own future. In practice, this meant returning to a general scheme of social insurance, with a large space left for occupational and private arrangements. At the same time, great emphasis was placed on the democratic nature of the new system and on the need for a large citizen participation in its management (Rys, 1993).

One of the first sectors to come under review was health care. In this case, the general trend favoured the transformation of the existing national health services into medical care insurance schemes. In Hungary, this had been somewhat surprisingly integrated into the general insurance scheme, before a law of July 1992 introduced a separate administration of this branch under its own governing body. In the Czech Republic, the National Health Insurance Fund became operational in January 1993, after a great deal of confusion and a year of administrative preparations; since then, two dozen other health insurance funds have come into being for the purpose of encouraging competition, with the resulting confusion greater than ever before. In Poland, meanwhile, the introduction of health insurance is considered an ultimate goal, but in the absence of a comprehensive concept of social policy, priority has been given to the improvement of the existing health services (Wlodarczyk and Mierzewski, 1991).

As for other social risks, a number of legislative acts passed in different countries dealt mainly with the elimination of the excessive measures of the previous regime, the adaptation of administrative structures, modifications in the system of financing and maintenance of the purchasing power of existing benefits. At the same time, considerable effort went into the preparation of social reform plans. In the blueprints produced during this period, the overall trend pointed towards the establishment of a general social insurance scheme covering old age, invalidity and survivors, as well as sickness (cash benefits) and work accidents. High hopes were being placed on the introduction of occupational pension schemes which were to help to reduce the expenditure going on basic state benefits. The trend in family allowances was to transform them into a state benefit subject to a means test.[4]

It was characteristic of this early period that a major social security reform was always imminent but never quite ready to go before parliament. In Hungary and Poland, the question of political divergences apart, the main reason was the progressive deterioration of the financial situation of the existing schemes, particularly in the field of pensions. In a generally unsettled economic situation, it was a question of common sense to place priority on the preservation of the basic functions of the existing arrangements before embarking on a major reform of the system. The situation was somewhat different in Czechoslovakia where, in the absence of a financial crisis of the existing scheme, the reform appeared to be dependent on technical matters regarding the progress of the economic reform; however, the real cause of the delay was probably the crystallization process of political attitudes, including those which led to the division of the state.

8.4 THE LESSONS OF EXPERIENCE

As time went on, the governments noted that, contrary to previous beliefs, there was perhaps no hurry to go ahead with the social reform which no longer seemed indispensable for the progress of the economic transformation. On the contrary, this could proceed better without unnecessary popular discontent likely to be raised by new and, by definition, more restrictive social legislation shaking even further an already precarious political stability.

Another feature of the original social reform blueprint to come under scrutiny was the call for democratization of social security administration. This became less perceptible after the social elections in Hungary had been won by the ex-Communist trade unions in May 1993. In a more striking manner, the Czech neo-Liberal Government – which could have been expected to maintain the line of reducing the role of the state – turned its back on administrative democracy only a few months after its official policy declaration and retained a state control of social security funds. Admittedly, as the introduction of social security contributions produced amounts far in excess of annual expenditure, it was tempting to keep the *status quo* rather than to get involved in discussions with social partners.

Even the original battle-cry 'away with state paternalism' had to undergo some soul-searching revision in so far as it covered both government supervision and financing. Already in 1992, at a meeting of directors of social security organizations from Central Europe, voices were heard expressing misgivings about the move away from state budget financing to autonomous social insurance funds; experience has shown that it was easier to get a deficit covered when social security was part of the state budget rather than an autonomous fund. Thus social security authorities in Bulgaria had to have recourse to bank loans, knowing perfectly well that they would never be in a position to pay back or even cover the market interest rate. The Hungarian social security bodies decided in 1993 to launch a public subscription in the form of social security bonds, and although these had been issued with state guarantee, there was no rush at the counter (*The Financing*, 1993: 15). The message received by governments through all these developments clearly pointed to the need for a careful handling of the social reform issue and for refraining from any legislation unless absolutely necessary.

8.5 DISMANTLING THE COMMUNIST WELFARE STATE – OR HOW TO WALK ON A TIGHTROPE

During the early years, an outside observer following social security developments in Central Europe discovered sooner or later a widely respected taboo: the official circles had carefully avoided any mention of the excessive social expenditure during the period of Communist rule. One reason for this was no doubt the fear of provoking popular unrest by pointing to the need for reducing social benefits; in another context, this could also amount to admitting the superiority of the Communist system in the social field. Yet another explanation is of a more human nature: those responsible for the past development of social security measures could hardly be expected to start denouncing what had generally been considered a meritorious achievement. Consequently, for many years, nobody dared or wished to tell the citizen the truth about the rotten foundations of the system. Most of the governments kept pretending that, somehow, the essential benefits can be preserved. This is an attitude which is at present fairly common in countries of Western Europe. Nevertheless, in some respect, due to the radical break with the past, the post-Communist governments have incomparably more elbow-room than their Western counterparts. This is well demonstrated by the story of unemployment benefits in the early nineties; we must, of course, bear in mind, that this benefit has never been part of the Communist system. In other respects, and this concerns mainly the adverse economic situation of these countries, the political choice of their governments is reduced to a bare minimum.

8.6 THE RISE AND FALL OF UNEMPLOYMENT BENEFITS

It may be useful to start by a brief look at Table 8.1 indicating the rate of unemployment in the countries concerned at the end of each given year during the period which is of interest to us.

Table 8.1 Rate of unemployment (in %)

	1989	1991	1993
Czech Republic	0	4	3
Hungary	1	10	12
Poland	0	11	15

The volume of unemployment in the Czech Republic, while obviously an exceptional case, has no impact on our argument because at the time it was taking the first measures in 1990, the government did not know how low the rate would be and, indeed, expected (some economists hoping for) a figure of around 8 per cent.

Regarding the evolution of the unemployment benefit, the general trend is surprisingly uniform. Having introduced extremely liberal benefits, in the spirit of the good old (Communist) times, the governments were called to order by harsh economic realities. Within a relatively short time, it became necessary to apply more severe eligibility criteria, reduce the amount and duration of benefits and review the system of financing. The Polish and Czech experience is particularly revealing as shown by the following summaries of the situation after the introduction of the first laws as compared with rules existing at the end of 1993.

Polish experience

December 1989:
Financing: Employer's contribution of 2% of salaries
Eligibility: All persons seeking employment
Duration: Without limit
Amount: 70% of last salary during first three months
50% during the next six months
40% after nine months

December 1993:
Financing: Employer's contribution of 3% of salaries
Eligibility: At least six months in employment
            No other household income
            No refusal of an employment offer
Duration: 12 months (18 months after 25 years of work)
Amount: 36% of a national average salary (flat rate)

Czech experience

December1990:
Financing: State budget
Eligibility: All persons seeking employment
Duration: 12 months
Amount: 65% of last salary during first six months
            60% after six months
            70% if following programme of retraining
            Cumulative with end of service benefit

December 1993:
Financing: Employer's contribution of 2.25% and
            employee's contribution of 0.75%
Eligibility: 12 months in employment over last three years
Duration: six months
Amount: 60% of last salary for first three months
            50% after three months, with maximum not to exceed the
            statutory subsistence mimimum
            No cumulation with end of service benefit

Hungary was the first Communist country to introduce unemployment insurance even before the fall of the regime (Ferge, 1992); consequently, the scheme adopted in February 1991 was more sophisticated and underwent relatively little change in the subsequent years. The only exception is financing, with a steep increase in employer's contribution from 1.5 per cent to 5 per cent, accompanied by an increase in employee's contribution from 0.5 per cent to 1.5 per cent.

The sociologists readily subscribe to the affirmation that the treatment of unemployment in society depends on the social perception of the phenomenon. Although this approach may find some justification even in a post-Communist society, in the absence of normally constituted social actors, social perception – whatever this may mean under such circumstances – stands hardly any chance of getting translated into the political action of the government in power.

The above-described experience of a drastic revision of unemployment benefits is more complicated than would seem and cannot be reduced to a simple question of available financial means. At the start of the process, there is a general awareness on the part of the population of the price to be paid for a market economy and fear on the part of governments as to what this unknown evil may do to people. The result is an overgenerous legislation drafted in an old-time spirit of meeting social needs regardless of available resources and in the absence of any technical knowledge of the problems of unemployment insurance.[5]

It is, however, the second stage which is of real interest. What has made the governments take such a harsh line in revising legislation adopted only several months ago without fear of a popular outburst? The economic imperatives are obvious and need not be enlarged upon. Furthermore, there may have initially been an underestimation of the capacity of other social security branches, and above all of old-age and invalidity insurance, to absorb potential victims of unemployment. In some countries an improved parental allowance has no doubt reduced the number of women seeking employment.

However, factors other than those mentioned above may be of equal if not greater importance. To the extent that the same causes tend to produce the same effects, benefits awarded in the spirit of old-time liberality provoke the same abuse of social legislation as in the past. Many people draw the unemployment benefit while working in another undertaking; in some countries, one gets the impression that the emergence of a new class of self-employed is financed by the abuse of unemployment benefits. The governments hence cannot fail to realize that they are acting in contradiction to their declared policy of moving away from state paternalism and making people responsible for their own existence.

But why has there not been a major social upheaval which would probably follow in similar circumstances in any Western country? Have governments initially overestimated the psychological impact of unemployment as social phenomenon hitherto unknown to the population? This is probably the case, but the main reason could be that people in their majority have approved of the government decision to revise the legislation. The need for an economic reform has never been contested and abuse of unemployment benefits has reminded them perhaps too much of the buried Communist past. Moreover, it should not be forgotten that over a period of 40 years these populations have grown used to harsh measures from above and acquired a high degree of resourcefulness and a capacity for 'getting by'. With social controls greatly relaxed, it is perhaps this mental heritage of the past which still enables many unemployed people in these countries to make ends meet in one way or another.

All this seems to indicate that a Western politician, trying to scale down even further the already meagre unemployment benefits offered by a market economy, would be ill-advised to take his cue from Central Europe. While the capacity of the Western employee to assume this risk has been remarkable, his long-term resistance is probably weaker than that of his Eastern colleague.

8.7 SOCIAL REFORM AND POLITICAL IDEOLOGY

As from the middle of 1993 the wind of political change starts blowing over Central Europe. Poland, soon followed by Hungary, takes a sharp turn left, while the Czech Republic abandons the left of centre position maintained under the former federation and embraces a right-wing neo-liberal policy. In all cases attempts are first made to develop social policy in line with the government's political ideology; in all cases these attempts fail to make headway. They are all related to the central question of this essay which is how to dismatle the Communist welfare state without committing political suicide. Examples of recent developments in the main countries of the region throw an interesting light on this issue.[6]

8.7.1 The Czech Republic

In the spring of 1993, the Czech Parliament was expected to adopt eagerly awaited legislation on supplementary pension schemes. The draft law which had been approved by social partners provided for the establishment of voluntary occupational pension funds based on collective bargaining. The tripartite General Agreement for 1993 dealing with social and economic policy was duly signed in the middle of March. However the relations between the government and the trade unions grew tense in the subsequent weeks, when it became clear that the government had no intention of going ahead with the occupational pension scheme and other questions of labour policy. By the end of June, the Prime Minister announced that the government would gradually withdraw from the existing tripartite system so as to ensure its right to make sovereign decisions on social and economic matters.

Later that year, on the occasion of a parliamentary debate concerning an increase in family allowances, the Prime Minister referred to a new social policy concept of the government. This policy should address only the needy, and not, in general, some particular groups of the population. There were a great many children in extremely rich families and hence a flat subsidy was a sheer waste of tax-payer's money. The government's policy aimed therefore at addressing specific family situations.[6]

At the beginning of 1994, the conflict with trade unions broke out again on account of several questions including a draft of the basic pension law. In the middle of February, without waiting for the draft, the parliament approved the *law on supplementary pensions*. Under this provision, an individual may take out voluntary insurance with an approved pension fund, established as a commercial shareholding company under the supervision of the Ministry of Finance. The insured person must pay a monthly contribution, which is not tax-deductible, but the state contributes directly to each individual according to the amount of his monthly contribution. The law stipulates that 10 per cent of the pension fund gains may be redistributed to shareholders. An outside observer could plainly see that the government used – or rather abused – this opportunity for adopting an excellent instrument of capital formation rather than one of social protection.

A month later, the government submitted draft principles of three social security laws (pensions, state social support and social aid) for examination by all parliament committees. The trade unions duly opposed these proposals, which, they argued, did not envisage the establishment of a social insurance scheme but the continuation of a state social security system. The funds collected from contributions would still be used without parliamentary approval and insured persons would have no means of expressing their views. However, their arguments made no impact on the committee hearings. As it happened, there was no coherent opposition stand in the committees and the trade union representatives stood little chance of influencing the vote. The official proposals were approved without change.

The first anti-government mass demonstration organized by the trade unions in the subsequent weeks gave the Prime Minister an opportunity to further elaborate his ideas on their role in society. In his view:

(a) trade unions belong to the sphere of employer–employee relations and not to that of social relations;
(b) the main platform for trade union activity is the enterprise and not the government level. This seems to indicate that throughout this period the government stakes were higher than one or another form of income maintenance; the central issue was, no doubt, the global reform of economic and social institutions of the country. The Prime Minister, a great admirer of Mancur Olson, sees in the institutions of civic society the expression of selfish partial interests which detract from the common good defended by the state; 'collectivism at a lower level' as practised in many Western societies is as detestable to him as the state collectivism of the Communist society.[7] His social policy

recognizes the principle of solidarity between those who have and those who have not and favours the idea of preservation of a minimum level of living. However, nobody else but the state may be the master of the necessary redistribution and only the needy may obtain help. Notions such as the prevention of need through social insurance, or equality of social rights based on citizenship have no place in this scheme.

If the trade unions lost the battle at the stage of the formulation of social reform principles, they made a considerable impact on the subsequent discussions of the full text of social reform laws. With the help of mass media, they managed to wake up public opinion and transfer the debate to the highest political level. This was not due to any action undertaken by the left-wing opposition parties, still incapable of producing a coherent social policy alternative to the government programme; it was the impact of their arguments on some of the government coalition partners which made the change. With the mid-1996 general elections looming on the horizon, one of the smaller partners, the Christian Democratic Union, suddenly discovered the social doctrine of the church and took sides with some of the trade union demands.

With regard to the *state social support system* the main argument concerned the issue of universality versus targeting of family allowances. When this began to threaten the government coalition, a special committee was established to co-ordinate different points of views. The end result was a compromise solution and the law, adopted in May 1995, provides that four of these benefits will be targeted but five will remain universal. Consequently, family allowances will be paid according to the age of the child and family income, the benefit being extinguished if income exceeds three times the official subsistence minimum.[8] On the other hand, a fairly high parental allowance will be maintained as a universal benefit and, surprisingly enough, the payment will be extended up to the age of four.

The controversy around the *basic pension law*, adopted a month later, revolved around two issues: firstly, the government proposal to increase the retirement age – over a period of 12 years – by two years for men (from 60 to 62) and by four years for women (who may now retire between the age of 57 to 61 according to the number of children); and secondly, the government refusal to establish a special pension fund. The first proposal was accepted, but there was a compromise again on the second point, the government having been forced to establish a special fund within the state budget. They saved the day, thanks solely to the last minute support of a small ethnic party which replaced the absent votes of Christian Democrats. Obviously, this result had relatively little to do with social policy principles.

For all practical purposes, it may thus be considered that the Czech neo-liberal experiment is over. There has been a certain return to reality in the Czech Republic implying that the country is turning its back on economic doctrine and ideology and facing the hard facts of life. Recent public opinion surveys in the country indicate that support for political parties is no longer formulated in terms of ideological preferences but in terms of personal losses or advantages arising out of legislative decisions (Hartl, 1994). The Prime Minister is no doubt a staunch supporter of neo-liberal theories, but he has also a sharp sense of political priorities. Consequently, he should not find it too difficult to continue compromising his economic and ideological principles should the programme of dismantlement of the Communist welfare state become too radical for his political partners. Even if the general line of reducing benefits is maintained, the process of reduction regarding different types of benefits will have to be fairly selective.

8.7.2 Hungary

In May 1994, the general elections in the country resulted in an overall victory of the Socialist (ex-Communist) party which obtained a 54 per cent majority in parliament; an agreement concluded with a small liberal party (Union of Free Democrats) gave the government coalition a total of 72 per cent of seats. At the beginning of his mandate the Prime Minister, Gyula Horn, appeared confident that he would manage to reconcile the task of building up capitalism with the maintenance of social advantages acquired during the previous decades. However, several weeks later, his finance minister Békesi declared that in spite of the promise made by the the previous right-wing government that pensions would be increased by 8 per cent, for lack of financial meant a rise amounting to only 5 per cent could be envisaged. In January 1995, following the presentation of a budget with drastically reduced social benefits, the Minister was forced to resign.

Nevertheless, in the following months, after many bitter and heated discussions within the ruling party, the government yielded to the pressure of harsh economic reality and agreed to reduce social expenditure. The Prime Minister admitted that the cuts were unavoidable since a country with such a high national debt as Hungary could not afford to spend 27 per cent of its annual GDP on welfare and social services.[9] The government hence adopted, in March 1995, a radical reform package introducing, among other reforms, the abolition of family allowances as a universal benefit,[10] a reduction of parental allowance and the elimination of dental care from sickness insurance coverage. Two ministers resigned from the government when the project, which provoked a huge popular outburst, was presented, in June of the same year, to parliament. Even some leading economists took the view that such dismantling of the Communist welfare state was premature.

It would have been a mistake to consider, at that stage, that the battle was over. In fact, a month later, the Constitutional Tribunal suspended the application of several measures of the reform package, including those on family allowances, not because of the substance of these proposals, but 'for little time given to society to prepare for them.'[11] In February 1996, the main protagonist of the drastic social reform, the Finance Minister, Bokros, resigned from the government 'fed up with bickering over his planned welfare overhaul, after nearly exchanging blows with a trade union leader at a stormy cabinet meeting.'[12] Undoubtedly, in spite of the pressure from the World Bank, and although general elections will take place only in 1998, the Prime Minister and other leaders of the Socialist party, whose popular support has fallen considerably in recent months, have decided to slow down the pace of reform so as to preserve their political future.

8.7.3 Poland

Recent developments in this country offer yet another example of conflicting political views on the question of what to do with the Communist welfare state.

Poland was the first country in Central Europe to take a left turn as a result of the victory of the Socialist party (ex-Communist) in the general elections in September 1993. Due to the neo-liberal orientation of the previous government applying the 'big bang' theory to the process of economic transition, the institutional structure of the inherited welfare state has remained practically untouched; it is still based on the enterprise with a single employer contribution representing some 45 per cent of the payroll. The earlier governments had little interest in conducting a major social reform and the subsequent aggravation of living conditions was bound to make any such attempt still more difficult (Ksiezopolski, 1994). The problems faced by the present left-wing government in scaling down the benefits of the Communist welfare state are very similar to those encountered by their colleagues in Hungary.

The episode which is of particular interest to us concerns the period situated shortly before the presidential elections of 1995. In September, the Polish Parliament adopted a law imposing a limit on the adjustment of pensions, so that these would increase by 2.5 per cent only instead of 12.5 per cent provided for under the existing rules. The government declared that such an extra expenditure would raise the budget deficit for

1996 from 2.8 per cent to 4.6 per cent and the annual inflation would reach 28 per cent instead of the estimated 17 per cent. This vote has provoked an institutional duel with President Walesa who opposed it with his veto pointing out that 'a pension increase of 2.5 per cent could not improve the standard of living of old-age pensioners who represent the group most affected by the cost of economic transformations of the country.'[13] In the following weeks, the parliament having rejected the presidential veto, Walesa appealed to the Constitutional Tribunal, according to the scenario well known in the post-Communist countries. The outcome of this episode has been lost in the commotion which followed the election of the new Polish president; it may be safely assumed that the Tribunal made no haste in giving a verdict. According to newspaper reports from Central Europe, the Polish parliament has approved, at the end of April 1996, a government plan for major social reform to be carried out over the course of the next 15 years. The reform of the pension system is likely to follow the neo-liberal model proposed in 1994 by the World Bank.[14]

This latest orientation of the left-wing Polish government thus confirms that the policies aimed at dismantling the Communist welfare state cut across all barriers of economic doctrine or political ideology.

8.8 CONCLUSIONS

The social security developments in Central Europe described above indicate the presence of one common feature. Whatever the political orientation or the economic situation of the country concerned, the government can no longer impose social policy measures based on political ideology and has to discuss or even negotiate them not so much with the opposition as with the leaders of the ruling party itself and with the coalition partners. The time when questions regarding social reform were essentially a matter for internal exchanges between various competent ministries is definitively over. Once a social policy issue becomes the focus of attention of the general public, ideology gives way to parliamentary debates and agreements between political parties, as has normally been the case in Western countries. This is a positive development because rigid ideological attitudes tend to make social policy discussions sterile and any consensual agreement more difficult to reach. Obviously, party political deals in Central Europe may not be beneficial to the formulation of a nation-wide social policy, but this is a question of developing a certain political culture which may take some time to take roots.

This *rapprochement* with regard to the situation in other Western democracies justifies our attempt to examine whether the process of dismantling the Communist welfare state in Central Europe is likely to provide some lessons for the West. There obviously exists one common starting point which is the acute awareness on both sides of the extreme importance of social policy for the political survival of the government in power. Central Europe has learned this lesson relatively recently but it has learned it well. Beyond that, any statement on this subject is of necessity of a highly speculative nature.

We have pointed out in dealing with the earlier case of unemployment benefits, that due to the sharp break with the past and to the overall feeling of advancement on the way to prosperity, Central European populations may be expected to accept more readily harsh measures which would be refused by the majority of the population in the West. However, any further comparison is distorted by the serious economic problems in most post-Communist countries. If a left-wing government in Central Europe decides in favour of a dramatic reduction of existing social benefits, it is because – in view of the extreme economic pressures from outside and from within – it has hardly any other choice. It hence becomes a question of how far it can go short of losing all political support in the population. Nevertheless, even this is part of the old game which consists in establishing, at the level of existing political forces in the country, the necessary consensus for a given policy. The lesson which may be derived from this by Western politicians is the revelation of the extreme brutality with which economic factors may enter into play and overrule most other ideologically or socially conditioned considerations.

The message which may come through in analysing the situation in the Czech Republic, that is a country in a relatively comfortable economic situation, is of a different nature. This experience points to the difficulty of recomposing a national social policy approach even among groups with close political ties. The long spell of life under Communism has practically destroyed any common approach to questions or ideas as simple to understand as, for instance, the principles of social insurance, in the sense of a large number of individuals pooling resources to benefit from the laws of statistical averages in the occurrence of risks. The neo-liberal approaches to social policy find thus in this population an extremely fertile ground for their experiments. Although this situation can hardly be reproduced in the Western environment, those in charge of future welfare state reforms may be well inspired to take a closer look at Central Europe, in case the continuing social disruption of Western society should yield similar results.

ENDNOTES

1. Throughout this paper our attention is concentrated essentially on the Czech Republic, Hungary and Poland. For a more recent summary of the social security legislation in these countries see *Restructuring Social Security in Central and Eastern Europe . . .* 1994.
2. Even the neo-liberal Prime Minister of the Czech Republic, Vaclav Klaus, firmly rebuffed criticism by Jeffrey Sachs accusing him of overly generous welfare state policies; Klaus pointed out that examples of Malaysia, Taiwan or Singapore simply did not apply in Central Europe (*Lidove noviny*, 5 June, 1995). On social results of shock therapy in Poland see Jonczyk 1993: 213.
3. The Czech Republic adopted new legislation in the middle of 1995 and a comparable Polish reform is now pending.
4. This particular trend should not be interpreted as a sign of some spontaneous convergence but rather as a result of the persuasive advice offered by the World Bank.
5. According to Tomes (1995), sickness insurance legislation has served as a model in some countries.
6. *Lidove noviny*, 11 September 1993.
7. *Lidove noviny*, 21 November 1994.
8. It has been estimated that 5 per cent of the total number of families would lose this allowance, while about 20 per cent would see their benefit reduced.
9. *The Economist*, 1 April 1995.
10. This allowance should be suppressed for two-children families whose income exceeds 17 000 forints; the measure would concern about 20 per cent of all families. However, the benefit remains unchanged for families with three children.
11. *Tribune de Genève*, 5 July 1995.
12. *The Economist*, 24 February 1996.
13. *Espace sociale européen* (Paris), 6 October 1995.
14. *MF Dnes* (Prague), 25 April 1996.

REFERENCES

Ferge, Z. (1992), 'Le chômage en Hongrie', *Revue française des Affaires sociales*, **1**, 81–98.

The Financing of Social Insurance in Central and Eastern Europe (1993) European Series **20**, Geneva: ISSA.

Hartl, P. (1994), 'Political context of the changing perception of social security (in Czech)', Prague: Start.

Jonczyk, J. (1993), 'Unemployment: the Polish case and its implications', *Reforms in Eastern and Central Europe*, EISS Yearbook 1992, Leuven, 211–24.

Ksiezopolski, M. (1994), 'Social security in Poland in the period of transformation to market economy', *Paper Presented to FISS Symposium*, Sweden: Sigtuna.

Restructuring social security in Central and Eastern Europe. A Guide to Recent Developments, Policy Issues and Options. (1994), Geneva: ISSA.

Rys, V. (1993), 'Social security reform in Central Europe: issues and perspectives', *Journal of European Social Policy*, **3**, 163–75.

Rys, V. (1995), 'Social security developments in Central Europe: a return to reality', *Czech Sociological Review*, **2**, 197–208.

Tomes, I. (1995), 'From waste to targeting in social security: a Central and Eastern European reflection', *Social Security Tomorrow: Permanence and Change*, Geneva: ISSA, 87–101.

Wlodarczyk, W.C. and Mierzewski, P. (1991), 'From words to deeds: Health service reform in Poland', *International Social Security Review*, **4**, 5–17.

9. The crisis of the welfare state: a game-theoretic interpretation[1]

Egon Matzner[2]

9.1 THE GUIDING IDEA: DURING EPOCHS OF CHANGE, FISCAL CRISES MANIFEST THEMSELVES ALSO AS CRISES IN APPLYING OLD METHODS

Twenty years ago, the Institute of Public Finance and Infrastructure of the University of Technology in Vienna began to study the reasons for the growth of state activity and public expenditures. The thesis guiding these investigations was taken from Schumpeter's work *The Crisis of the Tax State* (1954). It reads as follows:

> The public finances are one of the best starting points for an investigation of society, especially though not exclusively of its political life. The full fruitfulness of this approach is seen particularly at those turning points, or better epochs, during which existing forms begin to die off and to change into something new, and which always involve a crisis of the old fiscal methods. This is true both of the causal importance of fiscal policy (in so far as fiscal events are an important element in the causation of all change) and of the symptomatic significance (in so far as everything that happens has its fiscal reflection)'.

> (Schumpeter, 1954/1918)

Most of the insights gained and also discussed internationally have remained valid. They are summarized in section 9.2, 'Origins of the state and state activity'. However, today the picture must be supplemented by new factors of great consequence which have since begun to restrict the room of manoeuvre of the welfare state. This is done in section 9.3.1, 'From systems rivalry to competition among locations and national currencies'. Section 9.4 deals with the 'Prospering and decline of institutions', taking up ideas from the theory of strategic games developed by John von Neumann and Oskar Morgenstern (1947): the well-known model called the prisoners' dilemma is applied in a rather unconventional way, like an 'analytical simile' as suggested by Georgescu-Roegens (1971). Section 9.5

154

attempts to summarize the arguments presented and concludes that 'the staging of positive-sum games should become the primary objective in politics'.

9.2 ORIGINS OF THE STATE AND OF STATE ACTIVITY

The research started at the University of Technology in Vienna and continued at the Science Centre Berlin revealed that state activity and the growth of public expenditures going with it originate from three sources: (1) external ones, (2) internal ones and (3) a combination of (1) and (2) (see Matzner, 1982).

This was based on a functional analysis of the state consisting of a socio-genesis of the state and its tasks, and of an economic explanation of their development, continuation and decline. The results achieved enabled the formulation of concrete suggestions based on empirical evidence for the reorganization of dysfunctional forms of state activity.

9.2.1 External Sources

The *first* key to understanding the origin of the state and its activities was the model of the prisoners' dilemma. With this model it is possible to explain the origin of the state as conceived by Schumpeter, just as by Elias (1976). Even earlier conceptions of the state like those of Hobbes or Hume were based on ideas reflected in this model (Taylor, 1976). The prisoners' dilemma model (PDM) is thus able to explain the production of internal and external security. One example for this would be the arms race between states, particularly important during the cold war. PDM is also applicable to technological competition among firms, or to competition for locations among nations, regions and communities. Another case in point observed in the 1970s, which can be explained by PDM, are features of the business cycle like the profit-wage-price-spiral or the under-utilization of capacities. Lastly, the malign growth of negative external effects leading to 'public bads' like pollution, traffic congestion and so on, as well as the weakness of positive external effects in producing 'public goods' like health, education and so on, are both rooted in situations covered by the situational logic of PDM.

It is characteristic of these examples that their inherent situational logic causes state activity: to expand institutions safeguarding security, to step up the use of high technology (for example atomic energy, genetic engineering) or to offer better infrastructure and larger tax concessions to parties interested in establishing new enterprises. In most cases the state and/or other public bodies suffer losses by such arrangements in the form of larger expenditures and smaller revenues. Increased urbanization, more high tech including use of chemistry, and the like, lead to increased negative external effects such as mountains of waste materials, pollution of air and water, or damage to biological cycles. No wonder that the application of 'old methods . . . (leads to) financial crises' – to quote Schumpeter once more.

A prolific source of growth in public expenditures is the rising number of unemployed and poor persons. They are to a large extent the result of low economic growth. Weaker economic growth and rising unemployment cause larger transfers and reduce the funds available for public welfare. Increasing poverty not only increases the volume of benefits and compensations to be paid. It also causes larger expenditures connected with crime related to mass poverty which many of us erroneously regarded as definitely overcome.

The *second* key to explaining the growth of public expenditures is the theory of subjective uncertainty employed by Schönbäck (1980) in his investigations of the wide field of social-policy motivated public expenditures. Subjective uncertainty regarding the amount of resources needed in case of illness, inability to work due to old age, or unemployment, as well as uncertainty regarding the particular point in time when such resources will be needed, can in certain important cases not be counteracted by accumulating voluntary savings or by voluntary insurance. Public provisions are indispensable if poverty and social harm affecting a large number of citizens are to be avoided.

Lastly, the *third* state-external reason leading to higher state expenditures has been identified as Baumol's 'cost disease' of personal services (Baumol, 1967). Unlike industrial or agricultural production, they cannot be rationalized, at least not at the same pace. Therefore the cost of personal services tends to rise constantly. Since many activities of this kind, like those of teachers, nurses, judges, nursery-school staff and so on, belong to the public sector or are (co-)financed by it, the cost disease of personal services will make itself felt particularly there.

When listing the reasons for growth in public expenditure one often overlooks that state activity and its financing results in positive services: external or internal security, more 'public goods', fewer 'public bads', or financial safeguards to offset subjective existential uncertainty (such as the risk of falling ill or becoming unemployed). In the case of this by no means complete list of examples, state activity and state expenditure lead to higher (economic) value added and greater (political) consent. If this gain becomes smaller than the increase in expenditures for state activities, a crisis potential will arise. The crisis of the welfare state becomes manifest when tax increases become necessary to finance a decreasing volume of services whose quality is deteriorating.

9.2.2 Internal Sources

A number of factors *internal* to the state will additionally contribute to reaching the crisis level. Among the *objective* reasons there are the consequences of hierarchical organization, for example the burden of annual budgeting which can only be mitigated but not eliminated altogether, or problems related to the timing and co-ordination of activities that involve a number of public bodies but affect a multitude of them. Such objective reasons are also present in large enterprises. However, in contrast to enterprises which must bear some profit for their owners and which are subject to market competition, in the public sector there are no similar incentives limiting avoidable expenditures due to inefficient organization. The tyranny of hard budget constraints tends to become effective only after very prolonged periods of inefficiency. There are many indications that the objective reasons for the existence of avoidable public expenditures are reinforced by *subjective reasons* for public spending. Among them there is private interest on the part of actors in the public domain, that is of politicians, civil servants and other government employees.[3] What is meant here is not corruption, that is illegal behaviour, but actions in accordance with the law and even covered by new, special legislation. The 'public choice school' has paid particular attention to the motives for exaggerated activity by the state. Its insights are highly valid as long as one does not overlook that self-interest is very often only an additional factor. This is so, because self-interest presupposes that there are external reasons for the existence and continuation of state activity. The 'public choice school' deserves credit for having drawn attention to the fact that the current rules of the game customary in many branches of the public sector contain too few incentives for an efficient fulfilment of tasks.

9.2.3 Symbiosis of External and Internal Sources

A constellation which greatly contributes to increasing public expenditures is one where the interests of state-external actors located in enterprises and other private bodies coincide with those of actors in the public sector (politicians and civil servants). This results in a symbiotic relationship characteristic of the 'modern public sector' (Weidenbaum, 1969). An example would be if public service staff advocate the purchase of state-of-the-art equipment and tools. This is very common in the field of external and internal security, but also in the health, transport and education sectors. For a long time, symbiotic expenditure programmes were defended by the full employment argument. Today, that argument is mainly used to ward off public expenditure cuts. On a theoretical level it was

George J. Stigler who drew attention to this in his 'capture theory'. Projects which lie in the common interest of actors in both the state-internal and the state-external sphere need not necessarily be socially harmful. If they accomplish public tasks from which all individuals may profit, or which at least do not harm anybody else's interests, such behaviour may even be socially welcome. However, very often this is not the case, or doubtful, as witnessed by numerous projects in the fields of armament, health, the arts, the sciences, as well as in research, transport, the environment and so on. Their outcome is an economically, socially and politically harmful growth of state expenditures.

9.2.4 Reasons for the Growth of Public Expenditures – Ways out of Crisis

Our investigations inspired by Schumpeter conducted in the 1970s and 1980s already listed the reasons for financial crises, and they are still valid today. They can be summarized as follows:

1. Higher unemployment because of too little effective demand, and there-fore relatively low investment and growth. Because of this, larger social welfare expenditures and lower revenues from taxes as well as lower social security contributions. This constellation follows the situational logic of PDM.
2. Intensified competition among regions and cities induces the public sector actors to offer improved infrastructure and to make tax conces-sions to enterprises. Again this corresponds to a pattern of action described by PDM.
3. Increase in social and economic constellations corresponding to the situ-ational logic of PDM. They are related to urbanization, increased use of mechanical and chemical devices, motorization and so on, and result in further problems (pollution, traffic congestion, deterioration of public transport and so on), all causing public expenditures.
4. Growing significance of self-interest on the part of public sector actors manifested in partial oversupply and overregulation. This combines with the symbiotic interaction of self-interest on the part of private and public actors, which is not justifiable by efficiency criteria in administration.
5. Lastly, societies characterized by individual ownership show a clear pref-erence for problem solutions enhancing expenditures. State-financed expenditure programmes make it possible to preserve the decision-making autonomy of problem generators such as investors, car drivers, persons who are ill and, above all, producers of products causing health problems or curing them.

Functional analysis, supported by research conducted at the Science Centre Berlin, (Research Area Labour Market and Employment, Matzner and Streeck, 1991) and by the work of the Research Unit for Socio-economics of the Austrian Academy of Sciences, led to the insight that an effective *reform strategy* would have to consist of changing the particular *situational logic*[4] that was giving rise to problems. Through changes in incentives/sanctions and in the institutional framework, a *socio-economic context* (Matzner, 1994 and below) should be created which would make it possible that individual action, guided by self-interest, would still serve the previously defined concrete public interest. Functional analyses of the fulfilment of public tasks were done, *inter alia*, on public policy in the fields of economic growth, employment, the labour market, transport, control of water pollution, public health, social welfare policy, as well as agriculture. Further studies deal with Austrian security policy, public subsidization of housing construction, of energy conservation, of voluntary fire brigades, and of the theatre. The results are quite conclusive. Yet very little use has been made of them by the public actors. (Examples would be the introduction of a basic income for farmers combined with the simultaneous reduction of quantity bonuses, or the organization of a regional integrated transport system for the city of Graz and its surroundings.)

The theoretical and empirical analyses published during the 1970s by the Institute of Public Finance and Infrastructure Policy of the Vienna University of Technology may today be considered as quite ahead of their time or, at least, as state-of-the-art. Why did politicians make so little use of them? Their authors had expected and hoped that the political and civil service actors, faced with the inefficient fulfilment of tasks and with financial constraints, as well as burdened by additional new tasks (relating to drugs, AIDS, organized crime, terrorism, and above all, since 1980, migration and refugee problems making new demands on financial resources) would take up the idea of reorganizing the way in which public tasks were traditionally fulfilled. The authors hoped that the fiscal crises connected with the various 'old methods' employed would turn into incentives to reform them – to which the functional analysis suggested by the authors could have made significant contributions. These hopes were disappointed.

As stated above, much of the 'Entwurf eines zeitgemäßen Musters staatlicher Interventionen' (Outline of an updated pattern of state intervention – the subtitle of Matzner, 1982) is still valid today. However, in 1997, in order to keep abreast of our time, it is also necessary to take account of developments which were underestimated in 1982, or could not yet be observed then. Among them are the implosion of the Soviet Union, of which there had been certain foreboding but which still took both the scientific community and politicians by surprise. The same is true for restrictions of the possibility for public action arising from the establishment of the EU and the introduction of a common European currency. What had also not been dealt with in the past were the limitations placed on public action due to globalization, especially of financial markets, or due to the increasing wealth and longevity of a large number of people in the developed industrial countries. The great problem posed by the current dramatic increase in older age groups and the decrease of younger age groups within the age pyramid, with the resulting serious consequences for public budgets, cannot be dealt with here. If the present study were to look into this matter, most probably one would discover further proof for the usefulness of approaching fiscal problems by *functional analysis* and through the *socio-economic context*, that is in a Schumpeterian way.

9.3   THE NEW SOCIO-ECONOMIC CONTEXT

In order to understand and explain the decision-making and acting of actors it has proved useful to visualize the situational logic in which they find themselves when doing so. This also holds for actors in the public domain who are responsible for carrying out and financing public tasks.

As mentioned above, in order to describe and analyse any particular situational logic, the concept of functional analysis was expanded by the concept of socio-economic context (Matzner, 1994), which consists of at least four elements:

1. *World views* on which the decisions, actions and interests by the dominant actors are based.
2. *Institutions* (in the shape of governments, enterprises, the family; but also markets, laws, decrees, norms and even habits); available *technology* (ranging from simple tools to telecommunications) and the *knowledge* necessary to apply it.
3. *Relative* prices, income and costs, but also *relative* attention, which induce individual effort.
4. *Political instruments* available to influence the four elements.

In which way has the socio-economic context for action by the state changed since the 1970s? Let us imagine two individual actors like the minister of finance and the president of a central bank of an EU member country which is a net contributor to the Union. Our two actors still advocate full employment in a welfare state. Which features would strike them as significant?

9.3.1 From Systems Rivalry to Competition among Locations and National Currencies

The new feature in the current socio-economic context for action to be taken within the state, the economy, the arts and sciences and so on, is, above all, the disappearance of the Soviet system with all its consequences. The removal of external danger must be listed *first* and foremost. However, this basically positive development has a number of serious consequences, also for 'the West', which cannot all be considered welcome. It is true that the end of the arms race means an end to external military threat and the constant danger of nuclear war at a global level. However, the place of the arms race has been taken by the scramble for arms markets in the former Soviet and Yugoslav spheres of influence. The eastward enlargement of NATO is, above all, an expansion of markets captured by Western arms producers to the detriment of the arms industry of Russia and the other post-Soviet states. There have also been cuts in arms research and research connected with security issues, which used to provide employment for many social scientists and economists particularly in the USA. As long as the West viewed the Soviet Union as a serious competitor also in the civil sphere, it was possible to get many important economic, educational and welfare programmes approved (Prager, 1962). The European Reconstruction Programme known as Marshall Plan, under which the USA donated a total of US$13 billion[5] to the non-Communist European countries, was a programme aimed at fighting Communism. The 'Point 4 Program' directed at non-Communist regimes in underdeveloped countries had the same aim. US aid to Europe was only provided under stringent conditions. Among them were measures like the elaboration of infrastructure programmes and the obligation to participate in the multilateral settlement of payments, that is planned economy-type measures. Full employment and planned economic development in the Soviet Union and the countries within the Soviet sphere of influence, but also recollections of the world economic crisis in the period between the two world wars, made it possible for full employment and economic growth to become recognized as desirable political aims also in the West. Comprehensive social security in the Soviet Union facilitated the stepwise elaboration of social security systems and the perfection of the welfare state in the Western countries. The development and promotion of the education system, of higher learning and of research institutions, was sparked off by the 'sputnik shock' particularly in the USA, but also in the other OECD countries. Most probably certain excessive public expenditures must also be attributed to systems rivalry. Since such expenditures were considered as 'social armament' needed to compete with the rival system, it was very easy to get political approval for them, just like for all arms expenditures during the cold war. A programme of cuts in social welfare expenditures and the abrogation of social security legislation (example: abolishment of the ban on dismissals in enterprises with up to 11 employees), like the one presented by the German government in the summer of 1996, would have been very unlikely while the GDR still existed. To be sure, competition on welfare cuts as was taking place between the Democrats and the Republicans in the US presidential election campaign in 1996, could hardly have taken place two or three decades ago. This, however, does not mean that the welfare state could have remained as it was if the Soviet Union had continued to exist as a rival to market societies.

In the year 1989, the change from systems rivalry to competition among locations ('Standort-Konkurrenz') and national currencies has become definite. While the desire to surpass the (imagined) scientific and social welfare achievements of the Soviet Union stimulated, or perhaps even caused, the development of the welfare state, above all the expansion of social welfare and education programmes, (imagined) competition with the newly industrialized countries in East Asia and with the new cheap-labour countries in Central and Eastern Europe is taken as justification for attempting to dismantle the welfare state and social welfare programmes. This is happening now at a time when social security programmes are more necessary than ever since the world economic crisis.

9.3.2 International Monetary Order and Deregulation of Capital Markets

It is one of the peculiarities of the *international monetary order* established by the USA as victor in World War II that its rules of the game tend to restrict the demand for products and thus keep down employment. As is well known, it is the main purpose of the international monetary system to enable the international settlement of payments of the countries participating in world trade. For this purpose the member countries of the International Monetary Fund (IMF) are obliged to reduce excessive deficits in their current accounts. A country in deficit must curb its economic activity (for example by increasing interest rates and taxes, or by reducing public expenditures). This results in lower imports, but also in lower production and employment both domestically and in other countries, from where less is imported. The production, income and employment of both the country in deficit and its main trading partners are reduced by this *asymmetric adaptation mechanism*: the total sum or outcome is negative.[6] That such restrictive tendencies did not predominate during the post-war period must largely be attributed to systems rivalry. But this has changed in the meantime: restrictive tendencies are no longer counteracted by political efforts.

Another important restrictive impulse affecting public expenditure programmes originates in the deregulation of national capital markets, particularly foreign exchange markets, which has become prevalent in the past 15 years. This has considerably reduced the room of manoeuvre for conducting an effective national fiscal and monetary policy. Expansionary fiscal and central bank policy is guided by the need to keep domestic assets attractive for foreign investment. Foreign investors in their turn are guided by currency stability and return on investment, also that expected in the future. Expansionary expenditure programmes combined with rising public debt and low-interest policy aimed at stimulating growth tend to reduce the attractiveness of a national currency. Since this holds for all currencies, they will compete with each other on attractivity terms. This, however, results in a restrictive influence on production, growth and employment. In this way, the jurors of such *beauty contests* among national currencies (the metaphor goes back to Keynes), that is international investors (such as pension and investment funds, enterprises, but also private asset holders), exert an influence which is stronger than the preference of electorates for active employment, social welfare, education and cultural policies.

This situation is compounded by the fact that such beauty contests drive interest rates up. Consequently, profits on financial investment often become higher than profits on investment in production. Higher interest rates of course also mean that more interest is due on public debt. At periods when the target of monetary stability predominates, this furthermore means that higher interest payments will reduce or take the place of expenditures on other public tasks. Frequently this affects expenditures on social welfare and education benefiting social groups that are least able to defend their case.

It is remarkable that in the debate around 'Standort-Konkurrenz' (competition among locations), the higher interest paid by enterprises as a result of beauty contests among currencies has not appeared in the argument. The discussions keep revolving around the cost of labour, taxes and social security contributions, despite the fact that in the past 20 years interest rates have increased much more than the other cost factors just mentioned.

9.3.3 Surplus of Private Savings, Public Debt and the Erosion of the Multiplier Effect of Public Expenditures

Circular flow analysis reveals that private household savings out of current income (that is current income minus consumption) by definition constitute a loss of effective demand for goods and services currently produced. However, these surpluses – mostly with the credit sector acting as intermediary – are absorbed by financing private investment and the export surplus. If private savings surpass private investment plus the export surplus, and if nothing else happens, demand will go down by that difference called surplus of private savings. However, effective demand is not reduced to the full extent because due to lower demand production and employment decline. The income from taxes and social security contributions falls to the same extent as social welfare expenditures rise because of higher unemployment. The private savings surplus is then absorbed by this automatic increase in the budget deficit. In fact, the private savings surplus of Austrian households of ATS100 billion in the year 1994 corresponded to the Austrian net budget deficit.

That these important interrelations are much more than a tautology has been theoretically clarified by Steindl (1990) and empirically illustrated by Guger and Walterskirchen (1988). They are, as already predicted by Keynes in 1943 (1982), a consequence of the maturity of national economies. Since private savings are relatively stable, while private investment and exports are quite sensitive to variations in interest rates and effective demand, the socio-economic context of mature national economies is one that favours rising unemployment and growing public indebtedness. Measures to 'improve the attractiveness of locations', for example through tax relief for higher incomes or raising interest earnings on financial investment as a consequence of beauty contests, contribute to pushing up the private savings surplus even further, thereby aggravating the original problem.

This trend is additionally promoted by national tax policy. It is a well-known fact that income from property is being taxed less and less while income from work is taxed more and more. This is not only an outcome of 'Standort-Konkurrenz': to a considerable extent it is due to the dominant agents' changed world view and interests. Nowadays it is no longer a rare event that key representatives of trade unions, or of Socialist, Liberal or Social-Conservative parties reveal themselves as private 'rent seekers' neglecting the 'public purpose'.

Rising income disparities observed in the OECD countries in recent years are an indication that the ability of national governments to exert an influence through policy measures is diminishing. This is also manifested by the weaker stimulation of demand emanating from public expenditure impulses: the public expenditures' multiplier is losing effectiveness because rising savings' rates make domestic demand go down, and also because a larger share of demand will shift to other countries when the import rate is rising.

9.3.4 The Creation of the European Economic and Monetary Union

The creation of the EU through the Maastricht treaties, particularly the plan to introduce a single European currency, can in a wider sense be seen as a consequence of the end of the cold war. In a narrower sense, it has to be seen as a consequence of German unification. The convergence criteria to be fulfilled heighten the dominance of monetary stability targets already enforced by the IMF and by deregulated financial markets. The convergence criteria with respect to price levels, exchange rates and long-term interest rates are met by most EU member countries wishing to join EMU; but most of them have difficulties meeting the requirements regarding their respective shares of public net deficit, and of total debt in GDP. In view of well-known circular flow relationships, one cannot be surprised that the convergence criteria are not fulfilled at a time of recession and rising unemployment. The attempt to fulfil them nevertheless means pursuing stabilization policy under price stability. This will delay any economic upturn and improvement on labour markets.

Since the political arguments supporting the introduction of the Euro are very strong and since there are also enough positive economic arguments (an end to speculation and 'beauty contests' among the currencies being replaced by the euro, a uniform unit of account, the reduction of transaction costs), it would be desirable to introduce the euro as soon as possible, that is according to the existing timetable.

What will happen after the introduction of the single European currency is not entirely clear. National monetary policies will definitely cease to exist. Governments of member countries will definitely become dependent on capital markets in financing their deficits. Their creditworthiness will definitely be rated in a manner similar to that of enterprises. The room of manoeuvre for financing the welfare state will diminish. Its fate will be decisively influenced by European Central Bank policy. If the convergence criteria are upheld or if – as advocated by the Deutsche Bundesbank – they become even more exacting, one must expect the continuation of low economic growth and a further increase in the number of the unemployed and poor. Regional differences will become sharper. Nationalisms and xenophobia will continue to be on the rise. Crisis will push back the welfare state. One can only hope that under the pressure of the resulting problems the actors on the EU stage will gain greater insight and energy and become better able to solve their problems than is the case at present.

9.3.5 The Revival of *Laissez-faire* Ideology

Thanks to Albert O. Hirschman we know that citizens' involvement tends to shift between private interest and public action (Hirschman, 1982). If he is right, it should not come as a surprise that a changed dominant world view is one of the new elements in today's socio-economic context. This is crucial in trying to understand what causes the current crisis of the welfare state and in any attempt to overcome this crisis. Until the early 1970s the prevalent view in economics and the social sciences was that the programme of the welfare state was able to prevent economic crises, or at least to mitigate them. Today most actors believe that it is the welfare state itself which causes economic decline and unemployment. For the welfare state supposedly raises the comparative costs of a particular 'Standort', thus lowering its competitiveness. In this way, the welfare state is believed to undermine the very economic resources on which it rests. Consequently, people think that the competitiveness of a particular 'Standort' can only be maintained or regained by monetary discipline. If one includes the negotiation results reached by the representatives of the major social groups, that is collective bargaining agreements and labour legislation in one's concept of the 'welfare state', then monetary discipline must also become enforceable at enterprise level and allow wage cuts and the introduction of longer working hours without any negotiated compromise. In its radical form the 'roll back' from the welfare state (Atkinson, 1995) also includes the end of social partnership.

This 'monetarist revolution' was intellectually prepared by certain economists during the 1950s and 1960s. Starting from Chicago, its main ideas became the dominant doctrine of the 1970s and 1980s. Has this doctrine managed to ensure the triumph of the target of monetary stability over the aims of the welfare state in the real world? There are many indications to this effect: advocates of monetarism act as advisers to influential politicians and central bank presidents. Their views dominate commentaries in the media and thus enter the world view of large numbers of people. Yet, this would not have been enough. It was decisive for the victory of the 'monetarist revolution' both in the intellectual and the political arena that the policy of deregulation and monetary discipline which it inspired favours the dominant interests of financial capital (from large enterprises, to pension funds, down to small holders of financial assets). According to the now dominant doctrine, the losers of the game, that is unemployed persons or unsuccessful entrepreneurs, may be reminded of their personal responsibility for their own fate. In short: the power élites which dominate the economy have lost interest in the welfare of the weaker members of society (Bhaduri and Steindl, 1987). It was precisely the end of systems rivalry that has made such behaviour possible. These economists and social scientists, legitimizing such developments, have only been scripting the incidental music. The play itself is acted out by the political leaders.

But one may question whether the monetarist policy implemented in the UK and the USA has been a success. Important welfare indicators are negative, the number of destitute persons (including the 'working poor') is growing. In Europe there is economic stagnation. In the USA average incomes are falling, income disparities are growing and public infrastructure is in decay. The external reasons for state activity listed in section 9.2.1 of this study could not have led us to expect anything different in consequence of receding state influence.

And yet, in spite of all this, the political and intellectual dominance of monetarist *laissez-faire* ideology remains unbroken.[7] The political representatives of the welfare state, that is the social-democratic parties and trade unions, have for a long time opposed even justified reforms. They concerned not only 'state-internal' reasons for public expenditures (see section 9.2.3), but also injustices and malfunctioning of the welfare state itself. In certain instances politicians have played the part of rent seekers or corruptionists. Suggestions for the reorganization of the welfare state based on a functional analysis of the fulfilment of state tasks (see section 9.2.4) presented as long as 20 years ago, have largely been neglected. It is true that alternatives to monetarist *laissez-faire* ideology have not been sufficiently elaborated. This is, of course, a more demanding task than to make suggestions on deregulation and monetary discipline often based on unfounded theories, as Atkinson (1995) has pointed out.

9.3.6 The New Socio-economic Context

When trying to uphold the idea of full employment in a welfare state our two actors, the imaginary minister of finance and the central bank president, today face a situational logic which differs profoundly from that of the year 1980. The new elements of the situation can be captured by again referring to the four basic elements of a socio-economic context:

1. The *world view* of the dominant actors is that of the *homo oeconomicus* who is able to pursue his market-oriented self-interest, not threatened by systems rivalry, nor controlled by any regulations or institutions. His only constraint is monetary discipline.
2. *Institutions, technology, knowledge*: deregulation and the increasing obsolescence of national borders due to telecommunications has brought forth enterprises which are active on global markets, the latter dominated by capital markets.

3. *Relative prices, income, costs*: these have gained importance considering
   (1) and (2). Interest earnings make up an increasing share of higher
   incomes. Earning ratios are becoming more dominant because of international competition among currencies and locations.
4. *Political instruments*: the political instruments of the nation state have
   been weakened by factors (1) to (3) above as well as by the influence of
   IMF, World Trade Organization (WTO), EU and so on. The predominance of the monetary stability target is affecting all programmes of
   the welfare state negatively.

The (probably social-democratic) minister of finance and his colleague,
the central bank president, will only have the choice of either acting in
accordance with the changed situational logic or – of resigning.

Streeck (1995, p. 68) puts this as follows: instead of using national sovereignty to tame and correct the market forces in favour of some public
interest, '. . . the only political programme still implementable by glob-
alised national economies without jeopardising the nation state . . .'
would be to give up national sovereignty altogether.

However, if the former minister of finance would still wish to pursue
the aim of full employment in a welfare state, he ought to put his efforts
into creating a socio-economic context where this would be possible.
Which considerations could guide him?

9.4   ON THE PROSPERING AND DECLINE OF INSTITUTIONS

9.4.1 Which Institutions Survive?

The ideas developed so far are basically concerned with the expansion of
institutions like the state and its agencies of public welfare, and with their
decline. The present study also deals with the creation of institutions without which a uniform European currency is impossible, and thus it is also
concerned with relations between EU institutions on the one hand and
the institutions of EU member states on the other, which could complement (both sides prospering) or substitute each other (one side winning
what the other side would lose).

Is it possible to theoretically capture these diverse processes of institutional change, continuation and decline in a way leading to new insights
on future policies?

Institutional change as viewed by Karl Marx was determined by technology (the 'productive forces'). Technology induces the removal of the

institutional fetters ('production relations') holding back development through social struggle. A number of macro-developments can be explained in this way. In fact, it was technical progress in communication technology which has enabled globalization, particularly of capital markets. However, the expansion of capital markets cannot be called an example of the unleashing of *productive* forces, neither according to the Marxist model nor in a system of national accounts; on the contrary, the dominance of financial over real capital established in this way is obstructing economic growth.

A similar argument holds for the explanation of institutional growth proposed by New Institutional Economics. According to this theory, those institutions will survive which enable larger marginal returns than competing institutions (North and Thomas, 1973). However, it does not seem possible to explain the development of institutions, not even that of private property, in this way. Take the case of the expansion of capital markets: it can hardly be said to be the result of applying a marginal utility calculus. 'Marginal utility' is a concept yielding useful results in analysing *already existing* material production, particularly in agriculture. But what could a marginal utility calculation look like that would explain the *introduction* of a financial derivative or the *non-introduction* of another? Is the decision not more like that of a person choosing to play poker rather than scat? New players may join the dominant game or may try to play a not yet existing one. Such a decision is not based on a *marginal utility* calculation, neither *ex ante* nor *ex post*. *Innovation* is a matter of preferences, abilities and risk appraisals within a *total calculus*.

The expansion of capital markets, just as the development of globally active enterprises, can be better explained by Adam Smith's theory of 'increasing market size', which becomes possible through improvements in technology and cheaper means of communication. They open up *new possibilities* of making profits on the basis of existing interest differentials and profit margins, as convincingly demonstrated by Kregel (1994).

In the *functional analysis* of the state presented in section 9.2, the development of institutions is perceived as a response to pressure exerted by some problem. Thus, the continued existence of an institution is linked with expectations that it will contribute to solving the problem, while institutional decline is related to persistent disappointment of such expectations. According to this approach, those institutions will survive which sustain, either directly or indirectly, a larger value added (in national account terms) and to greater political consent (for example through increased productivity because employees are cared for by the welfare state), such that this gain is larger than the (transaction) cost of maintaining the respective institutions. Institutions will suffer a decline if this plus turns into a permanent minus. However, the expansion of the capital market cannot be explained in this way. Rather, like in the enterprise sector, it depends on the identification and realization of new profit chances, as stressed by Hayek (1978) following Adam Smith, and as demonstrated in concrete terms by Kregel.

Finally, the rise and fall of institutions decisively depends on the social interaction of the actors constituting them, but also on the (physical and legal) persons to whom these institutions render services, and whose expectations are or are not fulfilled. Jacob Burckhardt refers to this kind of interaction (quoted by Lendi, 1992) when concluding with respect to the historical example of the Italian city states that their rise and fall depended on their citizens' commitment. If the citizens 'inner commitment' was stronger than their 'inner retreat', both tending to take place continuously, the conditions were present for prosperous development. In the reverse case, that is when inner retreat was stronger than inner commitment, some 'external factor' was sufficient to set the decline of an institution in motion. Burckhardt's answer is simple and yet correct. It is important because it explains the evolution of institutions as a result of social interaction. This is an advantage over other types of explanation mentioned earlier which focus on motives (income opportunities) or results (development of the productive forces, larger marginal utility, a plus in value added and/or consent). Burckhardt's explanation is carried further by game theory which deals with social interactions in situations where the decision of one actor also depends on the decision(s) of (an)other actor(s). Such situations are very common and are becoming more frequent, as mentioned in section 9.2.1 dealing with the game-theoretic model of PDM.

9.4.2 An (Unconventional) Attempt in the Light of Game Theory

Human behaviour in social situations is almost always connected with the observation or breaking of rules (customs, habits, legal norms, or rules in games like, for example, poker). Institutions themselves are social entities characterized by rules. The state is regarded as an institution and so is the global foreign exchange market. The following attempt at interpreting social interaction embedded in social situations and social entities is inspired by game theory but does not, in certain important points, completely follow its conventions.

Actions taking place in social situations may be divided into two categories or types according to their respective effect:

- In the case of *type 1* the actors' decisions or actions do not have any effect on other actors.
- In the case of *type 2* the actors' decisions or actions have either a positive or a negative effect on others.

The subject of game theory is the analysis of social situations in which *type 2* actions occur. Furthermore, a distinction is made between co-operative and non-co-operative behaviour. In the case of co-operative behaviour, the result of the action taken by the actors does not harm any public interest or 'public purpose', that is some common concern of the individuals involved. Co-operative behaviour would be: not to break any law, agreement or binding rule, that is not to steal, or selfishly harm fellow human beings or the environment and so on. It would be non-co-operative behaviour to harm the public interest.

In conventional game theory (see Osborn and Rubinstein, 1994) a distinction is made between constant-sum games and non-constant-sum games. An example of a constant-sum game is the well-known zero-sum game: what one person wins, the other person loses. PDM, as mentioned earlier, is a non-constant-sum game: on the assumption that the pay-offs expected by the actors are additive, their sum will differ, depending on which decisions the actors took.

Following a suggestion by the Polish social psychiatrist, Ryskar Praszkier (1996), and based on a simple PDM-type game (see Table 9.1), we should introduce a special terminology. It will differ somewhat from the conventions of game theory just described. Within PDM, we distinguish between three sub-variants of the game:

1 *The positive-sum sub-variant* is one in which all actors co-operate and thus together contribute to the 'public purpose'. In PDM (see Table 9.1) this corresponds to the sum 5 + 5. This variant is characterized as a positive-sum one because *both* actors end up better in this case than with all other possible decision combinations.

Table 9.1 Pay-off matrix in a simple PDM game

		Agent B	
		Co-operation	Non-co-operation
Agent A	Co-operation	5, 5	1, 8
	Non-co-operation	8, 1	2, 2

2 The *negative-sum sub-variant* is one in which all actors do not co-operate with each other and thus damage the 'public purpose'. In PDM (see Table 9.1) this corresponds to the sum 2 + 2, which is obtained by non-co-operative behaviour on the part of A and B. This variant is characterized as a negative-sum one because *both* actors end up worse than with all other decision combinations.

3 The *zero-sum sub-variant* is one in which a number of actors co-operate and the remaining ones do not. Thus, the 'public purpose' is partly supported and partly 'damaged'. In PDM (see Table 9.1), the non-co-operative actor achieves the best result and the co-operative one the worst of all decision combinations. The constant sum in this sub-variant (see Table 9.1) is assumed to be 9.[8]

The introduction of sub-variants to non-constant-sum games of the PDM type defined by different decision combinations and corresponding 'pay-offs' (positive, zero and negative sums) is justified if portions of social reality can be better explained by them than before. The following text will show whether this is indeed the case.

One can certainly draw a line from Burckhardt's explanation of the rise and fall of Italian city republics, which was applied to the development of other institutions by Lendi (1992), to the game-theoretical interpretation attempted in the present study. 'Prospering' of institutions as a result of 'inner commitment' by the citizens corresponds to that variant of the positive-sum game within PDM which results from co-operative behaviour by perhaps not all actors, but at least by the decisive ones. It yields positive results for all actors. 'Decline' of institutions as a result of 'inner retreat' by the citizens corresponds to the negative-sum variant of the game which is caused by non-co-operative behaviour of the decisive actors. It results in a loss for all actors. Nothing in Jacob Burckhardt's or Martin Lendi's texts would correspond to the variant of the zero-sum game. However, this variant characterizes a precarious situation where a decision is called for and where the zero-sum game may easily switch into a positive-sum or negative-sum one. If the external environment remains constant, and if a strategy of 'tit for tat' is chosen within PDM, such a situation will tend towards co-operation and thus to the sub-variant of the positive-sum game (Axelrod, 1984).

At this point it is worth making the effort to recall the opinions held by classical liberal economists on this subject. They thought that the pursuit of self-interest, 'if unrestrained by suitable institutions, carries no guarantee of anything except chaos'. (Robbins, 1978). Adam Smith and the English classical liberal economists therefore attributed an active role in politics to the state. The 'invisible hand' they refer to is – according to

Robbins – that of the *law giver*. It is the task of the legislature to create a legal framework which will exclude selfish behaviour whose effect would harm public welfare (Robbins, 1978). The classical economists' programme of economic policy started from a divergence between private and public interest. They wanted to influence the conditions for decision-making and action in such a way that the pursuit of self-interest, taken all together, would correspond to the public interest, or at least would not harm it. (A game-theoretical explication of this is found in Holler, 1986.[9])

Translated into the language of game theory, this means that the classical liberal economists advocated the pursuit of self-interest and competition under conditions of a positive-sum game. In such a framework, according to Adam Smith, 'moral sentiments' certainly have their place. They correspond to what is called co-operation in game theory. Therefore, in summary, the classical economists' programme of social policy is: pursuit of self-interest under competition *plus* co-operation.

As we know from Jacob Burckhardt, besides co-operation ('inner commitment') and non-co-operation ('inner retreat'), the development of institutions depends on a third factor, an 'external factor' which may reinforce non-co-operation or co-operation, or may cause one to change into the other.

'Moral sentiments', the state and 'external factors' are therefore decisive for the dominance of positive- or negative-sum games. What role did they play in the twentieth century with respect to prosperity or decline in Europe?

9.4.3 Inter-war Period. World War II. Cold war. The End of the Post-war Period?

The *inter-war period* certainly was one of decline. It reached its lowest point during the world economic crisis and the World War II with its extreme and unprecedented destructiveness. Thinking of the magnitudes of human victims and material destruction, about which one cannot speak except in deeply emotional terms, it is dangerous to enter into an explanation of that period using the cool terminology of game theory. The term 'game' theory itself heightens this danger, since in everyday language this word is associated with sports and having fun. If a game-theoretical review of this historical period is nevertheless attempted, the reason is that it will reveal how non-co-operation and negative-sum games, which may start quite harmlessly, even like some masquerade, can turn into catastrophes.

There is no doubt that at the beginning of the period of decline called the inter-war-period, non-co-operation was slowly intensifying. The advocates of the dictatorship of the proletariat, just like those of a state led by a 'führer', demanded the (physical) elimination of their opponents. The less radical groups pursued somewhat similar aims by democratic means, at least without demanding the physical liquidation of opponents. However, they were unable to co-operate for some 'public interest' encompassing needs they all had in common. The 'external factor' was the Soviet Union whose followers in the European countries advocated the creation of Soviet Republics according to that model. The threatened elimination of 'class enemies', which was actually taking place in the Soviet Union, was bound to heighten the antagonism of the opposing groups. The 'external factor' thus reinforced non-co-operation and speeded up the downfall of democratic institutions.

World War II itself was the murderous extreme of non-co-operation. It culminated in the systematic annihilation of the Jews under the command of Nazi Germany, supported by stooges and collaborators of the same mind in the Nazi-occupied territories.

The *cold war* which followed the 'hot' one without interval marked a long period of growth in the OECD countries, consisting of roughly five years of reconstruction, 25 years of constant expansion with falling unemployment, followed by slower growth and rising unemployment.

The success story of the cold war period is that of co-operation within and among the non-communist countries, a sequence of positive-sum games. What motivated the decisive political, economic, social and intellectual actors to advocate co-operation and positive-sum games and to act accordingly? One can name *moral sentiments* which made co-operation appear desirable. The important role attributed to co-operation was the result of the lessons learned about the catastrophic consequences of non-co-operation in the form of the world economic crisis and World War II. Lessons were also learned from the peace treaties after World War I and the ill-fated League-of-Nations loans. As a consequence, the loser of the war, (West) Germany, hardly had to pay reparations, but instead *was donated* considerable sums under the Marshall Plan to finance its reconstruction like all OEEC countries. State intervention and regulation of the economy were, at that time, not frowned upon. They were, not very surprisingly in view of the debacle of the inter-war period, highly appreciated by politicians and scholars. The state acted as owner of sizeable portions of the economy. Full employment, access to health services, social security and free higher education for all gifted persons were considered important public tasks and a moral responsibility. There was widespread consensus about their desirability. In the case of important decisions, the needs of employees and farmers were voiced by their representative bodies and taken into consideration. There was nearly complete agreement about the desirability of the welfare state, or at least of publicly guaranteed social welfare.

Finally, an 'external factor' existed in the shape of the Soviet Union which had emerged stronger from World War II despite the great sacrifices it had had to make. This time, the external reason 'Soviet Union' worked as a threat which for a long time stimulated co-operation within the OECD countries. Under the impact of system competition with the Soviet Union, poverty disappeared in the OECD countries. Before that period and afterwards, in the traditional world view of the *homo oeconomicus*, this social task has been regarded as support of idleness. After the sputnik shock, the mobilization of talent was considered to be part of the arms race. In all OECD countries Keynesian monetary and fiscal policies were regarded as proper instruments for the stimulation of effective demand, that is of production, investment and employment.

However, the Soviet Union lost the competition between the two rival systems. That became obvious, at the latest, when the Conference on Security and Cooperation in Europe (CSCE) treaty was signed in Helsinki. It was intended to give international guarantees to the Soviet Union for its sphere of influence established by the agreements of Yalta and Potsdam. After 1975, the only threat left was a military one. Accordingly, the interest in co-operation and positive-sum games of dominant actors in politics, economics, society and research began to dwindle. The challenge posed by the existence of an attractive alternative model of society (or hope for one) no longer existed. Thus there is less pressure on decision-makers, for example owners of capital, to improve the social conditions in their immediate sphere of responsibility. This is what usually happens when there is no more competition for workers in short supply and a certain lack of 'moral sentiments' and of responsibility for the 'public purpose'.

The arms race between the Soviet Union and the USA was a prisoners' dilemma situation in which the two powers played the sub-variant of a zero-sum game. It ended with the exhaustion of the Soviet Union. The implosion of the Soviet Union was caused by the dominance of non-co-operation and negative-sum games in the Soviet Union itself and in the Council of Mutual Economic Assistance (COMECON) member countries. Large enterprises and combines in the centrally planned economies were constantly pursuing negative-sum strategies against the central authority. This involved having low target figures put in their plan, or obtaining larger allotments of raw materials, energy, machines and so on. Within enterprises, permanent negative-sum games were played against collective institutions both 'from above' by the nomenclatura and 'at the bottom' by the staff. This meant low productivity, theft of resources and so on. A sketch by the Soviet satirist Raikin entitled 'Everything depends on all of us' vividly describes this non-co-operation. The scene deals with two trees, the big tree of collective property and the tiny tree of private property. According to Raikin, since the big tree belongs to everybody and thus to nobody, everybody takes what he or she can grab. Some even get at the roots. Thus it becomes doubtful whether the collective tree will still be able to bear good fruit, too many people have snatched something from it; meanwhile, the little private tree thrives, blossoms, sprouts . . . . This satire was told in the 1970s. A similar constellation regarding decision-making was the case among the various Soviet Republics and within the CMEA. It contributed to the erosion of the Soviet system, which never succeeded in replacing Stalinist terror by co-operation (see Sen, 1973).

Since the *end of the post-war period* marked by the implosion of the Soviet Union, 'the West', whose economic doctrine is now also shaping the former Soviet bloc, does not have an 'external factor' that would counteract the inherent tendency for non-co-operation. Therefore non-co-operation and negative-sum games are becoming increasingly predominant. In the hemisphere formerly controlled by Moscow, the end of the duel between the superpowers has paved the way for a series of negative-sum 'games' in the form of wars of secession. The same is the case in former Yugoslavia, the country between the former opposing blocs. Wartime has replaced the post-war period also in Europe.

Are there any further negative- and zero-sum games contributing to the crisis of the welfare state?

9.5 THE PREDOMINANCE OF MONETARY STABILITY TARGETS AS MAIN DANGER TO THE WELFARE STATE

The downgrading of the classical task of full employment and of welfare policies observed since the end of systems' rivalry is pointing to the rise of negative-sum games. To this one must add the factors contributing to a changed socio-economic context (section 9.3.6).

The asymmetric adaptation mechanism, for example, forcing solely the country running a current account deficit to bring about its reduction (see section 9.3.2), corresponds to a negative-sum game. Yet the adaptation mechanism would also allow positive sums, if governments and central banks took other economic and social policy tasks besides stability, such as full employment, as their target. Under the predominance of monetary stability, however, negative-sum games are gaining ground, thus reducing effective demand, and therefore production and employment.

Something similar holds for currency competition among countries. The attractivity of a currency is influenced positively by price stability, a low budget deficit, an export surplus and high interest rates, that is factors that mostly affect effective demand, and thus production, investment and employment negatively. The attractivity contest forces all countries to move in the same direction. In the end, the world economy's effective demand will be lower than it would have been without the contest. This is again the result of a negative-sum game.

On the other hand *'Standort' – competition among governments*, related to the location of new enterprises usually has an expansionary effect and thus influences the state budget negatively, at least in the short run. The governments wanting to attract new enterprises must offer favourable conditions regarding infrastructure, which raises public expenditures, and must make tax concessions, which reduces public revenues. However, this 'competition' is itself a consequence of insufficient effective demand: the latter is not big enough to support higher production and employment in all locations, let alone in additional new ones. Nourished (*inter alia*) by the contractive effects of the asymmetric adaptation mechanism and of the convergence criteria, a negative-sum game is staged: only a few locations can win the competition and attract internationally active enterprises; the other players get nothing.

The demands made on the budget in the effort to attract new enterprises will have a negative effect on other tasks financed out of the state budget. Very often such expenditures concern benefits provided by the welfare state. This situation will be repeated, at the latest when, after the amortization of the invested capital, efforts must again be made to prevent the enterprise from moving elsewhere. However it is impossible to prevent this if there are locations offering far better conditions regarding labour costs for the same kind of production. Enterprises, in their turn, are locked in a prisoners' dilemma situation *vis-à-vis* their competitors in a given market. As soon as one competitor moves to a low-wage country, the others must do the same. This is compounded by the *introduction of the euro* under fulfilment of the convergence criteria: it is a negative-sum game that lowers effective demand (directly affected are public consumption and investment, private investment and demand for import goods; indirectly affected is private consumption). So far there is no system of incentives to compensate this reduction in demand.

The most serious threat to welfare, however, comes from making monetary stability the overriding political task. This is an expression of the present predominance of financial capital over the production sphere. It results in the spread of negative-sum games to all social and cultural spheres. The absolute priority given to monetary stability over other public tasks means that the latter are more difficult to fulfil as soon as, or as long as stability targets are not met. This primarily affects the targets of full employment and economic growth. Consequently the financial demands on the (welfare) state rise at the same time as its revenues are reduced. This triggers off a chain reaction of further zero and negative-sum games.

For example if more than two persons compete for one available job, this is the situation of a zero-sum game: only one can win, all others must lose. As is well known, at present the number of persons in the EU who are looking for jobs is more than ten times larger than the number of vacancies. Every cut made in social, health, education or cultural budgets due to the predominance of monetary stability gives rise to zero-sum games between those persons who just about received what they needed and those who did not make it. This creates an atmosphere discouraging co-operation in the sense of pursuit of a public task and means there is no sense of 'inner commitment'.

The basis of the welfare state, like of any other institution, is co-operation allowing (expectations of) positive-sum games that will encourage and reward those taking part in co-operation. This basis is seriously jeopardized by the inordinate growth of non-co-operation leading to negative-sum games.

9.6 THE STAGING OF POSITIVE-SUM GAMES AS PRIMARY OBJECTIVE IN POLITICS

9.6.1 Assigning New Tasks to Politics, Economics and Society

If the world view presented in this essay interprets the current situation correctly, if it is true that negative-sum games are currently replacing positive-sum ones, then it is clear what must be done. The overriding *political* task in our time must then be to stage positive-sum games.

The *humanities and social sciences* would be called upon to clarify the following questions: What are the consequences of non-co-operation? What are the preconditions for co-operation in different social situations? Above all: What are the conditions under which zero- or negative-sum games can be transformed into positive-sum ones? This constitutes a demanding research programme, a challenge to theory and to experimental economic and social science.

9.6.2 A New Agenda of Public Tasks

Co-operative behaviour presupposes that a public interest (or 'public purpose') exists which is adopted as public task. This public interest is harmed by the pursuit of self-interest. Behaviour is co-operative when the actors override their self-interest and act in accordance with the public interest. Fulfilment of the latter will in the longer run be to the advantage of all actors or participants in co-operative behaviour.

Whenever co-operative behaviour does not emerge spontaneously or in a self-organized way, this is reason for action by the state:[10] therefore, in order to make co-operative behaviour recognizable as such and to be able to organize positive-sum games, an *agenda of public tasks* is needed. Their fulfilment means satisfying the public interest. The best way of doing so is to create a socio-economic context in which the pursuit of self-interest coincides with the 'public purpose'. It is not well known that this idea goes back to Adam Smith and other English classical political economists (Robbins, 1978).

The *agenda of public tasks* should be permanently headed by a general procedure: the application of the co-operation mode. It should be applied to carry out, in turn, the public task or tasks that are most urgent at any particular moment: at periods of high inflation this would be currency stability; at times of high unemployment it would be the restitution of full employment. Any socially significant, serious problem that could not be solved under the unbridled rule of self-interest, and of the market forces because they themselves had caused it (see section 9.2.2), would be a suitable candidate for inclusion in the catalogue of (subjects for) public action. Problems of public interest for Europe as a whole would be, for example: slower economic growth, rising unemployment, increase in poverty and inequality, environmental damage, organized crime, drugs, as well as excessively high real interest rates, excessive public debt, and of course, whenever that is the case, inflation. This catalogue of problems is just a suggestion; it should be open to new as well as to old problems believed to have been solved already and of concern to all of Europe. The criterion for inclusion in an agenda of EU problems would be divergence between private and public interest, which is quite large in a number of EU member countries. Just as in the case of the convergence criteria, efforts should concentrate on the task or tasks generally regarded as most urgent.

The absolute priority of the target of monetary stability should only remain in force until the introduction of the euro. Thereafter it should become a public task besides others, whose place in the list of priorities would depend on to urgency attributed to it.

9.6.3 Five Difficulties in Introducing the Co-operation Mode

Anyone wishing to contribute to leaving the downward-sloping path of non-co-operation that leads to zero- and negative sums, and who would like to see the co-operation mode installed which promises positive-sums as a reward, should be prepared to encounter at least five difficulties.

The *first* one would be the difficulty of making the actors, but also a large number of persons affected by them, aware of the consequences of non-co-operation, and of giving them an insight into the long-term advantages of co-operation. One can only move from non-co-operative to co-operative behaviour if the idea of co-operation and of a positive-sum game is already present in the minds of the actors. For, as the social psychiatrist Praszkier from Warsaw so correctly remarked, one usually desires something one knows. He observed that the mind of the *homo post-sovieticus* is closed to the idea of the positive-sum game (Praszkier, 1996). Unfortunately this is also true for the *homo oeconomicus* in 'the West'. Romantic cultural pessimists are not alone in deploring the *erosion* of 'moral sentiments' dating back to the stock of cultural values of pre-industrial society (see Hirsch, 1976). Empirical investigations (for example Putnam, 1995 in the USA) have revealed a rapid decline of 'social capital', that is of people's ability to do something for other persons, to trust others (Davy, 1995) and to enter into exchange relationships with one another that are not determined by economic advantage. This dangerous tendency is also observable in many other countries. Making (non)-co-operation understood is of universal concern.

The *second* difficulty would be the one of explaining in concrete terms for every specific social situation what the results of non-co-operation and what the preconditions and advantages of co-operation would be. In this effort, the model of the prisoners' dilemma and other game-theoretical models, as well as the concept of socio-economic context, could be useful.

The *third* difficulty would be to *write the script*, as it were, for the co-operation mode in every concrete situation and for every institution in danger of disintegration, and then to stage the respective positive-sum games. The theoretical models and concepts mentioned under item two above could again be helpful in practical implementation.

The *fourth* difficulty would lie in making the actors and the persons affected by them accept the co-operation mode. This would not be easy since the end of the predominance of monetary stability would, overall, cause losses to investors on capital markets. Also the central banks would lose influence. Both investors and banks would fight to keep their advantages. Yet one should not conclude that the introduction of the co-operation mode would be impossible. There is a positive example supporting this hope: EU banks are advocating the introduction of the Euro, in spite of the fact that this will make them lose most of their profitable foreign exchange business. Therefore there is reason for hope and this is not just a necessary prerequisite.

The *fifth* difficulty would be to make the co-operation mode something worth reporting about in the media. This will not be easy at all. On the one hand, there is a lot of talk about co-operation today, but this term, just like the related term solidarity, is mostly used in a very diffuse way as part of everyday political rhetoric. This has nothing to do with the concept of co-operation presented in this study which is derived from the theory of strategic games and clearly defined in analytical terms. On the other hand, it will be hard to induce the media to take on the subject of the co-operation mode, because for the media in their present shape only 'bad news is good news'. Co-operation is hardly ever spectacular and thus uninteresting for the media, since it does not promise to attract much public attention. The same can be said of compromises reached in negotiations: they are only worth being publicized in a derogatory way, as 'bad news'. The co-operation mode can hardly compete with the duel, the most radical form of non-co-operation. The duel seems to be the show best suited to the binary age of electronic mass media, be it in the form of a box fight, a TV duel between politicians or an entertainment show of the kind *The winner takes all*. It has always been difficult to make the truth known, but one should not stop trying. The rise and fall of Mr Berlusconi demonstrates that quality of marketing will, even in the media, not always be able to replace the quality of what is being marketed.

Recognizing the possibilities embodied in positive-sum games, their conception, staging and acceptance did not fall from heaven either, as it were, during the long period after World War II, when positive-sum games were predominant. Yet they were then much easier to organize, since many people had personal experience of the consequences of non-co-operation ending in totalitarian dictatorship and the catastrophe of World War II. During that period co-operation was mostly threatened from 'outside'. Danger emanated from the Soviet System, but it simultaneously stimulated various kinds of co-operation as a form of defence inside the threatened countries. It was a period of reconstruction and expansion during which co-operative behaviour was stimulated and remunerated by rapidly increasing incomes and capital. At the end of the twentieth century the lessons learned from totalitarian dictatorship and World War II are steadily losing influence. The threat posed by the Soviet Union has disappeared altogether. Increases in income which are an important part of positive sums are becoming smaller. Values other than money or material goods would now (partly) need to take the place of the former incentives. Non-material values have so far only appeared in their destructive form within the positive sum. For example, a Bosnian (or Serb, or Croat) commander is said to have replied to the argument that continuation of the war would bring still more poverty and misery to more people: 'Even if the standard of living drops by another 50 per cent we will still be better off if we gain our national independence.'

Would it be impossible to introduce *non-monetary values* to the positive sum and to make them acceptable at times when incomes, having reached high levels, stagnate or begin to go down? Could personal satisfaction not be derived from doing something that is also useful for other persons?

It may still appear utopic today to suggest that co-operation should become the essence of politics. However it will perhaps be possible to defend this idea in the future by recalling its origin: it can at least draw on the political and social theories of classical liberal economists like Adam Smith, on classical philosophy like that of Immanuel Kant, on the core of socialist thought (leaving aside the Marxist world of historical subjects and depersonalized collective actors), on Christian conceptions of society, on encyclicals by the Pope, as well as recently on the communitarian 'I and we paradigm' (Etzioni, 1988).

The idea of politics as the staging of positive-sum games will not be utopic particularly if it is based on a realistic view of current problems. The pressure of the problems at hand should establish a suitable hierarchy of tasks to be put on the public agenda. So far, after monetary stabilization, mainly deregulation and privatization have been awarded the status of public tasks. If the 'mad cow' disease really turns into the catastrophe feared by some, this event could contribute to a revival of the priority of public interest (in this case for regulation in animal breeding and meat processing) over short-term private interests (in this case cost reduction through deregulation of animal breeding).

9.6.4 Contours of a Socio-economic Context Encouraging Co-operation

It would be justified to criticize the suggestions made in this essay as being utopic if they did not pay attention to the fact that human beings cannot be expected to constantly act against their own interest. This is why a socio-economic context would need to be created whose inherent logic has the effect of keeping the divergence between public and private interests as small as possible. In the ideal case it would have to contain incentives making it possible to mobilize self-interest for the fulfilment of a public task. In short such a socio-economic context would have to create opportunities for the fulfilment of public tasks beyond stability targets, for public action at the national level, but above all also at higher ones: that of the EU, OECD, UN, IMF, WTO and ILO (International Labour Office), as well as other supranational agencies. The new socio-economic context should also allow and stimulate renewed and increasing use of spontaneous and self-organized co-operation.

New elements in the envisaged situation can again be outlined by refer-ring to the four basic elements of socio-economic context:

1. According to the *new world view* the market will continue to play a cen-tral role in the fulfilment of individual and social needs. If unrestrained pursuit of private interest increasingly harms others and thus the public interest, it recognizes the need for regulation. The effectiveness of regu-latory institutions must therefore be restored. Monetary stability is not regarded as an intrinsic value, but one public task among others.
2. Restoration of the power of national, as well as sub- and supranational authority implies a reversal of the dominance of financial markets over product and labour markets. This presupposes reforms of important *institutions* like the IMF (for example change to a *symmetrical adaptation mechanism*) and capital markets. The speed of financial transactions would have to be lowered (for example by separating the execution of a transaction from the time it begins to bear interest).
3. *Relative prices, incomes, costs, non-monetary advantages* (for example prestige, attention) and so on are to be employed to fulfil other than monetary public tasks. For example the cost of financial transactions could be raised by putting a 'Tobin tax' on them (Tobin, 1982, and, elaborated further, Bhaduri and Matzner, 1990).
4. The effectiveness of *political instruments* must be increased and uti-lized. A catalogue of public tasks on and for all levels of political authority are to be drawn up. This is to be followed by the creation of conditions suitable for realizing them. By taking care of all this, politics would be following the call to contribute to the fulfilment of public tasks by staging positive-sum games.

If there were a guarantee that Hirschman's cycle of citizens' involvement – that is shifting between private interest and public action – exists, the future of the welfare state could be greeted with optimism. Such a guaran-tee, however, does not exist. The 'five difficulties' listed above should already have made this obvious. Optimism must rely on a less certain, yet quite promising argument: the future, that is the creation of a better socio-economic context, is not just a matter of forecasting; it still is made up of the sum of individual actions.

9.6.5 How to Continue from Here?

Today the creation of a socio-economic context that would stimulate co-operation transcends the possibilities of the nation state. Therefore this issue should be put on the agenda of political actors able to exert an influ-ence at a higher than the national level.

If the EU is to make staging the co-operation mode its overriding aim, research into specific subjects and problems will be as much needed as concerted political effort. In view of their great significance, positive-sum games should take the top position in a catalogue of European public tasks. What other framework would be more appropriate to elaborate these ideas than the constitution of the EU? That it would be desirable to adopt such a legal framework has long been recognized in discussions on European democracy. Political negotiations on a catalogue of top priority EU tasks would introduce concrete issues to the debate on an EU constitution and would take it out of its ivory tower.

The political actors will therefore have to realize that they will need to elaborate programmes consisting of various levels. They will have to distinguish between tasks that can *still* be carried out at the national level and others that will *only* be implementable at EU level, and yet others that will have to be tackled by *other* political arenas (for example the IMF, WTO, or IBM, Microsoft and so on), and finally others which under present conditions *cannot* be realized at all.

Returning to the beginning of this study, no doubt we currently find ourselves in an era of change during which, in Schumpeter's words, 'old methods run into crisis', which usually also manifests itself in financial crises. The crisis of the welfare state can certainly also be considered as a crisis of 'old methods', but not exclusively. Old and new methods practised by other institutions than the welfare state are making significant contributions.

Staging the co-operation mode and creating a socio-economic context favourable to co-operation are suggested as 'new methods' able to meet the challenges of the current period of change. That this idea, also applied to the welfare state itself, is not altogether new will become clear by reading one of the 'fathers' of the modern welfare state: Gunnar Myrdal (1958).

ENDNOTES

1. Written version of a lecture at the International Symposium 'Challenges to the Welfare State: Internal and External Dynamics for Change' organized by the Forum International des Sciences Humaines, Paris, and the Department of Economics, University of Navarra, Pamplona, Spain, 23–26 May 1996. Translated by Silvia Plaza.
2. The author would like to thank Karl S. Althaler (Vienna), Horst Grabert (Berlin), Max Haller (Graz), Stuart Holland (London), Hardy Hanappi (Vienna), Manfred J. Holler (Hamburg), Hans Keman (Amsterdam), Gabriele Matzner-Holzer (Vienna), Sabine Mayer (Vienna), Claus Noe (Hamburg), Sylvia Pintarits (Munich), Manfred Prisching (Graz and Harvard), Sonja Puntscher-Riekmann (Vienna), Hazel Rosenstrauch (Vienna) and Gunther Tichy (Graz and Vienna) for their encouragement and critical remarks. Responsibility for the text of course rests entirely with the author.

3. In view of the preponderance of selfish behaviour in governments and administrations, Musgrave (1996) recently coined the expression 'the flawed state' for the phase following the welfare state.
4. The notion 'situational logic' was inspired by Popper (1945) who speaks of 'the logic of situation'. In the view of Hedström and Swedberg (1996) the heurestic significance of Popper's idea was in social research so far almost entirely neglected.
5. In 1996 this corresponds to about US$64 billion. Considering the low standard of living at the time, this magnitude was of even greater significance. The largest donation per capita was made to the Austrian people. Why? Austria was threatened most seriously by Communism (Kennan, 1967).
6. The IMF terms of reference state as one of the fund's objective the reduction of *fundamental disequilibria* between countries. They also urge member countries to reduce their surpluses. In reality the elimination of deficits became the dominant policy.
7. It is true, however, that at present an increasing number of opposing voices can be heard (see, *inter alia*, Atkinson, 1995; Holland, 1994; Sinn, 1995; Scharpf, 1996; or Tichy, 1993).
8. Holler (1996) presents strict analytical definitions on this which largely correspond to the descriptions used here.
9. It is interesting to note that Hayek refers to a similar social situation in the following words: 'Modern game theory has, moreover, shown while some games lead to the gains of one side being evenly balanced by the gains of the other, other games may produce overall gains. The games of the extended structure of interaction was made possible by the individual's entry into the latter sorts of game, ones leading to overall increase of productivity'. (Hayek 1988, p. 154).
10. Commissioned by the World Bank, Stiglitz and a team of researchers investigated the role of the state under rapid economic growth in eight East Asian countries. He concludes that government policy was able to stimulate co-operation and to combine it with the advantages of competition. It thus contributed to strong growth (Stiglitz 1996). Heilbroner/Milberg (1995) develop a vision of a changed public sector coming close to Stiglitz's conception (1989) and research results (Stiglitz 1996).

REFERENCES

Atkinson, A.B. (1995), 'The economic consequences of rolling-back the welfare state', *Draft of Lectures at the Centre of Economic Studies*, University of Munich.

Axelrod, R. (1984), *The Evolution of Co-operation*, New York: Basic Books.

Baumol, W.J. (1967), 'Macroeconomics of unbalanced growth: the anatomy of urban crisis', *The American Economic Review*, 57.

Bhaduri, A. and Matzner, E. (1990), 'Relaxing the international constraints on full employment politics', *Banca Nazionale di Lavoro Review*, 172, March, 49–70.

Bhaduri, A. and Steindl, J. (1987), 'The Rise of Monetarism as a Doctrine', *Thames Papers in Political Economy*, Northeast London Polytechnic.

Davy, B. (1997), *Essential Injustice*, Vienna and New York: Springer Verlag.

Elias, N. (1976), *Über den Prozeß der Zivilisation. Zweiter Band: Die Sozio- und Psychogenese des Staates und des Steuermonopols*, Frankfurt/Main: Suhrkamp (first edition Bern 1939).

Etzioni, A. (1988), *The Moral Dimension. Towards a New Economics*, New York: Free Press.

Guger, A. and Walterskirchen, E. (1988), 'Fiscal and monetary policy in the Keynes–Kalecki tradition' in J.A. Kregel, E. Matzner and A. Roncaglia (eds), *Barriers to Full Employment*, Basingstoke and London: Macmillan, 103–32.

Hayek, F.A. v. (1978), 'Competition as a discovery procedure', in F.A. Hayek, *New Studies in Philosophy, Politics, Economics and the History of Ideas*, London: Routledge & Kegan Paul.

Hayek, F.A. v. (1988), 'Play, the school of rules', in *The Collected works of F.A. Hayek*, vol 1, London: Routledge & Kegan Paul.

Hedström, P. and Swedberg, R. (1996), 'Rational choice, empirical research and the sociological tradition, in *Working Paper number 34*, University of Stockholm: Department of Sociology.

Heilbroner, R. and Milberg, W. (1995), *The Crisis of Vision in Modern Economic Thought*, Cambridge: Cambridge University Press.

Hirsch, F. (1976), *Social Limits to Growth*, London: Routledge & Kegan Paul.

Hirschman, A.O. (1982), *Shifting Involvements. Private Interest and Public Action*, Princeton: University Press.

Holland, S. (1994), *Toward a New Bretton Woods. Alternatives for the Global Economy*, Nottingham: Spokesman.

Holler, M.J. (1986), 'Moral sentiments and self-interest reconsidered', in A. Diekman and P. Mitter (eds.), *Paradoxical Effects of Social Behaviour. Essays in Honour of Anatol Rapaport*, Vienna.

Holler, M.F. (1996), 'Personal letter' to the author.

Kennan, G.F. (1967), *Memoirs 1925–1950*, Boston: Little, Brown & Co.

Keynes, J.M. (1982), 'The long-term problem of full employment', *Collected Writings of John Maynard Keynes*, vol. 22, (first published in 1943) London: Macmillan.

Kregel, J.A. (1994), 'Capital flows: globalization of production and financing development', *UNCTAD Review*, 23–38.

Lendi, M. (1992), 'Der Beitrag der Schweiz an das neue Europa', in M. Lendi, *Bewährung des Rechts*, Zürich: Verlag der Fachuer Bände.

Matzner, E. (1982), *Der Wohlfahrtsstaat von Morgen. Entwurf eines zeitgemäßen Musters staatlicher Intervention*, Frankfurt/Main:Campus Verlag.

Matzner, E. (1991), 'Policies, institutions and employment performance', in E. Matzner and W. Streek (eds), *Beyond Keynesianism. The Socio-Economics of Production and Full Employment*, Aldershot: Edward Elgar.

Matzner, E. (1994), 'Instrument-targeting or context-making? A new look at the theory of economic policy', *Journal of Economic Issues*, **28** (2).

Musgrave, R.A. (1996), 'The role of the state in fiscal theory', *International Tax and Public Finance*, **3** (3), 247–58.

Myrdal, G. (1958), *Beyond the Welfare State*, London: Macmillan.

Neumann, J. von and Morgenstern O. (1947), *Theory of Games and Economic Behavior*, 2nd edition, Princeton: Princeton University Press.

North, D.C. and Thomas, P.R. (1973), *The Rise of the Western World: A New Economic History*, Cambridge: Cambridge University Press.

Osborn, M.J. and Rubinstein, A. (1994), *A Course in Game Theory*, Cambridge, MA: MIT Press.

Prager, T. (1962), *Wirtschaftswunder oder keines?* Wien: Europe Verlag.

Praszkier, R. (1996), 'Mental and cognitive factors in the transformation process', *Lecture at the 3rd AGENDA Workshop on Lessons from Transformation*, Austrian Academy of Sciences, Research Unit for Socio-Economics, Vienna, 12–14 April 1996.

Putnam, R.D. (1995), 'Tuning in, tuning out: the strange disappearance of social capital', *Political Science and Politics*, December 1995, 664–83.

Robbins, L.C. (1978), *The Theory of Economic Policy in English Classical Political Economy*, Philadelphia: Porcupine Press (1st edition 1952).

Scharpf, F.W. (1996), 'The impact of globalization on democracy and the welfare state', Founder's Prize Award Lecture to the *8th International Conference on Socio-Economics*. Geneva University, 12–14 July 1996.

Schönbäck, W. (1980), *Subjektive Unsicherheit als Gegenstand staatlicher Intervention*, Frankfurt/Main: Campus Verlag.

Schumpeter, J.A. (1954), 'The crisis of the tax state', *International Economic Papers*, 4.

Sen, A.K. (1973), *On Economic Inequality*, Oxford: Clarendon Press.

Sinn, H.-W. (1995), 'Theory of the welfare state', *Scandinavian Journal of Economics*, 4.

Steindl, H. (1990), 'The role of household savings in the modern economy', in J. Steindl, *Economic Papers 1941–1988*, New York: St Martin's Press.

Stiglitz, J.E. (1990), 'On the economic role of the state', in A. Heertje (ed.), *The Economic Role of the State*, Oxford: Basil Blackwell.

Stiglitz, J.E. (1996), 'Some lessons from the East Asian miracle', *The World Bank Research Observer*, **11** (2), 151–77.

Streeck, W. (ed.), *Beyond Keynesianism: The Socio-Economics of Production and Full Employment*, Aldershot: Edward Elgar.

Taylor, M. (1976), *Anarchy and Co-operation*, London: John Wiley & Sons.

Tichy, G. (1993), 'The credibility of monetary integration. The experience of European countries and some inferences for a greater Europe', *Research Memorandum 9305*, Department of Economics, University of Graz.

Tobin, J. (1982), 'Adjustment responsibilities of surplus and deficit countries', in J. Tobin (ed.), *Essays in Economics, Theory and Policy*, Cambridge, MA: University Press.

Weidenbaum, M.L. (1969), *The Modern Public Sector. The Ways of Doing the Government's Business*, New York: Basic Books.

10. Doing good without the idea of *Good*: on policies for 'the fight against poverty'

Philippe Bénéton

I

The social policies launched in the Western world in the 1960s were driven by a fighting spirit. Enlightened by the social sciences, public authority was henceforth regarded as capable of effectively combating the social ills that had until this time been considered inherent to the human condition. Unfortunately, such expectations have largely remained unfulfilled; even worse, the effects of the ensuing government initiated policies have often been contrary to their objectives. Indeed, we have only witnessed a decline in the quality of social life. Although in 1964 President Johnson promised a 'great society', 30 years later American society appeared rather to have become a 'demoralized society', (as it was referred to by G. Himmelfarb).[1] In some form, this trend is common to all Western societies. Clearly, social policy cannot be solely held responsible for the decline of society, but it has nevertheless played a significant role. In what ways? The failure of these policies can be attributed to two fundamental errors:

1. They have underestimated the strategic dimension of human actions and the vast scope of options which are ultimately available to the individual. In other words, they were fed on an illusion: the social world is easily malleable, enlightened reason coupled with good intentions can only lead to good results. That is to say, the objects of these well-meaning intentions are assumed to be passive individuals, their behaviour to be unchanging. This, however, is hardly the case: the measures called for by social policies impact the structure of incentives, and in so doing, the actions of those concerned. Individuals are not mere pawns; they react to situational changes using the scope of choices available to them. Inevitably then, policies often result in unforeseen and undesirable effects: aid to single mothers increases their number,

restrictions on the levels of rent discourages owners from renting, taxes perceived as excessive have incited fraud, various forms of financial assistance have given way to the refusal to work. Today these effects are better known and more readily taken into consideration, thanks to the lesson of experience as well as to a greater recognition of economic reasoning.

2. Social policies have ignored the moral dimension of human actions. A purely economic analysis, in its limited perspective, also contributes to this misconception. What has given way to such a restricted understanding of human actions? To begin with, moral relativism has become a dogma central to our society: each individual lives as he or she wishes and acts as the sole judge of his or her well-being; as a result, it is unacceptable to impose one's idea of good upon others. Secondly, scientism, which continues to dominate in our society, excludes any 'value judgements'. The question of good and evil is not a scientific one. Relativism and scientism have conjointly contributed to the transformation of the objectives of social policies: it has thus become a matter *of doing good without imposing an idea of what is good.* The question of good and evil is nonetheless still alive and well – how could it not be in matters of political action? – but it has been reformulated. The traditional question of living standards is no longer relevant, or more precisely, the question has been reduced to one of rights and means. The conception of good lacks any real substance. When applied on a large scale, such as to society, it tends to be equated to a sum of private and heterogeneous 'goods'. Social policies work toward creating a good society with little regard for the *bona vita.*

The *common man* however is no more indifferent than is the social science expert when it comes to himself. The moral significance of an act undoubtedly weighs on the actor's feelings. In his pursuit of recognition and prestige, does the *social scientist* indifferently choose between honest means and the manipulation of statistics and citations? Likewise, in his struggle to make ends meet, does the *common man* indifferently choose among various options such as holding a respectable job, receiving *welfare*, and dealing drugs? Should one consider that the *common man*, unlike the social scientist, lacks a moral conscience?

The rule of the relativist and the scientist forecloses moral distinctions among different types of behaviour. As a result, social policies have neglected to address the issue of differences in ways of living. What can be expected other than miscalculation from such negligence? Policies which have aimed to fight poverty provide a sad but vivid example.

II

A fundamental misconception is reflected by the official titles of the policies themselves: 'war on poverty', 'anti-poverty programmes', 'lutte contre la pauvreté'. almost all make reference to *poverty*, in the all-inclusive sense of the word. Yet this word, as it is employed in the singular, precludes a necessary deeper reflection. In reality, *there is not one but various forms of poverty*. Those who are commonly referred to as the poor are, in fact, a wide variety of individuals who live in a diversity of ways. As such, they need to be differentiated.

However this elementary truth remains unrecognized by many. The official and most widely held definition of poverty is a purely economic one; an established income level differentiates the poor from the rest of the population. International organizations, such as the EU, the USA, France (and so on) rely on a statistical criterion . Such a conception is appropriate when considering poverty in its most extreme form – a scarcity of the goods necessary to man's basic needs for survival. However, its application to the Western world takes another form: poverty is defined in reference to a *poverty line* which designates the minimal standard of living acceptable and which is determined in proportion to the average income or the minimum wage. Such pre-established levels are largely arbitrary; they create artificial categories, they fail to accurately reflect reality. In short, four criticisms can be directed at the use of a statistical criterion:

1. Income level is only one factor which determines living conditions. Any Welfare family in Harlem is perhaps not as poor as it was 20 years ago, but does this allow us to assert that living conditions have improved when fear prevents many from taking the subway at night, when there are drug dealers at every street corner, when the neighbourhood is made up of buildings in a state of dilapidation and ruin?
2. A statistical criterion disregards differing sources of poverty and the varying ways in which poverty is dealt with by its 'victims'. Should a family who honourably struggle to maintain a decent lifestyle be placed in the same category as professional bums? Should a victim of a series of unfortunate circumstances (illness, unemployment . . .) be regarded in an identical manner as an individual who has always refused to work? Should we consider poverty resulting from alcoholism or drug abuse to be of the same nature as that endured by a widow raising a child on her own? There is no such thing as *one* 'poverty culture'.[2] Irving Kristol tells of the street in which he lived in the 1970s:

There was a Chinese family, recent immigrants, who ran a basement laundry. The parents and their five children shared the two tiny rooms at the back of the tiny store, and I shudder to think what this family did to our poverty statistics. Still those parents expressed great confidence that their children would 'get ahead' – and in fact, all five ended up as college graduates. (...) In contrast, on that same street there were several welfare families whose incomes, in cash and kind and services, may well have been larger than that of our Chinese family, but who were in various stages of a dependency-induced corruption, with little family stability and with the children involved *in drugs and delinquency*.[3]

This example illustrates the heterogeneousness of the category of Americans designated as 'the poor'. In France, beneficiaries of the *Revenue Minimum d'insertion* (RMI) created in 1988,[4] constitute an equally diverse population: the young, the old, men, women, isolated individuals, families, those with a desire to change their situations and others who have already given up, 'expert' abusers of social assistance and others who are ashamed of their dependence. Or more concretely: an alcoholic who gives no sign of ambition to overcome his dependency, an unemployed artist who refuses to make any concessions in the name of his occupation, a farmer who is determined to survive a difficult phase, a divorcee with children, a misfit resolute on remaining inactive.[5]

3. A single criterion logically leads to a sole solution: policies created to combat poverty (in the singular form) use the same medicine to treat different illnesses. There are cases when financial assistance is a clear necessity and others when it only acts as a trap (*the poverty trap*). Therefore, distinctions need to be made, behaviour and its moral value must be taken into consideration. From this perspective, the problem which faces the American *underclass* today is above all a problem of behaviour (irresponsibility, the decline of the family, delinquency. . .). It is not just a matter of poverty but of pauperism (to make use of an old distinction). To reduce the question to a mere lack of money is to follow an erroneous line of reasoning and to mistake the symptom for the illness.

4. Finally, a statistical criterion is unreliable and easy to manipulate. In the USA as in France, official data are overridden with numerous approximations and are often missing facts: how can one evaluate the significance and the contribution of undeclared income, illegal income, free medical assistance, real and feigned cohabitation, family transfers. Bureaucratic systems of assistance are a prime target for abuse. One unfortunate provocation among others.

III

What are the consequences of such policies which fail to differentiate the poor? Across the Atlantic the perverse effects of *welfare* are well known.[6] The system encourages abuse, it provides a series of perverse incentives (the refusal to work, the refusal to marry and to take on family responsibilities, fraud). Combined with a view of the poor, and above all of poor blacks, as perpetual victims, it has significantly contributed to the development of the American *underclass* who lead, what can be characterized as, a dissolute lifestyle. However it would be erroneous to infer the overall condition of the poor from that of the *underclass*. There exists the official 'poor' who refuse to carry this title and who are unwilling to accept the assistance to which they have a 'right'; there also exists a considerable number of poor people who remain as such for only a very brief period of time and who are able to benefit from the system without becoming imprisoned in the *welfare trap*. Confronted with a uniformly applied policy of assistance, the heterogeneousness of the poor population has thus, at least partially, remained intact. If the preceding observations are accurate, it follows that the conservative thesis, as argued by Charles Murray (the system has trapped the poor), is not entirely true nor is the liberal thesis, in its most well-known version until recent years (the system has helped the poor), totally false. Once again, distinctions need to be made as an all-encompassing conception of *poverty* only tends to blur our vision of the veritable results of assistance.

An analysis of the effects of French policy leads to similar arguments: the results of the RMI are of a wide variety (even more so, it seems, than those observed in the USA). *In short, the system assists some and traps others.* It allows some to find a way out of a difficult situation, it locks others into laziness and irresponsibility. The practice of 'start-up' contracts varies considerably with the degree of the involvement of local communities and the type of poor people concerned: the majority of RMI beneficiaries receive assistance outside of any contract; among those contracts which are signed, some are authentic (part-time work, training positions. . .) and facilitate entry into or return to the working world, while others are invalid contracts and only give the appearance of offering pure and simple assistance. The French department boasting some of the most favourable results is *Ile-et-Vilaine*: in 1995 it witnessed 3071 'exits' from and 4031 'entries' into the system. Among those who left the system, that is those who ceased to receive the RMI, 644 or 21 per cent found jobs.[7] At the other extreme, the results of certain overseas departments are disastrous. In French Guiana, the native Indians, or those originally from Surinam, no longer hunt nor fish. Upon becoming beneficiaries of the

RMI, they buy transistors, rum, and guns and get those who do   not
yet receive any financial assistance to do the hunting for them. On
Réunion Island (1 per cent of the population which nonetheless accounts
for 10% per cent of all RMI beneficiaries), the people for cutting sugar-
cane has become increasingly difficult to find. Young people, who were
not so long ago bustling, are now found hanging about alongside of
roads. Indeed, the RMI releases people from the necessity to work[8] .

IV

What should be done? What solutions can be proposed? It is certainly
much easier to say what shouldn't be done than to suggest what should.
Nevertheless, two series of propositions can be drawn from experience:

1. In terms of assistance, the key objective is the following: the various
   forms that poverty take must be identified so as to adapt assistance to
   the actual needs (moral and material). But such a distinction is not a
   simple task, as Tocqueville states in his *Mémoire sur le pauperisme*
   (1835). As a result, it is impossible to accomplish this aim through
   administrative or impersonal means. Aside from particular cases when
   criteria are clear or relatively clear (aid to the elderly or to the dis-
   abled), experts and civil servants do not have the knowledge necessary
   to differentiate among the poor without floundering in uncertainty.
   Thus aid should be as decentralized as possible and make significant
   use of the services offered by volunteer organizations whose flexibility
   offers advantages that could never be provided by regulated forms of
   assistance. In sum, charity work is preferable to the distant benevolence
   of 'social problem' specialists.
2. These distinctions do not exclude the need for moral considerations
   (even if the risk of abuse obviously exists). This implies modifications
   in our use of vocabulary and a return to terms which express the moral
   signification of actions: laziness, courage, cheating, dignity, corruption,
   commitment. Today such a vocabulary is immediately denounced as
   'stigmatizing' certain individuals. But this external attitude of compassion and non-discrimination is counterproductive: concern for the
   well-being of others does not mean indifference to evil. It seems that
   the proper solution is found in the words of Saint-Augustin: 'Damnare
   errorem amare errantes'.[9] There is such a thing, as Tocqueville noted,
   as a coexistence of discipline and humanity.

These solutions have a general reach. The refusal to make moral or vital
distinctions has not only distorted policies concerning 'the poor', it has

also compromised or completely altered family policies (all forms of family life are considered equally valid), school policies (the difference between good and bad behaviour has lost its force), policies to fight AIDS (all 'sexual preferences' have become acceptable). Time and time again, experience has shown: we cannot do good while neglecting the very idea of *good*.

ENDNOTES

1. *The De-moralization of Society*, New York, A. Knopf, 1995.
2. As the following example illustrates: the landless Hungarian peasants before the war – whose life is described in a personal account by Margit Gari in *Le vinaigre et le fiel* (trans. Fr. Plon, 1963) – are more deprived than the poor of Mexico – whose experience is related by Oscar Lewis in *Les enfants de Sanchez* (trans. Fr., Paris, Gallimard, 1963) – and yet the former lead a much more structured and dignified lifestyle, due in great part to the women of the community who, instilled with a strong sense of faith, exhibit the admirable traits of resolution and bravery. This contrast portrays how one's mind determines one's existence. For other examples of the diversity of lifestyles of the poor, see (and compare) P.J. Helias, *Le cheval d'orgueil*, Paris, Plon, 1975; R. Hoggart, *La culture du pauvre*, (trans. Fr, Paris, éd. de Minuit, 1970); Ken Auletta, *The underclass,* New York, Random House, 1982.
3. *Reflection of a Neo-conservative*, New York, Basic Books, 1983, p. 196.
4. This system, which was put into place by the law of 1 December, 1988, consists of the following: anyone above the age of 25 (or having at least one child in their charge), who resides in France, and whose resources, including any received assistance, fall below a certain level, can benefit from the RMI. The monthly maximum an individual can receive is FFr 2374 for the first trimester of 1996 (approximately 38 per cent of the minimum salary in France), with a 50 per cent increase for a second person in the household, a 30 per cent increase for a third person, and a 40 per cent increase for each additional person (a family of four receives about the equivalent of the minimum salary in France). The RMI is a form of assistance which involves, at least in principle, an exchange: the beneficiary makes a commitment, in the form of a contract, to enter into a process (training periods, small jobs for the public interest. . .) whose objective is social and professional integration. In this way, this system attempts to avoid the classical perverse effects which often accompany assistance.
5. V.S. Paugam, 'Le revenue minimum d'insertion. Les leçons de l'expérience française', *Commentaire* 60, hiver 1992–1993, p. 901–910 ; M. Court and V. Duponchelle, 'Voyage chez les Rmistes', *Le Figaro*, 7, 8 and 9 janvier 1992.
6. The references are numerous. In particular, Charles Murray, *Losing Ground. American Social Policy* (1960–1980), New York, Basic Books, 1984; Nathan Glazer, *The Limit of Social Policy*, Harvard University Press, 1988; and numerous articles on the subject in *The Public Interest*. More detailed information in: 'Les pauvretés américaines', *Commentaire*, 38, été 1987, pp. 280–287.
7. Information provided by the departmental Mission of the RMI.
8. For the case of Guyane, V.M. Anselme, *Ces hommes qu'on achève*, (ed). du Rocher, 1991; for that of the Réunion, V.P. Robert-Diard, 'Les 'Rmistes' of the Réunion', *Le Monde*, 17 août 1990.
9. 'To condemn error, to love the erring.'

Index

Aid to Families with Dependent
   Children 10
Alber, J. 53, 54, 55, 57
Alesina, A. 126
Alt, J.E. 107
Asia 58, 73
   East 8, 50, 162
   South-East 55
asymmetric adaptation mechanism
   162, 176
Atkinson, A.B. 64, 166, 167
Australia
   employment distribution 84, 86
   government expenditures 25, 26, 27
   government services and growth 31
   household employment patterns 93
   'objective conditions' 29
   parties in government, impact of 39
   transfer payments and growth 32
Austria
   government expenditures 25, 27,
      112, 117
   government responsibility 101, 102
   government services and growth 31
   income inequality 115, 116
   'objective conditions' 30
   parties in government 39
   policy features 40
   socio-economic context 113, 164
   tax fairness 114
   transfer payments and growth 32
Axelrod, R. 172

backlash and tax revolt 98–121
   government overload 103–6
   government responsibility 101, 102
   government spending 105, 112, 117
   income differences 115–16
   legitimacy crisis 106–7
   middle mass 100–103
   new political agenda 108–10

rational choice revolt 107–8
socio-economic equality policies
   113
subtlety and sophistication 110–11
tax fairness 114
West European pattern 118–19
Baker, K.L. 109
Barr, N. 64
Baumol, W.J. 156
Békesi, Finance Minister 149
Belgium
   Christian democracy and Social
      democracy 37
   employment distribution 84, 86
   government expenditures 25, 26, 27
   household employment patterns 93
   policy features 40
   social security system 59
Benelux countries 59
Bénéton, P. 188–94
Berlusconi 181
Beveridgean (British) model 52
Bhaduri, A. 166, 183
Bismarckian countries 123
Bismarckian (German) model 52
Bokros, Finance Minister 150
Borre, O. 99, 104
Bossi, U. 134
Bradshaw, J. 64
Brittan, S. 1–6, 104
Budge, I. 35, 37, 109
Bulgaria 52, 142
Burckhardt, J. 170, 172, 173
Bush, G./administration 7, 17, 19

Cameron, D.R. 27, 34
Campbell, J. 53
Canada
   employment distribution 84, 86
   government expenditures 25, 26, 27
   government services and growth 31

195